The Ultimate Scene Study Series
Volume II

102 Scenes for Two Actors

The Ultimate Scene Study Series Volume II

102 Scenes for Two Actors

edited by Jocelyn A. Beard

SCENE STUDY SERIES

A SMITH AND KRAUS BOOK

Published by Smith and Kraus, Inc.
177 Lyme Road, Hanover, NH 03755
www.SmithKraus.com

Copyright © 2000 by Smith and Kraus, Inc.
All rights reserved
Manufactured in the United States of America

First Edition: May 2000
10 9 8 7 6 5 4 3 2 1

Library of Congress cataloguing in publication data
The ultimate scene study series / edited by Jocelyn A. Beard
p. cm. — (Scene study series)
Includes bibliographical references.
Contents: v.1. 101 scenes for groups — v.2. 102 short scenes for two actors — v.3. 103 scenes for three actors — v.4. 104 scenes for four actors.
ISBN 1-57525-153-1 (v.2)
1. Acting. 2. English drama. 3. American drama. 4. Drama—Translations into English.
I. Beard, Jocelyn. II. Series.

PN2080.U49 1999
808.82—dc21   99-089197

NOTE: These scenes are intended to be used for audition and class study; permission is not required to use the material for those purposes. However, if there is a paid performance of any of the scenes included in this book, please refer to the permission acknowledgment pages 287–300 to locate the source who can grant permission for public performance.

Contents

PART THREE: THE GLORIOUS 17TH CENTURY

PART FOUR: THE WICKEDLY ELEGANT 18TH CENTURY

PART FIVE: PASSION AND FANTASY IN THE 19TH CENTURY

PART SIX: THE EARLY 20TH CENTURY...
SEX AND POLITICS

PART SEVEN: THE LATE 20TH CENTURY... MILLENNIUM'S EDGE

Forword

When Marisa and Eric approached me about editing this book I said yes—very enthusiastically—hung up the phone and then groaned at my inexplicable penchant for self-torture.

I thought of the huge boxed collection of plays that I swore to never open again and the unbelievable effort that lay ahead. Those of you who are students know all too well how you have to scramble to read every assigned play in a semester. Try reading hundreds in that same amount of time. I won't lie to you, the book you're holding in your hand was a beast to put together. For the last year it has been my white whale as surely as I morphed into a kind of nasty post-feminist Ahab (or should that be "Ahabia?") in my pursuit of 102 scenes that could legitimately be called "ultimate."

A couple of words about the length of the scenes: Every single scene in this book can be done in two minutes or under by my reckoning. Those that were borderline were read aloud and timed. Now, we all know that a scene can be read faster than it can be performed, so I must beg your understanding and indulgence if you take a scene from this collection and find that it takes you two minutes and 37.567 seconds to perform. Before you get your dander up please remember that the timing standard was a brisk read. In other words, if a certain scene seems longer than two minutes, ask yourself how quickly it would go if it was performed by Kevin Spacey and Holly Hunter, rather than by Olivier and Streep. If nothing else this may open up an exciting dialogue with your fellow performers about the necessity of adhering to the laws of Pace, a god to whom all actors should pay homage from time to time.

I know talented young actors who have never heard of Ben Jonson or William Wycherley who are exposed to Shakespeare via the sweaty efforts of Leonard DiCapprio or Gwynneth Paltrow. This ain't right. Books like this one offer the student and lover of theatre an opportunity to enjoy a hearty taste of many of the important play-wrights who have gone before us. Nothing is more important to your understanding of theatre. Nothing.

I shall therefore, as always, close with the following plea: If you find a scene or two that tickles your fancy, for heaven's sake get ahold of the play and read it.

This book could not have been completed without the patience of both Smith and Kraus and to them I extend my grateful thanks. The reason this book looks so swell and is perhaps the most hand-some in your collection is because of the above and beyond work of the talented Julia Gignoux of Freedom Hill Designs; my thanks and admiration go to her as well as good luck wishes for her upcoming special project. Finally, I want to thank Heather McNeil from the bottom of my heart. Thanks for coming to my rescue and for making sure I actually finished the book.

The Ultimate Scene Study Series Vol.II: 102 Scenes for Two Actors is dedicated to the students of Bethel High School, Bethel, Connecticut.

Jocelyn Beard
The Brickhouse
Patterson, NY
Summer 1999

The Ultimate Scene Study Series
Volume II

102 Scenes
for Two Actors

PART ONE:

THE ANCIENTS

The Persians

Aeschylus, Translated by Philip Vellacott
472 BC

Scene: the royal court of the kingdom of Persia

Man and Woman

Atossa (40–50) Queen of the Persian Empire and Darius (50–60) the ghost of her late husband, the king.

> *Here, grieving Atossa tells her husband's ghost of their son's military disasters in Greece.*

DARIUS: Speak, Queen Atossa, royal partner of my bed;
    Cease these laments and tears, be plain. Grief is man's lot,
    And men must bear it. Sorrows come from sea and land;
    And mortal ills will multiply with mortal years.
ATOSSA: Surely your happiness excels all other men's:
    Blest in your life—who, while you still beheld the sun,
    Lived long unclouded years as Persia's envied god;
    And envied now in death, which has not suffered you
    To see the abyss of ruin. Then hear all in brief:
    Persia's great name and empire are laid low in dust.
DARIUS: But how? By stroke of pestilence? or civil war?
ATOSSA: No; but near Athens our whole army was destroyed.
DARIUS: Tell me, which of my sons campaigned so far afield?
ATOSSA: Xerxes, whose rashness emptied Asia of its men.
DARIUS: Poor fool! Was it by land or sea he attempted this?
ATOSSA: Both; he advanced two-fronted to a double war.
DARIUS: How could he, with so huge a land-force, cross the sea?
ATOSSA: He chained the Hellespont with ships, to make a road.
DARIUS: That was a feat! He closed the mighty Bosporus?
ATOSSA: He did. Doubtless some god helped him achieve his plan.
DARIUS: Some god, I fear, whose power robbed Xerxes of his wits.
ATOSSA: Too clearly true; witness the ruin he achieved.

DARIUS: What happened to his armies, that you weep for them?

ATOSSA: Disaster to the fleet destroyed his force on land.

DARIUS: Destroyed? Is our whole army killed to the last man?

ATOSSA: Such is the desolation for which Susa mourns.

DARIUS: A noble army lost, the safeguard of our land!

ATOSSA: And every Bactrian, all their flower of youth, is gone.

DARIUS: O wretched son, to lose so fine an allied force!

ATOSSA: Xerxes alone, we hear, with some few followers—

DARIUS: What fate fell to him in the end? Is he alive?

ATOSSA: He reached at last, with joy after despair, the bridge
    Yoking two continents—

DARIUS: Safe on to Asian soil?

ATOSSA: Safe, without doubt; the message vouches for his life.

DARIUS: How swiftly came fulfilment of old prophecies!
    Zeus struck within one generation: on my son
    Has fallen the issue of those oracles which I
    Trusted the gods would still defer for many years.
    But heaven takes part, for good or ill, with man's own zeal.
    So now for my whole house a staunchless spring of griefs
    Is opened; and my son, in youthful recklessness,
    Not knowing the gods' ways, has been the cause of all.
    He hoped to stem that holy stream, the Bosporus,
    And bind the Hellespont with fetters like a slave;
    He would wrest Nature, turn sea into land, manacle
    A strait with iron, to make a highway for his troops.
    He in his mortal folly thought to overpower
    Immortal gods, even Poseidon. Was not this
    Some madness that possessed him? Now my hard-won wealth,
    I fear, will fall a prey to the first plunderer.

ATOSSA: Xerxes the rash learnt folly in fools' company.
    They told him you, his father, with your sword had won
    Gold to enrich your children; while he, like a coward,
    Gaining no increase, played the warrior at home.
    He planned this march to Hellas, this vast armament,
    Swayed by the ceaseless slanders of such evil men.

DARIUS: Hence this disaster, unforgettable, complete;

Measureless, such as never yet made desolate
Our Persian land, since Zeus first gave this ordinance,
That one man, holding throne and sceptre, should be lord
Over all Asia's pastured plains.

Seven Against Thebes

Aeschylus, Translated by Philip Vellacott
467 BC

Scene: the bloody streets of Thebes, a city that has become a battle-ground

Two Women

Antigone (18–20) and Ismene (16–18) daughters of Oedipus.

Following the dreadful slaughter at Thebes, these grief-stricken sisters lament the deaths of those who gave their lives for their city, including their own dear brother.

(Antigone and Ismene now move to centre stage to mourn over the bodies.)

ANTIGONE: If you gave wounds, you also received wounds,
ISMENE: If you dealt death, you also suffered death.
ANTIGONE: With the spear you killed—
ISMENE: By the spear you died—
ANTIGONE: Pitiful in inflicting.
ISMENE: Pitiful in suffering.
ANTIGONE: Let the cry rise—
ISMENE: Let the tear fall—
ANTIGONE: For you who died.
ISMENE: For you who killed.
ANTIGONE: My heart is wild with sobs.
ISMENE: My soul groans in my body.
ANTIGONE: Brother, whom I weep for—
ISMENE: Brother, most pitiable—
ANTIGONE: You were killed by your brother.
ISMENE: You killed your brother.
ANTIGONE: Twofold sorrow to tell of—
ISMENE: Twofold sorrow to see—
ANTIGONE: Sorrow at the side of sorrow!

ISMENE: Sorrow brother to sorrow!
CHORUS: O Fate, whose gifts are cruel and grievous,
     O august shade of Oedipus,
     O dark Erinys, how great is your power!
ANTIGONE: This is a sad and terrible sight.
ISMENE: This is how I welcome him from exile.
ANTIGONE: And when he killed, he failed to gain his home.
ISMENE: And when he saved his home, he lost his life.
ANTIGONE: He lost his life.
ISMENE: And took his brother's.
ANTIGONE: O reckless sons!
ISMENE: O hopeless end!
ANTIGONE: The same sad name for both.
ISMENE: The same tears for a threefold agony.
CHORUS: O Fate, whose gifts are cruel and grievous,
     O august shade of Oedipus,
     O dark Erinys, how great is your power!
ANTIGONE: You know now that you sinned—
ISMENE: You learnt in the same moment
ANTIGONE: When you came back to Thebes.
ISMENE: When you chose to fight your brother.
ANTIGONE: How terrible a tale!
ISMENE: How terrible a sight!
ANTIGONE: Alas, for suffering!
ISMENE: Alas, for wrong done—
ANTIGONE: To the royal house and to Thebes—
ISMENE: To me even more.
ANTIGONE: Alas for the consummation of follies and miseries!
ISMENE: Alas for the most tormented of mankind—
ANTIGONE: Who in their folly—
ISMENE: Were like men possessed.
ANTIGONE: What place shall we find to bury them?
ISMENE: Where they will receive most honour.
ANTIGONE: Alas, alas!
     If they sleep by their father they will trouble him.

Antigone

Sophocles, Translated by Sir George Young
442 BC

Scene: Thebes

Man and Woman

Creon (40s–50s), conqueror of Thebes and Antigone (16–20) daughter of the deposed king; a defiant idealist.

> *Creon has ordered that the bodies of the slain Thebian soldiers who opposed him shall be left in the streets to rot. Here, fearless Antigone informs the tyrant that she intends to bury her brother, who fought bravely for their city to his death.*

ANTIGONE: Would you aught more
    Than take my life, whom you did catch?
CREON: Not I;
    Take that, take all.
ANTIGONE: Then why do you delay?
    Since naught is pleasing of your words to me,
    Or, as I trust, can ever please, so mine
    Must needs be unacceptable to you.
    And yet from whence could I have gathered praise
    More worthily, than from depositing
    My own brother in a tomb? These, all of them,
    Would utter one approval, did not fear
    Seal up their lips. 'Tis tyranny's privilege,
    And not the least—power to declare and do
    What it is minded.
CREON: You, of all this people,
    Are singular in your discernment.
ANTIGONE: Nay,
    They too discern; they but refrain their tongues
    At your behest.

CREON: And you are not ashamed
    That you deem otherwise?
ANTIGONE: It is no shame;
    To pay respect to our own flesh and blood.
CREON: And his dead foeman, was not he your brother
    As well?
ANTIGONE: Yes, the same sire's and mother's son.
CREON: Why pay, then, honours which are wrongs to him?
ANTIGONE: The dead clay makes no protest.
CREON: Not although
    His with a villain's share your reverence?
ANTIGONE: It was no bondman perished, but a brother.
CREON: Spoiling, I say, this country; while his rival
    Stood for it.
ANTIGONE: All the same, these rites are due
    To the underworld.
CREON: But not in equal measure
    Both for the good man and the bad.
ANTIGONE: Who knows
    This is not piety there?
CREON: The enemy
    Can never be a friend, even in death.
ANTIGONE: Well, I was made for fellowship in love,
    Not fellowship in hate.
CREON: Then get you down
    Thither, and love, if you must love, the dead!
    No woman, while I live, shall order me.

The Clouds

Aristophanes, Translated by T. Mitchell
423 BC

Scene: Athens

Two Men

Strepsiades (50–60), a man obsessed with current fashionable trends in philosophy and Pheidippides (20–30) his long-suffering son.

> Foolish Strepsiades has been studying au currant philosophy much to his son's dismay. Here, a family quarrel provides the older man with an opportunity to showcase his newly learned theories.

STREPSIADES: You swore but now by Jupiter—
PHEIDIPPIDES: I did.
STREPSIADES: Mark now what 'tis to have a friend like me—
    I tell you at a word there is no Jupiter.
PHEIDIPPIDES: How then?
STREPSIADES: He's off; I tell it you for truth;
    He's out of place, and Vortex reigns instead.
PHEIDIPPIDES: Vortex indeed! What freak has caught you now?
STREPSIADES: No freak, 'tis fact.
PHEIDIPPIDES: Who tells you this?
STREPSIADES: E'en Socrates the Melian,
    And Chærephon, the flea philosopher.
PHEIDIPPIDES: And are you so far gone in dotage, sir,
    As to be dup'd by men like them, fellows
    Whose bile has overflowed them?
STREPSIADES: Keep a good tongue;
    Take heed you slander not such worthy men,
    So wise withal and learned—men so pure
    And cleanly in their morals, that no razor
    Ever profan'd their beards; their unwash'd hides

Ne'er dabbled in a bath, nor wafted scent
Of od'rous unguent as they pass'd along.
But you, a prodigal fine spark, make waste
And havoc of my means, as I were dead
And out of thought—but come, turn in and learn.

PHEIDIPPIDES: What can I learn or profit from such teachers?

STREPSIADES: Thou canst learn everything that turns to profit;
But first and foremost thou canst learn to know
Thyself how totally unlearn'd thou art;
How mere a blockhead, and how dull of brain—
But wait awhile with patience— *(Enters the house hastily.)*

PHEIDIPPIDES: Woe is me!
How shall I deal with this old crazy father?
What course pursue with one, whose reason wanders
Out of all course? Shall I take out the statute,
And cite him for a lunatic; or wait
Till nature and his phrenzy, with the help
Of the undertaker, shall provide a cure?
(Strepsiades returns, with a cock in one hand and a hen in the other.)

STREPSIADES: Now we shall see! Lo! what have I got here?

PHEIDIPPIDES: A chicken—

STREPSIADES: Well and this?

PHEIDIPPIDES: A chicken also.

STREPSIADES: Are they the same then? Have a care, good boy
How you expose yourself, and for the future
Describe them cock and hen-chick severally.

PHEIDIPPIDES: Ridiculous! Is this the grand discovery
You have just borrow'd from these sons o' th' dunghill?

STREPSIADES: This, and a thousand others—but being old
And lax of memory, I lose it all
As fast as it comes in.

PHEIDIPPIDES: Yes, and methinks
By the same token you have lost your cloak.

STREPSIADES: No, I've not lost it; I have laid it out
Upon the arts and sciences.

PHEIDIPPIDES: Your shoes—
      They're vanish'd too. How have you laid them out?
STREPSIADES: Upon the commonwealth.
      —Like Pericles
      I'm a barefooted patriot.—Now no more;
      Do as thou wilt, so thou wilt but conform
      And humour me this once, as in times past
      I humour'd thee, and in thy playful age
      Brought thee a penny go-cart from the fair,
      Purchas'd with what my legal labours earn'd,
      The fee for my attendance.
      (Going towards the house of Socrates.)
PHEIDIPPIDES: You'll repent,
      My life upon 't; you will repent of this.

Oedipus at Colonus

Sophocles, Translated by E. F. Watling
c. 401 BC

Scene: Ancient Greece

Man and Woman

Antigone (16–20) daughter of Oedipus and Polynices (20s) her rash
brother.

> *Polynices has determined to return to Thebes to fight the usurper,
> Creon. Here, Antigone begs him not to go knowing that if he
> does so, he will surely die.*

POLYNICES: All this for nothing!
　　And worse than nothing. All those trusting friends,
　　And the high hopes in which we marched from Argos,
　　Brought to this end! An end I dare not name
　　To any of them. I cannot turn them back.
　　I must go on in silence to what awaits me.
　　But O my sisters, if all these pitiless curses
　　Which you have heard, fulfil themselves in act,
　　And if you ever come again to Thebes,
　　By all the gods, remember me with kindness.
　　Give me a grave, and reverent offices.
　　So to the commendation which you earn
　　For faithful service here, more may be added
　　By what you do for me.
ANTIGONE: O Polynices,
　　Do this one thing for me.
POLYNICES: What, dear Antigone?
ANTIGONE: Order your army back to Argos; now,
　　Before it is too late, to save yourself
　　And our city from destruction.
POLYNICES: That is impossible.
　　If I cry off this time, how can I ever

Lead them to battle again?

ANTIGONE: Again? But why?
Why need you fight again? What use is it
To make your home a ruin?

POLYNICES: Am I to endure
The insult of exile, and the mockery of a younger brother?

ANTIGONE: You are only hastening to its consummation
That double death your father prophesies.

POLYNICES: The deaths he hopes for! No, I'll not go back.

ANTIGONE: The more's the pity. How many of your men
Will follow when they hear what is foretold?

POLYNICES: They will not hear; I wouldn't tell such tales.
The careful leader does not spread alarm
By publishing bad news unnecessarily.

ANTIGONE: Then you're determined to do this?

POLYNICES: I am.
So let me go. I see my way before me,
Dark though it is and shadowed with grim shapes
Of vengeance answering to my father's prayers.
May yours be brighter, by God's mercy, sisters,
As you discharge that service at my death,
The last I shall require.
Now let me go.
This is good-bye for ever.

ANTIGONE: O my brother!

POLYNICES: Don't weep for me.

ANTIGONE: What can I do but weep,
Seeing you go like this to certain death?

POLYNICES: If certain, I must meet it.

ANTIGONE: Is there no other—?

POLYNICES: No other way that's right.

ANTIGONE: I cannot bear it!
To lose you!

POLYNICES: That must be as Fate decides.
Well...May the gods be good to you. God knows
You have deserved it.

The Madness of Hercules

Seneca, Translated by Dana Gioia
1st Century AD

Scene: the home of Hercules and Megara

Man and Woman

Megara (30s) faithful wife of Hercules and Lycus (30–50) her unwanted suitor and King of Thebes.

> *Hercules has been trapped in Hell for quite some time leaving Megara alone to fend off the persistent advances of Lycus. Here he asks Megara to become his queen.*

MEGARA: A chill of horror makes my body tremble.
    I can't believe your shameful proposition.
    When war erupted, I wasn't afraid.
    I faced each terror calmly—even when
    The fighting echoed round the city walls.
    But when you mention marriage, then I shudder.
    For the first time I truly realize
    I'm just another slave captured in war.
    Load me with chains or make me suffer death
    By slow starvation. No torture you devise
    Will break my loyalty to Hercules.
    If I must die, I swear I will die his.
LYCUS: Why waste your love on someone trapped in hell?
MEGARA: He challenged hell to earn a place in heaven.
LYCUS: But now the earth has crushed him with its weight.
MEGARA: No weight can crush a man who held up heaven.
LYCUS: What if I force you?
MEGARA: Force can only work
    On someone who is still afraid of death.
LYCUS: I can be generous. What wedding gift
    Shall I present my bride?

MEGARA: Your death or mine.

LYCUS: Have you gone crazy? Do you want to die?

MEGARA: In death at least I can rejoin my husband.

LYCUS: Why choose that slave when you can have a king?

MEGARA: That slave sent many vicious kings to death.

LYCUS: Why does he serve a king and do hard labor?

MEGARA: A hero earns his fame through valiant labor.

LYCUS: What valor comes from fighting animals?

MEGARA: Valor consists of conquering what men fear.

LYCUS: Why argue? Hercules is dead in hell.

MEGARA: One must risk death to merit immortality.

Medea

Seneca, Translated by Frank Miller
1st Century AD

Scene: Ancient Greece

Man and Woman

Creon (50s) a ruthless tyrant and Medea (20–30) a woman scorned
by an unfaithful husband.

> *When Jason falls in love with another woman, Creon demands
> that foreign Medea leave the kingdom and forfeit any claim to
> her two young sons. Medea has resolved to murder the boys
> rather than leave them with their father. Here, she persuades
> unsuspecting Creon to allow her to see the sleeping boys one
> final time before her departure.*

MEDEA: Thou bid'st me flee?
   Then give me back my bark wherein to flee. Restore
   The partner of my flight! Why should I flee alone?
   I came not thus. Or if avenging war thou fear'st,
   Then banish both the culprits; why distinguish me
   From Jason? 'Twas for him old Pelias was o'ercome;
   For him the flight, the plunder of my father's realm!
   My sire forsaken and my infant brother slain,
   And all the guilt that love suggests; 'twas all for him.
   Deep dyed in sin am I, but on my guilty soul
   The sin of profit lieth not.
CREON: Why seek delay
   By speech? Too long thou tarriest.
MEDEA: I go, but grant
   This last request: let not the mother's fall o'erwhelm
   Her hapless babes.
CREON: Then go in peace. For I to them
   A father's place will fill, and take them to my heart.

MEDEA: Now by the fair hopes born upon this wedding day,
  And by thy hopes of lasting sovereignty secure
  From changeful fate's assault, I pray thee grant from flight
  A respite brief, while I upon my children's lips
  A mother's kiss imprint, perchance the last.
CREON: A time
  Thou seek'st for treachery.
MEDEA: What fraud can be devised
  In one short hour?
CREON: To those on mischief bent, be sure,
  The briefest time is fraught with mischief's fatal power.
MEDEA: Dost thou refuse me, then, one little space for tears?
CREON: Though deep-ingrafted fear would fain resist thy plea,
  A single day I'll give thee ere my sentence holds.
MEDEA: Too gracious thou. But let my respite further shrink,
  And I'll depart content.
CREON: Thy life shall surely pay
  The forfeit if tomorrow's sun beholds thee still
  In Corinth But the voice of Hymen calls away
  To solemnize the rites of this his festal day.

PART TWO:

HOLY PLAYS FOR DARK TIMES LEAD TO THE EARLY RENAISSANCE STAGE

The Fall of Man

Anonymous
circa 1415

Scene: The Garden of Eden

Man and Woman

Satan (any age) and Eve (18–20).

> *Here the infamous serpent convinces innocent Eve to take a small bite of a certain apple.*

SATAN: Eve! Eve!
EVE: Who is there?
SATAN: I, a friend;
    And for thy good is the coming
    I hither sought.
    Of all the fruit that ye see hang
    In Paradise, why eat ye nought?
EVE: We may of them ilkane
    Take all that us good thought,
    Save a tree out is ta'en,
    Would do harm to nigh it aught.
SATAN: And why *that* tree—that would I wit—
    Any more than all other by?
EVE: For our Lord God forbids us it,
    The fruit thereof, Adam nor I,
    To nigh it near;
    And if we did, we both should die,
    He said, and cease our solace sere.
SATAN: Yea, Eve, to me take tent;
    Take heed, and thou shalt hear
    What that the matter meant
    He moved on that manner.

To eat thereof he you defend,
I know it well; this was his skill,
Because he would none other kenned
These great virtues that long theretill.
For wilt thou see,
Who eats the fruit, of good and ill
Shall have knowing as well as he.

EVE: Why, what kin thing art thou
That tells this tale to me?

SATAN: A worm, that woteth well how
That ye may worshipped be.

EVE: What worship should we win thereby?
To eat thereof us needeth it nought;
We have lordship to make mastery
Of all thing that in earth is wrought.

SATAN: Woman, do way!
To greater state ye may be brought,
And ye will do as I shall say.

EVE: To do is us full loath
That should our God mispay.

SATAN: Nay, certes, it is no wothe:
Eat it safely ye may.
For peril right none therein lies,
But worship and a great winning;
For right as God ye shall be wise,
And peer to him in all kin thing:
Ay, gods shall ye be,
Of ill and good to have knowing,
For to be as wise as he.

EVE: Is this sooth that thou says?

SATAN: Yea, why trowest thou not me?
I would by no kins ways
Tell nought but truth to thee.

EVE: Then will I to thy teaching trust,
And fang this fruit unto our food.
(And then she must take the apple.)

SATAN: Bite on boldly, be not abashed,
   And bear Adam to amend his mood
   And eke his bliss. *(Then Satan retires.)*

Abraham and Isaac

Anonymous
Late 15th Century

Scene: Ancient Judea

Two Men

Abraham (50s) a faithful patriarch and Isaac (12–18) his beloved son.

*When God commands Abraham to sacrifice Isaac, the dutiful
believer has no choice but to obey. Here, he prepares to take his
son's life in the name of God.*

ISAAC: Iwis, father, I am sorry to grieve you.
    I cry you mercy of that I have done,
    And of all trespass that ever I did move you;
    Now, dear father, forgive me that I have done.
    God of heaven be with me!
ABRAHAM: Ah, dear child, leave off thy moans!
    In all thy life thou grieved me never once;
    Now blessed be thou, body and bones,
    That ever thou were bred and born!
    Thou hast been to me child full good.
    But iwis, child, though I mourn never so fast,
    Yet must I needs here at the last
    In this place shed all thy blood.
    Therefore, my dear son, here shall thou lie;
    (Lifts him on to the altar.)
    Unto my work I must me stead.
    Iwis I had as lief myself to die,
    If God will be pleased with my deed,
    And my own body for to offer.
ISAAC: Ah, mercy, father, mourn ye no more!
    Your weeping maketh my heart sore,
    As my own death that I shall suffer.
    Your kerch, fader, about my eyes ye wind.

ABRAHAM: So I shall, my sweetest child in earth.

ISAAC: Now yet, good father, have this in mind,
    And smite me not often with your sharp sword,
    But hastily that it be sped.
    (Here Abraham laid a cloth on Isaac's face, thus saying.)

ABRAHAM: Now farewell, my child, so full of grace.

ISAAC: Ah, father, father, turn downward my face,
    For of your sharp sword I am ever adread.

ABRAHAM: To do this deed I am full sorry,
    But, Lord, thy hest I will not withstand.

ISAAC: Ah, Father of heaven, to thee I cry:
    Lord, receive me into thy hand!

ABRAHAM: Lo, now is the time come, certain,
    That my sword in his neck shall bite.
    Ah, Lord, my heart riseth thereagain;
    I may not find it in my heart to smite;
    My heart will not now thereto.
    Yet fain I would work my Lord's will;
    But this young innocent lieth so still,
    I may not find it in my heart him to kill.
    Oh, Father of heaven, what shall I do?

ISAAC: Ah, mercy, father, why tarry ye so,
    And let me lie thus long on this heath?
    Now would I to God the stroke were do!
    Father, I pray you heartily, short me of my woe,
    And let me not look after my death.

ABRAHAM: Now, heart, why wouldest not thou break in three?
    Yet shall thou not make me to my God unmild.
    I will no longer let for thee,
    For that my God aggrieved would be;
    Now hold the stroke, my own dear child.

Bilora

Angelo Beolco, Translated by Babette and Glenn Hughes
1527

Scene: 16th Century rural Italy

Man and Woman

Bilora (20s–30s) a simple man in pursuit of his wife, Dina (20s) a young woman with lofty goals.

> *Dina has allowed herself to be stolen away by a wealthy older man. Here, she and her cuckolded husband bicker over her willingness to be abducted.*

DINA: *(From within.)* Who's knocking at the door? A beggar? Go in peace.

BILORA: I am a beggar all right, but you can't get rid of me that way. I'm a friend of yours. Open the door! It's me.

DINA: What friend? Who are you? Messire is not at home. Go in peace.

BILORA: Go on Dina, open the door for me. It's me, confound it! You didn't recognize me, did you, you silly!

DINA: *(Appearing at the window.)* I tell you to get away from here. I don't know you. Messire is not at home. If you don't want to cause trouble, go on about your business.

BILORA: Damnation but you're mean! Listen! Come here; I want to have a little confidential talk with you. No use making a fuss; it is really me. Come now, Dina. You can see I am Bilora. I am your good husband.

DINA: All the worse for me! Just think of that! But what have you come here for?

BILORA: Eh? What's that you say? Come down a minute so I can see you.

DINA: I'm coming.

BILORA: *(Alone, speaking to himself.)* Now watch! I may be able to snatch some trinkets off her hands, or pinch some small change. I think my luck is turning. And a moment ago I was in despair!

DINA: *(From behind the door.)* But...you won't hit me if I open the door?

BILORA: Why should you expect me to hit you? You didn't follow him here of your own free will. Come on outside. I give you my word that I'll gladly take you back as my helpmeet and my darling, as though nothing had happened.

DINA: *(Coming from the house.)* Hello. Now tell me, how did you find your way here, and how are you, anyway? Are you well?

BILORA: I'm all right. And how about yourself? You're looking well.

DINA: God help me, I don't feel any too well, to be honest with you. I'm about fed up, living with this old fellow.

BILORA: I believe it. Why, he can hardly get around. Besides, the young don't get on well with the old. You and I make a much better match.

DINA: By heaven, he's half sick. All night he tossed like a dying sheep. He never slept a wink, but spent every minute hugging and kissing me. And I suppose he thought I liked it. God knows I wish I never had to see him again!

BILORA: His breath stinks worse than a dungheap; you can smell his rotten carcass for a thousand miles; and he's as filthy in front as he is behind.

DINA: How excited you are! You're saying very nasty things.

BILORA: Come on now; tell me. Do you want to go home with me, or do you want me to go and leave you here with the old man?

DINA: For my own part I'd like to go back with you, but he doesn't want me to, and I'm sure he'd never allow it. If you could see the way he caresses me you would have a fit. Good heavens, how he loves me! And I certainly live well here.

BILORA: Just listen to you! "He doesn't want me to!" Damn it, you'd drive a person crazy. What if he doesn't want you to go? Can't you want to, yourself? You'll make me swear myself into hell! Come on, now; what do you say?

DINA: On my faith, I don't know. I'd like to, and yet...I wouldn't.

BILORA: Oh! If Fate isn't plaguing me to-night! Will it be long before he comes home? Do you think he'll come soon?

DINA: Pretty quick. He can never wait to get home. And I'd just as soon he didn't see us here talking together. Run along now, like a dear. Then after he gets here you can come back, and maybe you both can agree after all.

BILORA: We'll agree in the buttocks! And watch out for yourself if we don't agree. By the blood of Christ, if I get started I will do more damage than a soldier. I have a feeling that you're putting a trick over on me. But you oughtn't to go on living like this with another man. It's rotten. You're a filthy woman.

DINA: I wouldn't gain anything by going back to you! Now remember, he has a very quick temper. Listen! Honestly, I'm not joking. Go away for a while, and then, when he has got home, come and knock at the door and say you wish to talk with Messire. Tell him first thing that you want me to go back home with you. You can see what he says. If he consents, everything is all right; and if he refuses, I will go anyway.

BILORA: Honestly, will you go with me even if he objects?

DINA: I tell you, yes! I swear I will! Now go, so he won't find you here!

Lena

Ludovico Ariosto, Translated by Barbara Reynolds
1528

Scene: the town of Ferrara, Italy

Man and Woman

Fazio (40–50) a merchant and Lena (30s) his fiery mistress.

> *Lena is sick and tired of being miserly Fazio's kept woman and here tells him so in no uncertain terms.*

FAZIO: Good morning, Lena.

LENA: Good morning and much good luck to follow, Fazio.

FAZIO: You're up early, Lena! It looks bad…looks bad.

LENA: Yes, of course it would be much more fitting, since you clothe me so splendidly and maintain me in such lavish style, if I were to lie in bed until noon, and spend the whole day in idleness.

FAZIO: I do what I can Lena. It would take a bigger income than mine to set you up like that; but I do make a point of giving you all the help that lies within my means.

LENA: *What* help?

FAZIO: You're always like that—always forgetting what I do for you. You show gratitude only at the moment when I'm giving you something. As soon as you've got it, it's a very different story.

LENA: And what have you ever given me? Are you going to bring up the rent-free house again?

FAZIO: And is that so little in your eyes? It's worth twelve *lire* a year in actual money, without counting the convenience of having me for a neighbour. But I won't say too much about that, because I don't want to throw it in your face.

LENA: Throw *what* in my face? The odd plate of soup or broth which you send me sometimes, when you've got more than you need?

FAZIO: No, something else, Lena.

LENA: Or the gift of two or three loaves of bread a month? or a small bottle of sour wine? or letting me take a couple of sticks when a cart-load of firewood arrives for you?

FAZIO: That's not all you have!

LENA: What else do I have from you? Come on, tell me! Robes of satin? Gowns of velvet?

FAZIO: You wouldn't be allowed to wear them, and I wouldn't be able to give them to you.

LENA: Show me an ordinary dress that you ever gave me.

FAZIO: I prefer not to answer.

LENA: You do give me the odd pair of clumsy old shoes or slippers for Pacifico, when they're well down at heel and full of holes.

FAZIO: And I give you new shoes for yourself!

LENA: Yes, but I'm lucky if I get three pairs in four years. And what about the accomplishments your daughter is learning from me, and has been for years past? Aren't they worth anything?

FAZIO: They're worth a lot, I won't deny it.

LENA: And when I came here, she couldn't spell out the Our Father in her first reader, and she didn't know how to hold a needle.

FAZIO: That's true

LENA: And she couldn't handle a spindle. Now she can say the office, and sew and embroider as well as any girl in Ferrara. What's more, she can copy any stitch at sight, no matter how difficult it may be.

FAZIO: I admit all this. I don't want to be like you, denying my obligations. But I will say this: if you hadn't taught her, someone else would have done it, and only charged ten *giulii* a year. That's a lot less than the twelve *lire* you cost me!

LENA: And haven't I ever done anything else for you, to make up the difference? Why, devil take it, if you gave me twelve *lire* twelve times a year, it wouldn't make up for the disgrace you've brought upon me; for the neighbours say openly that I'm your whore. God curse you for a scabby old miser for putting me in a hovel like that! But I won't stay there any longer—you can give it to someone else.

FAZIO: Be careful what you say.

LENA: Go on, give it to someone else! I'm tired of having it rammed down my throat that I live in your house and don't pay you any rent. Even if I have to take a place in the Gambaro or the Paradiso, I'm moving out of here!

FAZIO: Think it over, and let me know what you decide.

LENA: I've thought it over. Give the place to whoever you like!

FAZIO: I'd rather sell it…that's what I'll do.

LENA: Do what you like with it! Sell it, give it away, set fire to it! I'll find somewhere else.

Friar Bacon and Friar Bungay

Robert Greene
1589

Scene: the study of Friar Bacon

Two Men

Friar Bacon (any age) a dabbler in the black arts and Miles (any age) his incompetent servant.

> *Friar Bacon has created a Brazen Head that will supposedly reveal cosmic truths and arcane knowledge to him. When the head actually speaks, Miles gets the message all mixed up.*

MILES: Master, master, up! Hell's broken loose; your head speaks; and there's such a thunder and lightning, that I warrant all Oxford is up in arms. Out of your bed, and take a brown-bill in your hand; the latter day is come.

BACON: Miles, I come. *(Rises and comes forward.)* O, passing warily watched! Bacon will make thee next himself in love.
When spake the head?

MILES: When spake the head! Did not you say that he should tell strange principles of philosophy? Why, sir, it speaks but two words at a time.

BACON: Why, villain, hath it spoken oft?

MILES: Oft! ay, marry, hath it, thrice; but in all those three times it hath uttered but seven words.

BACON: As how?

MILES: Marry, sir, the first time he said "Time is," as if Fabius Commentator should have pronounced a sentence; the second-time he said "Time was"; and the third time, with thunder and lightning, as in great choler, he said, "Time is past."

BACON: 'Tis past indeed. Ah, villain! time is past.
My life, my fame, my glory, all are past.
Bacon, the turrets of thy hope are ruined down,

Thy seven years' study lieth in the dust;
Thy Brazen Head lies broken through a slave
That watched, and would not when the head did will.
What said the head first?

MILES: Even, sir, "Time is."

BACON: Villain, if thou hadst called to Bacon then,
If thou hadst watched, and waked the sleepy friar,
The Brazen Head had uttered aphorisms,
And England had been circled round with brass;
But proud Asmenoth, ruler of the north,
And Demogorgon, master of the fates,
Grudge that a mortal man should work so much.
Hell trembled at my deep-commanding spells,
Fiends frowned to see a man their over-match;
Bacon might boast more than a man might boast.
But now the braves of Bacon have an end,
Europe's conceit of Bacon hath an end,
His seven years' practice sorteth to ill end:
And, villain, sith my glory hath an end,
I will appoint thee to some fatal end.
Villain, avoid! Get thee from Bacon's sight!
Vagrant, go roam and range about the world,
And perish as a vagabond on earth!

MILES: Why, then, sir, you forbid me your service?

BACON: My service, villain, with a fatal curse,
That direful plagues and mischief fall on thee.

MILES: 'Tis no matter, I am against you with the old proverb,—The
more the fox is cursed, the better he fares. God be with you, sir.
I'll take but a book in my hand, a wide-sleeved gown on my back,
and a crowned cap on my head, and see if I can want promotion.

BACON: Some fiend or ghost haunt on thy weary steps,
Until they do transport thee quick to hell;
For Bacon shall have never merry day,
To lose the fame and honor of his head.

The Jew of Malta

Christopher Marlowe
c. 1590

Scene: Malta

Two Men

Barabas (50s) a wealthy businessman and Ithamore (any age) his faithful slave.

Barabas has made a fortune selling his beautiful young daughter, Abigail to different suitors. When Ithamore informs him that Abigail has joined the convent and converted to Christianity, Barabas plots to kill all the nuns in the convent as an act of revenge.

ITHAMORE: Here 'tis, master.
BARABAS: Well said, Ithamore! What, hast thou brought
　　The ladle with thee too?
ITHAMORE: Yes, sir. The proverb says, he that eats with the devil had need of a long spoon; I have brought you a ladle.
BARABAS: Very well, Ithamore; then now be secret;
　　And for thy sake, whom I so dearly love,
　　Now shalt thou see the death of Abigail,
　　That thou mayst freely live to be my heir.
ITHAMORE: Why, master, will you poison her with a mess of rice-porridge that will preserve life, make her round and plump, and batten more than you are aware?
BARABAS: Ay, but Ithamore, seest thou this?
　　It is a precious powder that I bought
　　Of an Italian in Ancona once,
　　Whose operation is to bind, infect,
　　And poison deeply, yet not appear
　　In forty hours after it is ta'en.
ITHAMORE: How, master?

BARABAS: Thus, Ithamore:
  This even they use in Malta here,—'tis call'd
  Saint Jaques' Even, and then, I say, they use
  To send their alms unto the nunneries:
  Among the rest, bear this, and set it there:
  There's a dark entry where they take it in,
  Where they must neither see the messenger,
  Nor make inquiry who hath sent it them.
ITHAMORE: How so?
BARABAS: Belike there is some ceremony in't.
  There, Ithamore, must thou go place this pot:
  Stay, let me spice it first.
ITHAMORE: Pray, do, and let me help you, master.
  Pray, let me taste first.
BARABAS: Prithee, do.
  (Ithamore tastes.)
BARABAS: What say'st thou now?
ITHAMORE: Troth, master, I'm loath such a pot of pottage should be
  spoiled.
BARABAS: Peace, Ithamore! 'tis better so than spar'd. (Puts the powder
  into the pot.)
  Assure thyself thou shalt have broth by the eye.
  My purse, my coffer, and myself is thine.
ITHAMORE: Well, master, I go.
BARABAS: Stay, first let me stir it, Ithamore.
  As fatal be it to her as the draught
  Of which great Alexander drunk and died;
  And with her let it work like Borgia's wine,
  Whereof his sire the Pope was poisoned!
  In few, the blood of Hydra, Lerna's bane,
  The juice of hebon, and Cocytus' breath,
  And all the poisons of the Stygian pool,
  Break from the fiery kingdom, and in this
  Vomit your venom, and envenom her
  That, like a fiend, hath left her father thus!

ITHAMORE: *(Aside.)* What a blessing has he given't! Was ever pot of
   rice-porridge so sauced?—What shall I do with it?
BARABAS: O my sweet Ithamore, go set it down;
   And come again as soon as thou hast done,
   For I have other business for thee.
ITHAMORE: Here's a drench to poison a whole stable of
   Flanders mares: I'll carry't to the nuns with a powder.
BARABAS: And the horse-pestilence to boot. Away!
ITHAMORE: I am gone:
   Pay me my wages, for my work is done. *(Exit with the pot.)*
BARABAS: I'll pay thee with a vengeance, Ithamore! *(Exit.)*

Dido, Queen of Carthage

Christopher Marlowe
c. 1595

Scene: a cave during a terrible storm

Man and Woman

Dido (20s) a passionate young queen and Æneas (20s) the man she loves.

> *During a storm, Dido is forced to take refuge in a cave where she encounters Æneas, a man with whom she has secretly been in love for some time. Emboldened by the raging tempest, Dido here confesses her feelings.*

DIDO: Æneas!
ÆNEAS: Dido!
DIDO: Tell me, dear love, how found you out this cave?
ÆNEAS: By chance, sweet queen, as Mars and Venus met.
DIDO: Why, that was in a net, where we are loose;
    And yet I am not free,—O, would I were!
ÆNEAS: Why, what is it that Dido may desire
And not obtain, be it in human power?
DIDO: The thing that I will die before I ask,
    And yet desire to have before I die.
ÆNEAS: It is not aught Æneas may achieve?
DIDO: Æneas, no, although his eyes do pierce.
ÆNEAS: What, hath Iarbas anger'd her in aught?
    And will she be avenged on his life?
DIDO: Not anger'd me, except in angering thee.
ÆNEAS: Who, then, of all so cruel may he be
    That should detain thy eye in his defects?
DIDO: The man that I do eye where'er I am,
    Whose amorous face, like Paean, sparkles fire,
    Whenas he butts his beams on Flora's bed.

Prometheus hath put on Cupid's shape,
And I must perish in his burning arms.
Æneas, O Æneas, quench these flames!

ÆNEAS: What ails my queen? Is she faln sick of late?

DIDO: Not sick, my love; but sick I must conceal
The torment that it boots me not reveal.
And yet I'll speak,—and yet I'll hold my peace.
Do shame her worst, I will disclose my grief:
Æneas, thou art he—what did I say?
Something it was that now I have forgot.

ÆNEAS: What means fair Dido by this doubtful speech?

DIDO: Nay, nothing; but Æneas loves me not.

ÆNEAS: Æneas' thoughts dare not ascend so high
As Dido's heart, which monarchs might not scale.

DIDO: It was because I saw no king like thee,
Whose golden crown might balance my content;
But now that I have found what to affect,
I follow one that loveth fame 'fore me,
And rather had seem fair (in) Sirens' eyes,
Than to the Carthage queen that dies for him.

ÆNEAS: If that your majesty can look so low
As my despised worths that shun all praise,
With this my hand I give to you my heart,
And vow, by all the gods of hospitality,
By heaven and earth, and my fair brother's bow,
By Paphos, Capys, and the purple sea
From whence my radiant mother did descend,
And by this sword that sav'd me from the Greeks,
Never to leave these new-upreared walls,
Whiles Dido lives and rules in Juno's town,
Never to like or love any but her!

DIDO: What more than Delian music do I hear,
That calls my soul from forth his living seat
To move unto the measures of delight?
Kind clouds, that sent forth such a courteous storm
As made disdain to fly to fancy's lap!

Stout love, in mine arms make thy Italy,
Whose crown and kingdom rests at thy command:
Sichaeus, not Æneas, be thou call'd;
The king of Carthage, not Anchises' son:
Hold, take these jewels at thy lover's hand,
(Giving jewels, etc.)
These golden bracelets, and this wedding-ring,
Wherewith my husband woo'd me yet a maid,
And be thou king of Libya by my gift.
(Exeunt to the cave.)

Arden of Feversham
Anonymous
1592

Scene: rural England

Man and Woman

Alice (18–20) an unfaithful young wife and Mosbie (20s) her lover.

Here, the unscrupulous pair plot to murder Alice's devoted husband, Arden.

ALICE: Mosbie, my love!
MOSBIE: Away, I say, and talk not to me now.
ALICE: A word or two, sweet heart, and then I will.
    'Tis yet but early days, thou needst not fear.
MOSBIE: Where is your husband?
ALICE: 'Tis now high water, and he is at the quay.
MOSBIE: There let him be; henceforward know me not.
ALICE: Is this the end of all thy solemn oaths?
    Is this the fruit thy reconcilement buds?
    Have I for this given thee so many favours,
    Incurred my husband's hate, and, out alas!
    Made shipwreck of mine honour for thy sake?
    And dost thou say "henceforward know me not"?
    Remember, when I lock'd thee in my closet,
    What were thy words and mine; did we not both
    Decree to murder Arden in the night?
    The heavens can witness, and the world can tell,
    Before I saw that falsehood look of thine,
    'Fore I was tangled with thy 'ticing speech,
    Arden to me was dearer than my soul,—
    And shall be still: base peasant, get thee gone,
    And boast not of thy conquest over me,
    Gotten by witchcraft and mere sorcery!

For what hast thou to countenance my love,
Being descended of a noble house,
And matched already with a gentleman
Whose servant thou may'st be!—and so farewell.

MOSBIE: Ungentle and unkind Alice, now I see
That which I ever feared, and find too true:
A woman's love is as the lightning-flame,
Which even in bursting forth consumes itself.
To try thy constancy have I been strange;
Would I had never tried, but lived in hope!

ALICE: What need'st thou try me whom thou ne'er found false?

MOSBIE: Yet pardon me, for love is jealous.

ALICE: So lists the sailor to the mermaid's song,
So looks the traveller to the basilisk:
I am content for to be reconciled,
And that, I know, will be mine overthrow.

MOSBIE: Thine overthrow? first let the world dissolve.

ALICE: Nay, Mosbie, let me still enjoy thy love,
And happen what will, I am resolute.
My saving husband hoards up bags of gold
To make our children rich, and now is he
Gone to unload the goods that shall be thine,
And he and Franklin will to London straight.

MOSBIE: To London, Alice? if thou'lt be ruled by me,
We'll make him sure enough for coming there.

ALICE: Ah, would we could!

MOSBIE: I happened on a painter yesternight,
The only cunning man of Christendom;
For he can temper poison with his oil,
That whoso looks upon the work he draws
Shall, with the beams that issue from his sight,
Suck venom to his breast and slay himself.
Sweet Alice, he shall draw thy counterfeit,
That Arden may, by gazing on it, perish.

ALICE: Ay, but Mosbie, that is dangerous,
For thou, or I, or any other else,
Coming into the chamber where it hangs, may die.

MOSBIE: Ay, but we'll have it covered with a cloth
    And hung up in the study for himself.
ALICE: It may not be, for when the picture's drawn,
    Arden, I know, will come and show it me.
MOSBIE: Fear not; we'll have that shall serve the turn.
    (They cross the stage.)
MOSBIE: This is the painter's house; I'll call him forth.
ALICE: But, Mosbie, I'll have no such picture, I.
MOSBIE: I pray thee leave it to my discretion.

Doctor Faustus

Christopher Marlowe
c. 1592

Scene: the study of Dr. Faustus

Two Men

Mephistophilis (any age) a demon and Faustus (30s) a man obsessed with gaining power through the study of arcane arts.

> *Faustus has conjured demonic Mephistophilis in hopes of subjugating Satan's powerful underling to his will. Here, the demon explains his allegiance to the devil and the nature of his fall from grace.*

MEPHISTOPHILIS: Now, Faustus, what would'st thou have me do?
FAUSTUS: I charge thee wait upon me whilst I live,
　　To do whatever Faustus shall command,
　　Be it to make the moon drop from her sphere,
　　Or the ocean to overwhelm the world.
MEPHISTOPHILIS: I am a servant to great Lucifer,
　　And may not follow thee without his leave;
　　No more than he commands must we perform.
FAUSTUS: Did not he charge thee to appear to me?
MEPHISTOPHILIS: No, I came now hither of mine own accord.
FAUSTUS: Did not my conjuring raise thee? speak.
MEPHISTOPHILIS: That was the cause, but yet *per accidens,*
　　For, when we hear one rack the name of God,
　　Abjure the Scriptures and his Saviour Christ,
　　We fly, in hope to get his glorious soul;
　　Nor will we come, unless he use such means
　　Whereby he is in danger to be damn'd.
　　Therefore the shortest cut for conjuring
　　Is stoutly to abjure the Trinity,
　　And pray devoutly to the prince of hell.

FAUSTUS: So Faustus hath
  Already done; and holds this principle,
  There is no chief but only Belzebub;
  To whom Faustus doth dedicate himself.
  This word 'damnation' terrifies not me,
  For I confound hell in Elysium:
  My ghost be with the old philosophers!
  But, leaving these vain trifles of men's souls,
  Tell me what is that Lucifer thy lord?
MEPHISTOPHILIS: Arch-regent and commander of all spirits.
FAUSTUS: Was not that Lucifer an angel once?
MEPHISTOPHILIS: Yes, Faustus, and most dearly lov'd of God.
FAUSTUS: How comes it then that he is prince of devils?
MEPHISTOPHILIS: O, by aspiring pride and insolence;
  For which God threw him from the face of heaven.
FAUSTUS: And what are you that live with Lucifer?
MEPHISTOPHILIS: Unhappy spirits that fell with Lucifer,
  Conspir'd against our God with Lucifer,
  And are for ever damn'd with Lucifer.
FAUSTUS: Where are you damn'd?
MEPHISTOPHILIS: In hell.
FAUSTUS: How comes it then that thou art out of hell?
MEPHISTOPHILIS: Why this is hell, nor am I out of it:
  Think'st thou that I, that saw the face of God,
  And tasted the eternal joys of Heaven,
  Am not tormented with ten thousand hells,
  In being depriv'd of everlasting bliss?
  O, Faustus, leave these frivolous demands,
  Which strikes a terror to my fainting soul!
FAUSTUS: What, is great Mephistophilis so passionate
  For being deprived of the joys of heaven?
  Learn thou of Faustus manly fortitude,
  And scorn those joys thou never shalt possess.
  Go bear these tidings to great Lucifer:
  Seeing Faustus hath incurr'd eternal death
  By desperate thoughts against Jove's deity,

Say, he surrenders up to him his soul,
So he will spare him four-and-twenty years,
Letting him live in all voluptuousness;
Having thee ever to attend on me,
To give me whatsoever I shall ask,
To tell me whatsoever I demand,
To slay mine enemies, and to aid my friends,
And always be obedient to my will.
Go, and return to mighty Lucifer,
And meet me in my study at midnight,
And then resolve me of thy master's mind.
MEPHISTOPHILIS: I will, Faustus.

Every Man In His Humour

Ben Jonson
1598

Scene: London

Two Men

Brainworm (30–50) a servant and Stephen (20s) a country fool.

Following a quarrel with a servant, rash Stephen searches for his escaped opponent but is here waylaid by Brainworm.

STEPHEN: O, Brainworm, didst thou not see a fellow here in a what-sha-call-him doublet? he brought mine uncle a letter e'en now.

BRAINWORM: Yes, Master Stephen, what of him?

STEPHEN: O, I ha' such a mind to beat him. Where is he, canst thou tell?

BRAINWORM: Faith, he is not of that mind: he is gone, Master Stephen.

STEPHEN: Gone! which way? When went he? How long since?

BRAINWORM: He is rid hence; he took horse at the street-door.

STEPHEN: And I staid i' the fields! Whoreson Scanderbag rogue! Oh that I had but a horse to fetch him back again!

BRAINWORM: Why, you may ha' my master's gelding, to save your long-ing, sir.

STEPHEN: But I ha' no boots, that's the spite on't.

BRAINWORM: Why, a fine wisp of hay, rolled hard, Master Stephen.

STEPHEN: No faith, it's no boot to follow him now. Let him e'en go and hang. 'Pray thee, help to truss me a little. He does so vex me—

BRAINWORM: You'll be worse vexed when you are trussed, Master Stephen. Best keep unbraced and walk yourself till you be cold; your choler may founder you else.

STEPHEN: By my faith, and so I will, now thou tell'st me on't. How dost thou like my leg, Brainworm?

BRAINWORM: A very good leg, Master Stephen! But the woolen stock-ing does not commend it so well.

STEPHEN: Foh! the stockings be good enough, now summer is coming on, for the dust. I'll ha' a pair of silk again winter, that I go to dwell i' the town. I think my leg would show in a silk hose.

BRAINWORM: Believe me, Master Stephen, rarely well.

STEPHEN: In sadness, I think it would. I have a reasonable good leg.

BRAINWORM: You have an excellent good leg, Master Stephen, but I cannot stay to praise it longer now, and I am very sorry for't.

PART THREE:

THE GLORIOUS 17TH CENTURY

The Shoemaker's Holiday

Tomas Dekker
1600

Scene: a garden

Two Women

Rose (18–20) a young woman in love and Sybil (20–30) a servant of
the household.

When Sybil returns from London, Rose summons her to the gar-
den to deliver a report on the young man with whom she is in
love.

SYBIL: Good morrow, young mistress. I am sure you make that garland
for me; against I shall be Lady of the Harvest.

ROSE: Sybil, what news at London?

SYBIL: None but good; my lord mayor, your father, and Master Philpot,
your uncle, and Master Scott, your cousin, and Mistress
Frigbottom by Doctors' Commons, do all, by my troth, send you
most hearty commendations.

ROSE: Did Lacy send kind greetings to his love?

SYBIL: O yes, out of cry, by my troth. I scant knew him; here 'a wore a
scarf; and here a scarf, here a bunch of feathers, and here precious stones and jewels, and a pair of garters,—O, monstrous!
like one of our yellow silk curtains at home here in Old Ford
house, here in Master Bellymount's chamber. I stood at our door
in Cornhill, looked at him, he at me indeed, spake to him, but he
not to me, not a word; marry go-up, thought I, with a wanion!
He passed by me as proud—Marry foh! are you grown humor-
ous, thought I; and so shut the door, and in I came.

ROSE: O Sybil, how dost thou my Lacy wrong!
My Rowland is as gentle as a lamb,
No dove was ever half so mild as he.

SYBIL: Mild? yea, as a bushel of stamped crabs.

He looked upon me as sour as verjuice. Go thy ways, thought I; thou may'st be much in my gaskins, but nothing in my nether-stocks. This is your fault, mistress, to love him that loves not you; he thinks scorn to do as he's done to; but if I were as you, I'd cry: Go by, Jeronimo, go by!

I'd set mine old debts against my new driblets,
And the hare's foot against the goose giblets,
For if ever I sigh, when sleep I should take,
Pray God I may lose my maidenhead when I wake.

ROSE: Will my love leave me then, and go to France?

SYBIL: I know not that, but I am sure I see him stalk before the soldiers. By my troth, he is a proper man; but he is proper that proper doth. Let him go snick-up, young mistress.

ROSE: Get thee to London, and learn perfectly,
Whether my Lacy go to France, or no.
Do this, and I will give thee for thy pains
My cambric apron and my Romish gloves,
My purple stockings and a stomacher.
Say, wilt thou do this, Sybil, for my sake?

SYBIL: Will I, quotha? At whose suit? By my troth, yes I'll go. A cambric apron, gloves, a pair of purple stockings, and a stomacher! I'll sweat in purple, mistress, for you; I'll take anything that comes a God's name. O rich! a cambric apron! Faith, then have at 'up tails all'. I'll go jiggy-joggy to London, and be here in a trice, young mistress.

ROSE: Do so, good Sybil. Meantime wretched I
Will sit and sigh for his lost company,

A Woman Killed With Kindness

Thomas Heywood
1603

Scene: Yorkshire

Man and Woman

Sir Charles (20s) a desperate man and Susan (18-20) his unfortunate
    sister.

> *Sir Charles owes a debt of 500 pounds to Sir Francis Acton for*
> *bailing him out of prison. Here, he approaches his sister with a*
> *vile plan to repay his benefactor.*

SUSAN: Brother, why have you tricked me like a bride?
    Bought me this gay attire, these ornaments?
    Forget you our estate, our poverty?
SIR CHARLES: Call me not brother, but imagine me
    Some barbarous outlaw or uncivil kern,
    For if thou shut'st thy eye and only hear'st
    The words that I shall utter, thou shalt judge me
    Some staring ruffian, not thy brother Charles.
    O Susan!
SUSAN: O brother, what doth this strange language mean?
SIR CHARLES: Dost love me, sister? Wouldst thou see me live
    A bankrupt beggar in the world's disgrace
    And die indebted to my enemies?
    Wouldst thou behold me stand like a huge beam
    In the world's eye, a byword and a scorn?
    It lies in thee of these to acquit me free,
    And all my debt I may outstrip by thee.
SUSAN: By me? Why I have nothing, nothing left;
    I owe even for the clothes upon my back;
    I am not worth—
SIR CHARLES: O sister, say not so.

It lies in you my downcast state to raise,
To make me stand on even points with the world.
Come, sister, you are rich! Indeed you are,
And in your power you have without delay
Acton's five hundred pound back to repay.

SUSAN: Till now I had thought you loved me. By mine honour—
Which I had kept as spotless as the moon—
I ne'er was mistress of that single doit
Which I reserved not to supply your wants.
And do you think that I would hoard from you?
Now by my hopes in Heaven, knew I the means
To buy you from the slavery of your debts,
Especially from Acton, whom I hate,
I would redeem it with my life or blood.

SIR CHARLES: I challenge it, and kindred set apart,
Thus ruffian-like I lay siege to your heart.
What do I owe to Acton?

SUSAN: Why, some five hundred pounds, toward which I swear
In all the world I have not one denier.

SIR CHARLES: It will not prove so. Sister, now resolve me:
What do you think—and speak your conscience—
Would Acton give might he enjoy your bed?

SUSAN: He would not shrink to spend a thousand pound
To give the Mountfords' name so deep a wound.

SIR CHARLES: A thousand pound! I but five hundred owe;
Grant him your bed, he's paid with interest so.

SUSAN: O brother!

SIR CHARLES: O sister! Only this one way,
With that rich jewel you my debts may pay.
In speaking this my cold heart shakes with shame,
Nor do I woo you in a brother's name,
But in a stranger's. Shall I die in debt
To Acton, my grand foe, and you still wear
The precious jewel that he holds so dear?

SUSAN: My honour I esteem as dear and precious
As my redemption.

SIR CHARLES: I esteem you, sister,
   As dear for so dear prizing it.
SUSAN: Will Charles
   Have me cut off my hands and send them Acton?
   Rip up my breast, and with my bleeding heart
   Present him as a token?
SIR CHARLES: Neither, sister,
   But hear me in my strange assertion.
   Thy honour and my soul are equal in my regard,
   Nor will thy brother Charles survive thy shame.
   His kindness like a burden hath surcharged me,
   And under his good deeds I stooping go,
   Not with an upright soul. Had I remained
   In prison still, there doubtless I had died;
   Then unto him that freed me from that prison
   Still do I owe that life. What moved my foe
   To enfranchise me? 'Twas, sister, for your love!
   With full five hundred pounds he bought your love,
   And shall he not enjoy it? Shall the weight
   Of all this heavy burden lean on me,
   And will not you bear part? You did partake
   The joy of my release; will you not stand
   In joint-bond bound to satisfy the debt?
   Shall I be only charged?
SUSAN: But that I know
   These arguments come from an honoured mind,
   As in your most extremity of need
   Scorning to stand in debt to one you hate—
   Nay, rather would engage your unstained honour
   Than to be held ingrate—I should condemn you.
   I see your resolution and assent;
   So Charles will have me, and I am content.
SIR CHARLES: For this I tricked you up.
SUSAN: But here's a knife
   To save mine honour shall slice out my life.

The Malcontent

John Marston
1604

Scene: Genoa, the court of Duke Pietro Jacomo

Two Men

Pietro Jacomo (30–40) Duke of Genoa and Malevole (30s) the former
duke, masquerading as an interfering buffoon.

Here, Malevole exposes treachery in the Duke's court.

MALEVOLE: Duke, thou art a becco, a cornuto.
PIETRO: How?
MALEVOLE: Thou art a cuckold.
PIETRO: Speak; unshale him quick.
MALEVOLE: With most tumbler-like nimbleness.
PIETRO: Who?—by whom? I burst with desire.
MALEVOLE: Mendoza is the man makes thee a horn'd beast; Duke, 'tis
    Mendoza cornutes thee.
PIETRO: What conformance?—relate! short, short!
MALEVOLE: As a lawyer's beard.
    There is an old crone in the court, her name is Maquerelle,
    She is my mistress, sooth to say, and she doth ever tell me.
    Blurt a rhyme, blurt a rhyme; Maquerelle is a cunning bawd, I am
    an honest villain, thy wife is a close drab, and thou art a notori-
    ous cuckold, farewell, Duke.
PIETRO: Stay, stay.
MALEVOLE: Dull, dull Duke, can lazy patience make lame revenge? O
    God, for a woman to make a man that which God never created,
    never made!
PIETRO: What did God never make?
MALEVOLE: A cuckold: to be made a thing that's hudwinkt with kind-
    ness whilst every rascal philips his brows; to have a coxcomb, with
    egregious horns, pinn'd to a Lord's back, every page sporting

himself with delightful laughter, whilst he must be the last man know it. Pistols and poniards, pistols and poniards.

PIETRO: Death and damnation!

MALEVOLE: Lightning and thunder!

PIETRO: Vengeance and torture!

MALEVOLE: Catzo!

PIETRO: O revenge!

MALEVOLE: Nay, to select among ten thousand fairs
A lady far inferior to the most,
In fair proportion both of limb and soul:
To take her from austerer check of parents,
To make her his by most devoutful rites,
Make her commandress of a better essence
Than is the gorgeous world, even of a man:
To hug her with as rais'd an appetite,
As usurers do their delv'd up treasury,
(Thinking none tells it but his private self,)
To meet her spirit in a nimble kiss,
Distilling panting ardour to her heart:
True to her sheets, nay, diets strong his blood,
To give her height of Hymeneal sweets—

PIETRO: O God!

MALEVOLE: Whilst she lisps, & gives him some court *quelquechose*,
Made only to provoke, not satiate:
And yet even then, the thaw of her delight
Flows from lewd heat of apprehension,
Only from strange imagination's rankness,
That forms the adulterer's presence in her soul,
And makes her think she clips the foul knave's loins.

PIETRO: Affliction to my blood's root!

MALEVOLE: Nay think, but think what may proceed of this,
Adultery is often the mother of incest.

PIETRO: Incest!

MALEVOLE: Yes, incest: mark, Mendoza of his wife begets perchance a daughter: Mendoza dies. His son marries this daughter. Say you?

Nay, 'tis frequent, not only probable, but no question often acted, whilst ignorance, fearless ignorance clasps his own seed.

PIETRO: Hideous imagination!

MALEVOLE: Adultery? why, next to the sin of simony, 'tis the most horrid transgression under the cope of salvation!

PIETRO: Next to simony?

MALEVOLE: Ay, next to simony, in which our men in next age shall not sin.

PIETRO: Not sin? Why?

MALEVOLE: Because (thanks to some church-men) our age will leave them nothing to sin with. But adultery—O dulness!—should show exemplary punishment, that intemperate bloods may freeze, but to think it. I would dam him and all his generation, my own hands should do it: ha, I would not trust heaven with my vengeance any thing.

PIETRO: Any thing, any thing, Malevole, thou shalt see instantly what temper my spirit holds; farewell, remember I forget thee not, farewell.

The Insatiate Countess

William Barksted and Lewis Machin from a draft by John Marston
1610

Scene: the court of the Countess of Swevia, Italy

Two Women

Abigail (20s) and Thais (20s) two best friends with a big problem.

*Abigail and Thais have been best friends since they were children
but have married two men involved in a serious feud. Here, they
decide that their friendship is more important than their husbands' quarrel.*

ABIGAIL: Well, Thais, O you're a cunning carver. We two that any time
these fourteen years have called sisters, brought and bred up
together; that have told one another all our wanton dreams,
talked all night long of young men, and spent many an idle hour;
fasted upon the stones on Saint Agnes' night together, practised
all the petulant amorousnesses that delights young maids; yet
have you concealed not only the marriage but the man. And well
you might deceive me, for I'll be sworn you never dreamed of
him, and it stands against all reason you should enjoy him you
never dreamed of.

THAIS: Is not all this the same in you? Did you ever manifest your
sweetheart's nose, that I might nose him by 't? Commended his
calf, or his nether lip?—apparent signs that you were in love or
wisely covered it. Have you ever said, 'Such-a-man goes upright'
or 'has a better gait than any of the rest'; as indeed, since he is
proved magnifico, I thought thou wouldst have put it into my
hands whate'er 't had been.

ABIGAIL: Well, wench, we have cross fates: our husbands such inveter-
ate foes, and we such entire friends. But the best is, we are neighbours, and our back-arbours may afford visitation freely. Prithee

let us maintain our familiarity still, whatsoever thy husband do unto thee, as I am afraid he will cross it i' the nick.

THAIS: Faith, you little one, if I please him in one thing, he shall please me in all, that's certain. Who shall I have to keep my counsel if I miss thee? Who shall teach me to use the bridle when the reins are in mine own hand? What to long for, when to take physic, where to be melancholy? Why, we two are one another's grounds, without which would be no music.

ABIGAIL: Well said, wench, and the prick-song we use shall be our husbands'.

THAIS: I will long for swine's flesh o' th' first child.

ABIGAIL: Wilt 'ou, little Jew? And I to kiss thy husband upon the least belly-ache. This will mad 'em.

THAIS: I kiss thee, wench for that, and with it confirm our friendship.

The Maid's Tragedy
Francis Beaumont and John Fletcher
1611

Scene: the court of the king of Rhodes

Man and Woman

Evadne (20s) a woman wronged and Melantius (20s) her wrathful
brother.

*Melantius has long suspected that his sister's honor has been
compromised. Here, he confronts her with his suspicions and is
shocked to learn that the man who has used her so poorly is the
king himself.*

MELANTIUS: Up, and begin your story.
EVADNE: O, I am miserable.
MELANTIUS: 'Tis true, thou art; speak truth still.
EVADNE: I have offended; noble sir, forgive me.
MELANTIUS: With what secure slave?
EVADNE: Do not ask me, sir;
    Mine own remembrance is a misery
    Too mighty for me.
MELANTIUS: Do not fall back again;
    My sword's unsheathed yet.
EVADNE: What shall I do?
MELANTIUS: Be true, and make your fault less.
EVADNE: I dare not tell.
MELANTIUS: Tell, or I'll be this day a-killing thee.
EVADNE: Will you forgive me then?
MELANTIUS: Stay, I must ask mine honour first.
    I have too much foolish nature in me.
    (He sheathes his sword) Speak.
EVADNE: Is there none else here?
MELANTIUS: None but a fearful conscience; that's too many.
    Who is't?

EVADNE: O hear me gently: it was the King.

MELANTIUS: No more. My worthy father's and my services
    Are liberally rewarded. King, I thank thee:
    For all my dangers and my wounds, thou hast paid me
    In my own metal. These are soldier's thanks.
    How long have you lived thus, Evadne?

EVADNE: Too long. Too late I find it.

MELANTIUS: Can you be sorry?

EVADNE: Would I were half as blameless.

MELANTIUS: Evadne,
    Thou wilt to thy trade again.

EVADNE: First to my grave.

MELANTIUS: Would gods thou hadst been so blessed.
    Dost thou not hate this king now? Prithee hate him.
    He's sunk thy fair soul. I command thee curse him,
    Curse till the gods hear and deliver him
    To thy just wishes. Yet I fear, Evadne,
    You had rather play your game out.

EVADNE: No, I feel
    Too many sad confusions here to let in
    Any loose flame hereafter.

MELANTIUS: Dost thou not feel amongst all those one brave anger
    That breaks out nobly, and directs thine arm
    To kill this base king?

EVADNE: All the gods forbid it!

MELANTIUS: No, all the gods require it:
    They are dishonoured in him.

EVADNE: 'Tis too fearful.

MELANTIUS: You're valiant in his bed, and bold enough
    To be a stale whore, and have your madam's name
    Discourse for grooms and pages, and hereafter,
    When his cool majesty hath laid you by,
    To be at pension with some needy sir
    For meat and coarser clothes; thus far you knew no fear.
    Come, you shall kill him.

EVADNE: Good sir!

MELANTIUS: An 'twere to kiss him dead, thou'd'st smother him.
　　Be wise and kill him. Canst thou live and know
　　What noble minds shall make thee see thyself,
　　Found out with every finger, made the shame
　　Of all successions, and in this great ruin
　　Thy brother and thy noble husband broken?
　　Thou shalt not live thus. Kneel and swear to help me
　　When I shall call thee to it; or, by all
　　Holy in heaven and earth, thou shalt not live
　　To breathe a full hour longer, not a thought.
　　Come, 'tis a righteous oath. Give me thy hand,
　　And, both to heaven held up, swear by that wealth
　　This lustful thief stole from thee, when I say it,
　　To let his foul soul out.
EVADNE: Here I swear it,
　　And all you spirits of abusèd ladies,
　　Help me in this performance.
MELANTIUS: Enough. This must be known to none
　　But you and I, Evadne; not to your lord,
　　Though he be wise and noble, and a fellow
　　Dare step as far into a worthy action
　　As the most daring, ay, as far as justice.
　　Ask me not why. Farewell.

A Chaste Maid In Cheapside

Thomas Middleton
1613

Scene: London

Two Men

Yellowhammer (40–50) a man scheming to wed his daughter to a wealthy knight and Allwit (20–30) a man seeking revenge upon the same knight.

Here, the wronged Allwit presents himself to Yellowhammer masquerading as a distant cousin and surreptitiously reveals that the knight the older man's daughter is about to marry already has a wife.

YELLOWHAMMER: You're welcome sir, the more for your name's sake.
Good Master Yellowhammer, I love my name well,
And which o'the Yellowhammers take you descent from,
If I may be so bold with you, which, I pray?
ALLWIT: The Yellowhammers in Oxfordshire,
Near Abbington.
YELLOWHAMMER: And those are the best Yellowhammers, and truest bred: I came from thence myself, though now a citizen: I'll be bold with you: you are most welcome.
ALLWIT: I hope the zeal I bring with me shall deserve it.
YELLOWHAMMER: I hope no less; what is your will sir?
ALLWIT: I understand by rumours, you have a daughter,
Which my bold love shall henceforth title cousin.
YELLOWHAMMER: I thank you for her sir.
ALLWIT: I heard of her virtues, and other confirmed graces.
YELLOWHAMMER: A plaguy girl sir.
ALLWIT: Fame sets her out with richer ornaments
Than you are pleased to boast of; 'tis done modestly;
I hear she's towards marriage.

YELLOWHAMMER: You hear truth sir.

ALLWIT: And with a knight in town, Sir Walter Whorehound.

YELLOWHAMMER: The very same sir.

ALLWIT: I am the sorrier for't.

YELLOWHAMMER: The sorrier Why cousin?

ALLWIT: 'Tis not too far past is't? It may be yet recalled?

YELLOWHAMMER: Recalled, why good sir?

ALLWIT: Resolve me in that point, ye shall hear from me.

YELLOWHAMMER: There's no contract passed.

ALLWIT: I am very joyful sir.

YELLOWHAMMER: But he's the man must bed her.

ALLWIT: By no means coz, she's quite undone then,
    And you'll curse the time that e'er you made the match;
    He's an arrant whoremaster, consumes his time and state,
    —whom in my knowledge he hath kept this seven years,
    Nay coz, another man's wife too.

YELLOWHAMMER: O abominable!

ALLWIT: Maintains the whole house, apparels the husband,
    Pays servants' wages, not so much, but—

YELLOWHAMMER: Worse and worse, and doth the husband know this?

ALLWIT: Knows? Ay and glad he may too, 'tis his living;
    As other trades thrive, butchers by selling flesh,
    Poulters by venting conies, or the like coz.

YELLOWHAMMER: What an incomparable wittol's this?

ALLWIT: Tush, what cares he for that?
    Believe me coz, no more than I do.

YELLOWHAMMER: What a base slave is that?

ALLWIT: All's one to him; he feeds and takes his ease,
    Was ne'er the man that ever broke his sleep
    To get a child yet by his own confession,
    And yet his wife has seven.

YELLOWHAMMER: What, by Sir Walter?

ALLWIT: Sir Walter's like to keep 'em, and maintain 'em,
    In excellent fashion, he dares do no less sir.

YELLOWHAMMER: Life has he children too?

ALLWIT: Children? Boys thus high,
    In their Cato and Cordelius.

YELLOWHAMMER: What, you jest sir!

ALLWIT: Why, one can make a verse,
     And is now at Eton College.

YELLOWHAMMER: O this news has cut into my heart coz.

ALLWIT: It had eaten nearer if it had not been prevented.
     One Allwit's wife.

YELLOWHAMMER: Allwit? Foot I have heard of him,
     He had a girl kursened lately?

ALLWIT: Ay, that work did cost the knight above a hundred mark.

YELLOWHAMMER: I'll mark him for a knave and villain for't,
     A thousand thanks and blessings, I have done with him.

ALLWIT: *(Aside.)* Ha, ha, ha, this knight will stick by my ribs still,
     I shall not lose him yet, no wife will come,
     Where'er he woos, I find him still at home, ha, ha! *(Exit.)*

The Tragedy of Valentinian

John Fletcher
1614

Scene: the Imperial Court of Valentinian

Two Women

Claudia (any age) and Marcellina (any age) ladies in waiting to a
chaste Roman lady.

*Here, two servants gossip and speculate about recent visitors to
their mistress.*

CLAUDIA: Sirrah, what ails my lady, that of late
    She never cares for company?
MARCELLINA: I know not,
    Unless it be that company causes cuckolds.
CLAUDIA: That were a childish fear.
MARCELLINA: What were those ladies
    Came to her lately? From the court?
CLAUDIA: The same, wench,
    Some grave instructors, on my life. They look
    For all the world like old hatched hilts.
MARCELLINA: 'Tis true, wench,
    For here and there (And yet they painted well too)
    One might discover, where the gold was worn,
    Their iron ages.
CLAUDIA: If my judgement fail not,
    They have been sheathed like rotten ships.
MARCELLINA: It may be.
CLAUDIA: For if ye mark their rudders, they hang weakly.
MARCELLINA: They have passed the line, belike. Wouldst live, Claudia,
    Till thou wert such as they are?
CLAUDIA: Chimney-pieces.
    Now heaven have mercy on me, and young men,

I had rather make a drollery till thirty,
While I were able to endure a tempest,
And bear my fights out bravely, till my tackle
Whistled i' th' wind, and held against all weathers,
While I were able to bear with my tires,
And so discharge 'em; I would willingly
Live, Marcellina, not till barnacles
Bred in my sides

MARCELLINA: Thou art i' th' right, wench.
For who would live (whom pleasures had forsaken),
To stand at mark and cry, 'A bow, short, signor'?
Were there not men came hither too?

CLAUDIA: Brave fellows.
I fear me, bawds of five i' th' pound.

MARCELLINA: How know you?

CLAUDIA: They gave me great lights to it.

MARCELLINA: Take heed, Claudia.

CLAUDIA: Let them take heed, the spring comes on.

MARCELLINA: To me, now,
They seemed as noble visitants.

CLAUDIA: To me, now,
Nothing less, Marcellina, for I mark 'em,
(And by this honest light, for yet 'tis morning),
Saving the reverence of their gilded doublets
And Milan skins.

MARCELLINA: Thou art a strange wench, Claudia.

CLAUDIA: Ye are deceived, they showed to me directly
Court crabs that creep a side way for their living.

The Duchess of Malfi

John Webster
1623

Scene: the court of Malfi

Man and Woman

The Duchess (20–30) a woman prepared to defy all for love and
  Antonio (30s) her steward and future husband.

*An attractive young widow, the Duchess has fallen in love with
Antonio, her faithful steward. Here, she finally declares her feelings.*

DUCHESS: What do you think of marriage?
ANTONIO: I take 't, as those that deny purgatory:
    It locally contains or heaven or hell;
    There's no third place in 't.
DUCHESS: How do you affect it?
ANTONIO: My banishment, feeding my melancholy,
    Would often reason thus:—
DUCHESS: Pray, let's hear it.
ANTONIO: Say a man never marry, nor have children,
    What takes that from him? Only the bare name
    Of being a father, or the weak delight
    To see the little wanton ride-a-cock-horse
    Upon a painted stick, or hear him chatter
    Like a taught starling.
DUCHESS: Fie, fie, what's all this?
    One of your eyes is blood-shot; use my ring to 't.
    They say 't is very sovereign. 'T was my wedding-ring,
    And I did vow never to part with it
    But to my second husband.
ANTONIO: You have parted with it now.
DUCHESS: Yes, to help your eye-sight.

ANTONIO: You have made me stark blind.

DUCHESS: How?

ANTONIO: There is a saucy and ambitious devil
    Is dancing in this circle.

DUCHESS: Remove him.

ANTONIO: How?

DUCHESS: There needs small conjuration, when your finger
    May do it: thus. Is it fit?
    (She puts the ring upon his finger; he kneels.)

ANTONIO: What said you?

DUCHESS: Sir,
    This goodly roof of yours is too low built;
    I cannot stand upright in 't nor discourse,
    Without I raise it higher. Raise yourself;
    Or, if you please my hand to help you: so! *(Raises him.)*

ANTONIO: Ambition, madam, is a great man's madness.
    That is not kept in chains and close-pent rooms,
    But in fair lightsome lodgings, and is girt
    With the wild noise of prattling visitants,
    Which makes it lunatic beyond all cure.
    Conceive not I am so stupid but I aim,
    Whereto your favours tend: but he's a fool
    That, being a-cold, would thrust his hands i' th' fire
    To warm them.

DUCHESS: So, now the ground's broke,
    You may discover what a wealthy mine
    I make you lord of.

ANTONIO: O my unworthiness!

DUCHESS: You were ill to sell yourself:
    This dark'ning of your worth is not like that
    Which tradesmen use i' th' city; their false lights
    Are to rid bad wares off: and I must tell you,
    If you will know where breathes a complete man
    (I speak it without flattery), turn your eyes,
    And progress through yourself.

ANTONIO: Were there nor heaven nor hell,

I should be honest: I have long serv'd virtue,
And never ta'en wages of her.
DUCHESS: Now she pays it.
The misery of us that are born great!
We are forc'd to woo, because none dare woo us;
And as a tyrant doubles with his words
And fearfully equivocates, so we
Are forc'd to express our violent passions
In riddles and in dreams, and leave the path
Of simple virtue, which was never made
To seem the thing it is not. Go, go brag
You have left me heartless; mine is in your bosom:
I hope 't will multiply love there. You do tremble:
Make not your heart so dead a piece of flesh,
To fear more than to love me. Sir, be confident:
What is 't distracts you? This is flesh and blood, sir;
'T is not the figure cut in alabaster
Kneels at my husband's tomb. Awake, awake, man!
I do here put off all vain ceremony,
And only do appear to you a young widow
That claims you for her husband, and, like a widow,
I use but half a blush in 't.
ANTONIO: Truth speak for me:
I will remain the constant sanctuary
Of your good name.

Women Beware Women
Thomas Middleton
1623

Scene: the Ducal palace in Florence

Man and Woman

Leantio (18–25) a man betrayed by his young wife, Bianca (16).

> *Leantio leaves his new bride, Bianca, at home with his scheming
> mother while he travels the land as a factor. In his absence, his
> mother takes lovely Bianca to the palace of the Duke, knowing of
> his legendary lechery. Indeed the duke becomes smitten with
> Bianca and takes her for his own. Here, the cuckolded husband
> pays a visit to his now-haughty wife.*

BIANCA: How now! What silkworm's this, i'th'name of pride?
    What, is it he?
LEANTIO: A bow i'th'ham to your greatness;
You must have now three legs, I take it, must you not?
BIANCA: Then I must take another, I shall want else
    The service I should have; you have but two there.
LEANTIO: Y'are richly plac'd.
BIANCA: Methinks y'are wondrous brave, sir.
LEANTIO: A sumptuous lodging.
BIANCA: Y'ave an excellent suit there.
LEANTIO: A chair of velvet.
BIANCA: Is your cloak lin'd through, sir?
LEANTIO: Y'are very stately here.
BIANCA: 'Faith, something proud, sir.
LEANTIO: Stay, stay, let's see your cloth-of-silver slippers.
BIANCA: Who's your shoemaker? h'as made you a neat boot.
LEANTIO: Will you have a pair?
    The Duke will lend you spurs.
BIANCA: Yes, when I ride.

LEANTIO: 'Tis a brave life you lead.

BIANCA: I could nev'r see you
    In such good clothes in my time.

LEANTIO: In your time?

BIANCA: Sure I think, sir,
    We both thrive best asunder.

LEANTIO: Y'are a whore.

BIANCA: Fear nothing, sir.

LEANTIO: An impudent spiteful strumpet.

BIANCA: Oh sir, you give me thanks for your captainship;
    I thought you had forgot all your good manners.

LEANTIO: And to spite thee as much, look there, there read, *(Gives letter.)*
    Vex, gnaw, thou shalt find there I am not love-starv'd.
    The world was never yet so cold, or pitiless,
    But there was ever still more charity found out
    Than at one proud fool's door; and 'twere hard, 'faith,
    If I could not pass that. Read to thy shame there;
    A cheerful and a beauteous benefactor too,
    As ev'r erected the good works of love.

BIANCA: *(Aside.)* Lady Livia!
    Is't possible? Her worship was my pandress.
    She dote, and send and give, and all to him!
    Why, here's a bawd plagu'd home.—Y'are simply happy, sir,
    Yet I'll not envy you.

LEANTIO: No, court-saint, not thou!
    You keep some friend of a new fashion;
    There's no harm in your devil, he's a suckling,
    But he will breed teeth shortly, will he not?

BIANCA: Take heed you play not then too long with him.

LEANTIO: Yes, and the great one too: I shall find time
    To play a hot religious bout with some of you,
    And perhaps drive you and your course of sins
    To their eternal kennels; I speak softly now,
    'Tis manners in a noble woman's lodgings,
    And I well know all my degrees of duty.
    But come I to your everlasting parting once,
    Thunder shall seem soft music to that tempest.

BIANCA: 'Twas said last week there would be change of weather,
    When the moon hung so, and belike you heard it.
LEANTIO: Why, here's sin made, and nev'r a conscience put to't;
    A monster with all forehead, and no eyes.
    Why do I talk to thee of sense or virtue,
    That art as dark as death? and as much madness
    To set light before thee, as to lead blind folks
    To see the monuments, which they may smell as soon
    As they behold; marry, oft-times their heads,
    For want of light, may feel the hardness of 'em.
    So shall thy blind pride my revenge and anger,
    That canst not see it now; and it may fall
    At such an hour, when thou least seest of all;
    So to an ignorance darker than thy womb
    I leave thy perjur'd soul: a plague will come.
BIANCA: Get you gone first, and then I fear no greater,
    Nor thee will I fear long; I'll have this sauciness
    Soon banish'd from these lodgings, and the rooms
    Perfum'd well after the corrupt air it leaves:
    His breath has made me almost sick in troth:
    A poor base start-up! Life! because he's got
    Fair clothes by foul means, comes to rail, and show 'em.

The Lady of Pleasure

James Shirley

1635

Scene: the Strand, London

Man and Woman

Celestina (20–30) an attractive widow and Lord Unready (20–30) her
aptly named suitor.

*Courtly love is the fashion of the day. Here, Lord Unready pro-
poses that Celestina become his platonic mistress—a notion that
she ultimately rejects.*

LORD: If you can love, I'll tell your ladyship.
CELESTINA: I have a stubborn soul else.
LORD: You are all
    Composed of harmony.
CELESTINA: What love d'ee mean?
LORD: That which doth perfect both. Madam, you have heard
    I can be constant, and if you consent
    To grace it so, there is a spacious dwelling
    Prepared within my heart for such a mistress.
CELESTINA: Your mistress, my good lord?
LORD: Why, my good lady,
    Your sex doth hold it no dishonour
    To become mistress to a noble servant
    In the now court Platonic way. Consider
    Who 'tis that pleads to you: my birth and present
    Value can be no stain to your embrace;
    But these are shadows when my love appears,
    Which shall in his first miracle return
    Me in my bloom of youth and thee a virgin,
    When I within some new Elysium
    (Of purpose made and meant for us) shall be

In everything Adonis, but in his
Contempt of love, and court thee from a Daphne.
(Hid in the cold rind of a bashful tree)
With such warm language and delight till thou
Leap from that bays into the queen of love
And pay my conquest with composing garlands
Of thy own myrtle for me.

CELESTINA: What's all this?

LORD: Consent to be my mistress, Celestina,
And we will have it springtime all the year,
Upon whose invitations, when we walk,
The winds shall play soft descant to our feet
And breathe rich odours to repure the air,
Green bowers on every side shall tempt our stay,
And violets stoop to have us tread upon 'em.
The red rose shall grow pale (being near thy cheek)
And the white blush (o'ercome with such a forehead).
Here laid, and measuring with ourselves some bank,
A thousand birds shall from the woods repair
And place themselves so cunningly behind
The leaves of every tree, that while they pay
Us tribute of their songs, thou shalt imagine
The very trees bear music and sweet voices
Do grow in every arbour. Here can we
Embrace and kiss, tell tales, and kiss again,
And none but heaven our rival.

CELESTINA: When we are
Weary of these, what if we shift our paradise,
And through a grove of tall and even pine
Descend into a valley that shall shame
All the delights of Tempe, upon whose
Green plush the graces shall be called to dance
To please us, and maintain their fairy revels
To the harmonious murmurs of a stream
That gently falls upon a rock of pearl.
Here doth the nymph, forsaken Echo, dwell,

To whom we'll tell the story of our love
Till, at our surfeit and her want of joy,
We break her heart with envy. Not far off
A grove shall call us to a wanton river
To see a dying swan give up the ghost,
The fishes shooting up their tears in bubbles
That they must lose the genius of their waves—
And such love, linsey-woolsey, to no purpose.

LORD: You chide me handsomely. Pray, tell me how
 You like this language. *(Offering to embrace her.)*

CELESTINA: *(Resisting him.)* Good my lord, forbear.

LORD: You need not fly out of this circle, madam.
 (Aside.) These widows are so full of circumstance.
 (To Celestina.) I'll undertake, in this time I ha' courted
 Your ladyship for the toy, to ha' broken ten,
 Nay twenty colts (virgins, I mean) and taught 'em
 The amble or what pace I most affected.

CELESTINA: Y'are not my lord again—the lord I thought you—
 And I must tell you now, you do forget
 Yourself and me.

LORD: You'll not be angry, madam.

CELESTINA: Nor rude (though gay men have a privilege)
 It shall appear. There is a man, my lord,
 Within my acquaintance, rich in worldly fortunes—
 But cannot boast any descent of blood—
 Would buy a coat of arms.

LORD: He may, and legs
 Booted and spurred to ride into the country.

CELESTINA: But these will want antiquity, my lord,
 The seal of honour. What's a coat cut out
 But yesterday to make a man a gentleman?
 Your family, as old as the first virtue
 That merited an escutcheon, doth owe
 A glorious coat of arms; if you will sell now
 All that your name doth challenge in that ensign,
 I'll help you to a chapman that shall pay
 And pour down wealth enough for't.

LORD: Sell my arms?
  I cannot, madam.
CELESTINA: Give but your consent.
  You know not how the state may be inclined
  To dispensation; we may prevail
  Upon the heralds' office afterward.
LORD: I'll sooner give these arms to th'hangman's axe—
  My head, my heart, to twenty executions—
  Than sell one atom from my name.
CELESTINA: Change that,
  And answer him would buy my honour from me:
  Honour that is not worn upon a flag
  Or pennon (that without the owner's danger
  An enemy may ravish and bear from me),
  But that which grows and withers with my soul;
  Beside the body's stain, think, think my lord,
  To what you would unworthily betray me.
  If you would not for price of gold, or pleasure
  (If that be more your idol), lose the glory
  And painted honour of your house—I ha' done.
LORD: Enough to rectify a satyr's blood.
  Obscure my blushes here.

The King, The Greatest Alcade

Lope Felix de Vega, Translated by John Underhill
1636

Scene: Spain

Man and Woman

Don Tello (30–50) ruthless and immoral and Elvira (20) virtuous and
innocent.

> *Don Tello has kidnapped beautiful Elvira with nothing but the
> worst of intentions. Here, the desperate young woman does her
> best to resist his advances.*

ELVIRA: To what end, Tello, would you torture me
With such dire cruelty? Do you not know
I prize my honor? Further to persist
But wearies you and wearies me.

DON TELLO: Enough
Or you will slay me, being so rough and hard.

ELVIRA: Return me to my husband, Tello

DON TELLO: No,
For he is not your husband, nor may a clown
Though fortunate, deserve such passing worth;
But were I Sancho, and he in turn were I,
How then, Elvira, could your cruel rage
Treat me thus foully? Cannot your rigor see
That this is love?

ELVIRA: Never, my Lord; for love
That is deficient in a true respect
For honor is but vile desire, not love;
And being evil, love never can be called.
For love is born of loving what one loves
In mad desire;
And love that is not chaste

By no name of love is graced
Nor ever can to love's estate aspire.

DON TELLO: How so?

ELVIRA: But would you have me make it plain?
Last night you saw me, Tello, for the first;
Why, then, your love was such a sudden thing
That you had scarce a moment to consider
What that thing was which you so much desired;
Yet in that knowledge all true love resides.
For love is born of a great-grown desire,
And love goes mounting then the steps of favor
Even to its own end and exercise.
So this you feel was never love we see
In simple truth—mad lust and longing rather
To snatch from me my whole, my heart of life
By heaven confided to me in pure honor;
But you would seek to load me with dishonor
And I defend my life.

DON TELLO: But my excuse
Is your intelligence, as in your arms.
Listen to reason.

ELVIRA: There is no argument
Can vanquish my assured intent.

DON TELLO: But how?
Do you maintain it is impossible
To see, desire and love, all at first sight?

ELVIRA: True.

DON TELLO: Then answer:
How can the basilisk, ungrateful girl,
Contrive to kill, and only with a glance?

ELVIRA: It is an animal.

DON TELLO: And so your beauty;
It is the basilisk.

ELVIRA: You argue falsely
As prompted by your wit.

DON TELLO: I argue falsely?

ELVIRA: The mortal basilisk kills with a look,
    Because his mind is wholly set to kill,
    Which reason is so evident and plain
    We could not say that he had power to kill
    Did he but look upon us with affection.
    Let us have no more arguments, my lord;
    I am a woman and I am in love,
    Nor have you aught to hope from me.
DON TELLO: How is it possible a country wench
    Should answer in this wise? Confess to me
    You are a fool, proving yourself discreet;
    Because, when I behold your full perfection,
    The more its sum, so much the more my love.
    Oh, would to God you were my equal now!
    But you know well the baseness of your state
    Affronts my noble blood. Ill were it done
    To join the brocade with the coarse homespun!
    God knows what might of love now drives me on,
    And turns to evil all my good intent!
    The world made these vile laws in ages gone,
    And I must yield to them, obedient.

Tartuffe

Molière, Translated by Richard Wilbur
1669

Scene: Paris

Two Women

Dorine (20s) a wily maid and Mariane (16–18) an obedient daughter.

Mariane's father, Orgon, has been taken-in by the charlatan, Tartuffe. When Orgon declares that Mariane shall marry the greedy interloper, Dorine tries her best to spur the docile girl to revolt.

DORINE: *(Returning.)* Well, have you lost your tongue, girl? Must I play
    Your part, and say the lines you ought to say?
    Faced with a fate so hideous and absurd,
    Can you not utter one dissenting word?
MARIANE: What good would it do? A father's power is great.
DORINE: Resist him now, or it will be too late.
MARIANE: But…
DORINE: Tell him one cannot love at a father's whim;
    That you shall marry for yourself, not him;
    That since it's you who are to be the bride,
    It's you, not he, who must be satisfied;
    And that if his Tartuffe is so sublime,
    He's free to marry him at any time.
MARIANE: I've bowed so long to Father's strict control,
    I couldn't oppose him now, to save my soul.
DORINE: Come, come, Mariane. Do listen to reason, won't you?
    Valere has asked your hand. Do you love him, or don't you?
MARIANE: Oh, how unjust of you! What can you mean
    By asking such a question, dear Dorine?
    You know the depth of my affection for him;
    I've told you a hundred times how I adore him.

DORINE: I don't believe in everything I hear;
  Who knows if your professions were sincere?
MARIANE: They were, Dorine, and you do me wrong to doubt it;
  Heaven knows that I've been all too frank about it.
DORINE: You love him, then?
MARIANE: Oh, more than I can express.
DORINE: And he, I take it, cares for you no less?
MARIANE: I think so.
DORINE: And you both, with equal fire,
  Burn to be married?
MARIANE: That is our one desire.
DORINE: What of Tartuffe, then? What of your father's plan?
MARIANE: I'll kill myself, if I'm forced to wed that man.
DORINE: I hadn't thought of that recourse. How splendid!
  Just die, and all your troubles will be ended!
  A fine solution. Oh, it maddens me
  To hear you talk in that self-pitying key.
MARIANE: Dorine, how harsh you are! It's most unfair.
  You have no sympathy for my despair.
DORINE: I've none at all for people who talk drivel
  And, faced with difficulties whine and snivel.
MARIANE: No doubt I'm timid, but it would be wrong…
DORINE: True love requires a heart that's firm and strong.
MARIANE: I'm strong in my affection for Valere,
  But coping with my father is his affair.
DORINE: But if your father's brain has grown so cracked
  Over his dear Tartuffe that he can retract
  His blessing, though your wedding-day was named,
  It's surely not Valere who's to be blamed.
MARIANE: If I defied my father, as you suggest,
  Would it not seem unmaidenly, at best?
  Shall I defend my love at the expense
  Of brazenness and disobedience?
  Shall I parade my heart's desires and flaunt…
DORINE: No, I ask nothing of you. Clearly you want
  To be Madame Tartuffe, and I feel bound

Not to oppose a wish so very sound.
What right have I to criticize the match?
Indeed, my dear, the man's a brilliant catch.
Monsieur Tartuffe! Now, there's a man of weight!
Yes, yes Monsieur Tartuffe, I'm bound to state,
Is quite a person; that's not to be denied;
'Twill be no little thing to be his bride.
The world already rings with his renown;
He's a great noble—in his native town;
His ears are red, he has a pink complexion,
And all in all, he'll suit you to perfection.

MARIANE: Dear God!

DORINE: Oh, how triumphant you will feel
At having caught a husband so ideal!

MARIANE: Oh, do stop teasing, and use your cleverness
To get me out of this appalling mess.
Advise me, and I'll do whatever you say.

DORINE: Ah no, a dutiful daughter must obey
Her father, even if he weds her to an ape.
You've a bright future; why struggle to escape?
Tartuffe will take you back where his family lives,
To a small town aswarm with relatives—
Uncles and cousins whom you'll be charmed to meet.
You'll be received at once by the elite,
Calling upon the bailiffs wife, no less—
Even, perhaps, upon the mayoress,
Who'll sit you down in the *best* kitchen chair.
Then, once a year, you'll dance at the village fair
To the drone of bagpipes—two of them, in fact—
And see a puppet-show, or an animal act.
Your husband…

MARIANE: Oh, you turn my blood to ice!
Stop torturing me, and give me your advice.

The Gentleman Dancing Master

William Wycherley

1670

Scene: London

Two Women

Hippolyta (14) the pampered daughter of a wealthy Spanish merchant and Prue (16–18) her maid.

> *Hippolyta has been cloistered in London until the arrival of her father from Spain. Here, she and Prue bemoan their shared fate.*

HIPPOLYTA: To confine a woman just in her rambling age! Take away her liberty at the very time she should use it! Oh barbarous aunt! Oh unnatural father! To shut up a poor girl at fourteen, and hinder her budding! All things are ripened by the sun. To shut up a poor girl at fourteen!

PRUE: 'Tis true, miss, two poor young creatures as we are!

HIPPOLYTA: Not suffered to see a play in a twelvemonth!

PRUE: Nor to go to Ponchinello nor Paradise!

HIPPOLYTA: Nor to take a ramble to the park nor Mulberry Gar'n!

PRUE: Nor to Tatnam Court nor Islington!

HIPPOLYTA: Nor to eat a sillabub in New Spring Gar'n with a cousin!

PRUE: Nor to drink a pint of wine with a friend at the Prince in the Sun!

HIPPOLYTA: Nor to hear a fiddle in good company!

PRUE: Nor to hear the organs and tongs at the Gun in Moorfields!

HIPPOLYTA: Nay, not suffered to go to church, because the men are sometimes there! Little did I think I should ever have longed to go to church.

PRUE: Or I either, but between two maids.

HIPPOLYTA: Not see a man!

PRUE: Nor come near a man!

HIPPOLYTA: Nor hear of a man!

PRUE: No, miss; but to be denied a man, and to have no use at all of a man!

HIPPOLYTA: Hold, hold. Your resentment is as much greater than mine, as your experience has been greater. But all this while, what do we make of my cousin, my husband elect (as my aunt says)? We have had his company these three days. Is he no man?.

PRUE: No faith, he's but a *monsieur.* But you'll resolve yourself that question within these three days, for by that time he'll be your husband, if your father come tonight—

HIPPOLYTA: Or if I provide not myself with another in the mean time! For fathers seldom choose well, and I will no more take my father's choice in a husband, than I would in a gown or a suit of knots. So that if that cousin of mine were not an ill-contrived, ugly, freakish fool—in being my father's choice, I should hate him. Besides, he has almost made me out of love with mirth and good humour, for he debases it as much as a jack-pudding, and civility and good breeding more than a City dancing-master.

PRUE: What, won't you marry him then madam?

HIPPOLYTA: Wouldst thou have me marry a fool? An Idiot?

PRUE: Lord, 'tis a sign you have been kept up indeed, and know little of the world, to refuse a man for a husband only because he's a fool. Methinks he's a pretty, apish kind of a gentleman, like other gentlemen, and handsome enough to lie with in the dark, when husbands take their privileges; and for the day-times, you may take the privilege of a wife.

HIPPOLYTA: Excellent governess, you do understand the world, I see.

PRUE: Then you should be guided by me.

HIPPOLYTA: Art thou in earnest then, damned jade? Wouldst thou have me marry him? Well—there are more poor young women undone and married to filthy fellows, by the treachery and evil counsel of chambermaids, than by the obstinacy and covetous-ness of parents.

PRUE: Does not your father come on purpose out of Spain to marry you to him? Can you release yourself from your aunt or father any other way? Have you a mind to be shut up as long as you live? For my part, though you can hold out upon the lime from the walls here, salt, old shoes, and oatmeal, I cannot live so. I must confess my patience is worn out—

HIPPOLYTA: Alas, alas, poor Prue! Your stomach lies another way. I will take pity of you, and get me a husband very suddenly, who may have a servant at your service. But rather than marry my cousin, I will be a nun in the new Protestant nunnery they talk of, where (they say) there will be no hopes of coming near a man.

PRUE: But you can marry nobody but your cousin, miss. Your father you expect tonight, and be certain his Spanish policy and wariness, which has kept you up so close ever since you came from Hackney School, will make sure of you within a day or two at farthest—

HIPPOLYTA: Then 'tis time to think how to prevent him. Stay—

PRUE: In vain, vain miss!

HIPPOLYTA: If we knew but any man, any man, though he were but a little handsomer than the devil, so that he were a gentleman...

PRUE: What if you did know any man? If you had an opportunity, could you have confidence to speak to a man first? But if you could, how could you come to him, or he to you? Nay, how could you send to him? For though you could write, which your father in his Spanish prudence would never permit you to learn, who should carry the letter? But we need not be concerned for that, since we know not to whom to send it.

The Country Wife

William Wycherley

1675

Scene: London

Man and Woman

Pinchwife (20s–30s) a boorish and selfish husband and Mrs. Pinchwife (20s) his unhappy spouse.

Absurd Pinchwife has forced his wife to entertain a dalliance with another man in order to maintain a fashionable and sophisticated air for their marriage. Here, he interrogates the poor woman following an afternoon spent with the other man.

PINCHWIFE: Come, tell me, I say.

MRS. PINCHWIFE: Lord! han't I told it an hundred times over?

PINCHWIFE: *(Aside.)* I would try, if in the repetition of the ungrateful tale, I could find her altering it in the least circumstance; for if her story be false, she is so too.—Come, how was't, baggage?

MRS. PINCHWIFE: Lord, what pleasure you take to hear it, sure!

PINCHWIFE: No, you take more in telling it, I find; but speak, how was't?

MRS. PINCHWIFE: He carried me up into the house next to the Exchange.

PINCHWIFE: So, and you two were only in the room!

MRS. PINCHWIFE: Yes, for he sent away a youth that was there, for some dried fruit, and China oranges.

PINCHWIFE: Did he so? Damn him for it—and for—

MRS. PINCHWIFE: But presently came up the gentlewoman of the house.

PINCHWIFE: Oh, 'twas well she did; but what did he do whilst the fruit came?

MRS. PINCHWIFE: He kissed me an hundred times, and told me he fancied he kissed my fine sister, meaning me, you know, whom he said he loved with all his soul, and bid me be sure to tell her so, and to desire her to be at her window, by eleven of the clock this morning, and he would walk under it at that time.

PINCHWIFE: *(Aside.)* And he was as good as his word, very punctual; a pox reward him for't.

MRS. PINCHWIFE: Well, and he said if you were not within, he would come up to her, meaning me, you know, bud, still.

PINCHWIFE: *(Aside.)* So he knew her certainly; but for this confession, I am obliged to her simplicity.—But what, you stood very still when he kissed you?

MRS. PINCHWIFE: Yes, I warrant you; would you have had me discover myself?

PINCHWIFE: But you told me he did some beastliness to you, as you call it; what was't?

MRS. PINCHWIFE: Why, he put—

PINCHWIFE: What?

MRS. PINCHWIFE: Why, he put the tip of his tongue between my lips, and so moused me—and I said, I'd bite it.

PINCHWIFE: An eternal canker seize it, for a dog!

MRS. PINCHWIFE: Nay, you need not be so angry with him neither, for to say truth, he has the sweetest breath I ever knew.

PINCHWIFE: The devil! you were satisfied with it then, and would do it again?

MRS. PINCHWIFE: Not unless he should force me.

PINCHWIFE: Force you, changeling! I tell you, no woman can be forced.

MRS. PINCHWIFE: Yes, but she may sure, by such a one as he, for he's a proper, goodly, strong man; 'tis hard, let me tell you, to resist him.

PINCHWIFE: *(Aside.)* So, 'tis plain she loves him, yet she has not love enough to make her conceal it from me; but the sight of him will increase her aversion for me and love for him, and that love instruct her how to deceive me and satisfy him, all idiot as she is. Love! 'twas he gave women first their craft, their art of deluding. Out of Nature's hands they came plain, open, silly, and fit for slaves, as she and Heaven intended 'em; but damned Love— well—I must strangle that little monster whilst I can deal with him—Go fetch pen, ink, and paper out of the next room.

MRS. PINCHWIFE: Yes, bud. *(Exit.)*

PINCHWIFE: Why should women have more invention in love than men? It can only be because they have more desires, more soliciting passions, more lust, and more of the devil.

The Virtuoso

Thomas Shadwell
1676

Scene: London

Man and Woman

Longvil (20s) a gentleman of wit and sense in love with Miranda
(18–20) a young woman in love with someone else.

*Longvil here endeavors to declare his love to Miranda who in turn
endeavors to resist.*

LONGVIL: Dear madam, tender the life and welfare of a poor, humble
lover.

MIRANDA: What! A fashionable gentleman of this age and a lover! It is
impossible. They are all keepers, and transplant tawdry things
from the Exchange or the playhouse, and make the poor creatures run mad with the extremity of the alteration, as a young
heir being kept short does at the death of his father.

LONGVIL: I was never one of those, madam; nothing but age and impo-
tence can reduce me to that condition. I had rather kill my own
game than send to a poulterer's. Besides, I never eat tame things
when wild of the same kind are in season. I hate your coop'd,
cramp'd lady; I love 'em as they go about, as I do your barndoor
fowl.

MIRANDA: 'Tis more natural indeed.

LONGVIL: But had I been ne'er so wicked, you have made such an
absolute whining convert of me that, forgetting all shame and
reproach from the wits and debauchees of the town, I can be a
martyr for matrimony.

MIRANDA: Lord! That you should not take warning! Have not several of
your married friends, like those upon the ladder, bidden all good
people take warning by them.

LONGVIL: For all that, neither lovers nor malefactors can take it: one will make experiment of marriage and th'other of hanging, at their own sad costs. Neither of the executions will e'er be left off.

MIRANDA: They are both so terrible to women, 'tis hard to know which to choose.

LONGVIL: If you ladies were willing, we men are apt to be civil upon easier terms.

MIRANDA: No, those terms are harder than the other.

LONGVIL: You are so nimble a man knows not which way to catch you.

MIRANDA: Once for all I assure you, I will never be catch'd any way by you.

LONGVIL: Do not provoke love thus, lest he should revenge his cause and make you dote upon some nauseous coxcomb whom all the town scorns.

MIRANDA: Let love do what it will, I neither dare nor will talk on't any longer.

LONGVIL: You are afraid of talking of love as some are of reading in a conjuring book, for fear it should raise the devil.

MIRANDA: Whatever you can say will as soon raise one as the other in me. But I must take leave of you and your similes. My uncle will want you.

LONGVIL: Will you not in charity afford me one interview more this afternoon?

MIRANDA: Provided I hear not one word of love and my uncle and aunt be secure. I shall be in the walk on the east side of the garden an hour hence. *(Aside.)* But, by your leave, I shall meet another there. *(Exit Miranda.)*

LONGVIL: A thousand thanks for the honor.—Yonder comes Bruce and Clarinda. I'll retire. *(Exit Longvil.)*

The Plain Dealer

William Wycherley

1677

Scene: London

Man and Woman

Captain Manly (late 20s–30) a plain dealer and Fidelia (18–20) a woman masquerading as a cabin boy on his ship.

Manly is obsessed with fickle Olivia, who has jilted him for another. Determined to have her at any cost, Manly here commissions loyal Fidelia to court Olivia on his behalf, unaware that his handsome young cabin boy is, in fact, a beautiful young woman and desperately in love with him.

FIDELIA: Sir, good sir, generous captain.

MANLY: Prithee, kind impertinence, leave me. Why shouldst thou follow me, (flatter my generosity now,) since thou know'st I have no money left? If I had it, I'd give it thee, to buy my quiet.

FIDELIA: I never followed yet, sir, reward or fame but you alone, nor do I now beg anything but leave to share your miseries. You should not be a niggard of 'em, since methinks you have enough to spare. Let me follow you now because you hate me, as you have often said.

MANLY: I ever hated a coward's company, I must confess.

FIDELIA: Let me follow you till I am none then, for you, I'm sure, will through such worlds of dangers that I shall be inured to 'em; nay, I shall be afraid of your anger more than danger and so turn valiant out of fear. Dear captain, do not cast me off till you have tried me once more. Do not, do not go to sea again without me.

MANLY: Thou to sea! To court, thou fool. Remember the advice I gave thee; thou art a handsome spaniel and canst fawn naturally. Go, busk about and run thyself into the next great man's lobby; first fawn upon the slaves without and then run into the lady's bed-chamber; thou may'st be admitted at last to tumble her bed. Go seek, I say, and lose me, for I am not able to keep thee; I have not bread for myself.

FIDELIA: Therefore I will not go, because then I may help and serve you.

MANLY: Thou!

FIDELIA: I warrant you, sir, for at worst I could beg or steal for you.

MANLY: Nay, more bragging! Dost thou not know there's venturing your life in stealing? Go, prithee, away. Thou art as hard to shake off as that flattering effeminating mischief, love.

FIDELIA: Love, did you name? Why you are not so miserable as to be yet in love, sure!

MANLY: No, no, prithee away, be gone, on— *(Aside.)* I had almost discovered my love and shame. Well, if I had? That thing could not think the worst of me—or if he did?—No—yes, he shall know it—he shall—but then I must never leave him, for they are such secrets that make (parasites and) pimps lords of their masters, for any slavery or tyranny is easier than love's.—Come hither. Since thou art so forward to serve me, hast thou but resolution enough to endure the torture of a secret? For such to some is insupportable.

FIDELIA: I would keep it as safe as if your dear precious life depended on't.

MANLY: Damn your dearness. It concerns more than my life, my honour.

FIDELIA: Doubt it not, sir.

MANLY: (And do not discover it by too much fear of discovering it,) but have a great care you let not Freeman find it out.

FIDELIA: I warrant you, sir. I am already all joy with the hopes of your commands (and shall be all wings in the execution of 'em.) Speak quickly, sir.

MANLY: You said you would beg for me.

FIDELIA: I did, sir.

MANLY: Then you shall beg for me.

FIDELIA: With all my heart, sir.

MANLY: That is, pimp for me.

FIDELIA: How, sir?

MANLY: D'ye start! Thinkst thou, thou couldst do me any other service? Come, no dissembling honour. I know you can do it handsomely; thou wert made for't. You have lost your time with me at sea; you must recover it.

FIDELIA: Do not, sir, beget yourself more reasons for your aversion to me and make my obedience to you a fault. I am the unfittest in the world to do you such a service.

MANLY: Your cunning arguing against it shows but how fit you are for it. No more dissembling. Here, I say, you must go use it for me to Olivia.

FIDELIA: To her, sir?

MANLY: Go flatter, lie, kneel, promise, anything to get her for me. I cannot live unless I have her. Didst thou not say thou wouldst do anything to save my life? And she said you had a persuading face.

FIDELIA: But did not you say, sir, your honour was dearer to you than your life? And would you have me contribute to the loss of that and carry love from you to the most infamous, most false and—

MANLY: And most beautiful! *(Sighs aside.)*

FIDELIA: Most ungrateful woman that ever lived, for sure she must be so that could (desert you so soon,) use you so basely, (and so lately too.) Do not, do not forget it, sir, and think—

MANLY: No, I will not forget it but think of revenge. I will lie with her, out of revenge. Go, be gone, and prevail for me or never see me more.

FIDELIA: You scorned her last night.

MANLY: I know not what I did last night. I dissembled last night.

FIDELIA: Heavens!

MANLY: Be gone, I say, and bring me love or compliance back, hopes at least, or I'll never see thy face again. By—

FIDELIA: O do not swear, sir. First hear me.

MANLY: I am impatient. Away. You'll find me here till twelve. *(Turns away.)*

FIDELIA: Sir—

MANLY: Not one word, [no insinuating argument more or soothing persuasion; you'll have need of all your rhetoric with her.] strive to alter her, not me. Be gone.

The Rival Queens

Nathaniel Lee

1677

Scene: Babylon, the palace of Alexander the Great

Two Women

Queen Statira (30s) first wife of Alexander the Great and Roxana (18–20) his vengeful younger wife.

Roxana craves the power that comes with being the first wife. To that end she has plotted to murder Statira so that she can take her place in the court and in the bed of their shared husband. Here, the rival queens face-off.

ROXANA: Where is my rival?
    Appear, Statira, now no more a queen,
    Roxana calls. Where is your majesty?
STATIRA: *(Coming forward).* And what is she who with such tow'ring pride
    Would awe a princess that is born above her?
ROXANA: I like the port imperial beauty bears;
    It shows thou hast a spirit fit to fall
    A sacrifice to fierce Roxana's wrongs.
    Be sudden then, put forth these royal breasts,
    Where our false master has so often languished,
    That I may change their milky innocence
    To blood, and dye me in a deep revenge.
STATIRA: No, barb'rous woman! Though I durst meet death
    As boldly as our lord, with a resolve
    At which thy coward heart would tremble,
    Yet I disdain to stand the fate you offer,
    And therefore, fearless of thy dreadful threats,
    Walk thus regardless by thee.
ROXANA: Ha! So stately!
    This sure will sink you.

STATIRA: No, Roxana, no.

    The blow you give will strike me to the stars,

    But sink my murd'ress in eternal ruin.

ROXANA: Who told you this?

STATIRA: A thousand spirits tell me.

    There's not a god but whispers in my ear

    This death will crown me with immortal glory;

    To die so fair, so innocent, so young,

    Will make me company for queens above.

ROXANA: Preach on.

STATIRA: While you, the burden of the earth,

    Fall to the deep so heavy with thy guilt

    That hell itself must groan at thy reception;

    While foulest fiends shun thy society,

    And thou shalt walk alone, forsaken fury.

ROXANA: Heav'n witness for me, I would spare thy life

    If anything but Alexander's love

    Were in debate. Come, give me back his heart,

    And thou shalt live, live empress of the world.

STATIRA: The world is less than Alexander's love,

    Yet, could I give it, 'tis not in my power.

    This I dare promise, if you spare my life,

    Which I disdain to beg, he shall speak kindly.

ROXANA: Speak! Is that all?

STATIRA: Perhaps at my request,

    And for a gift so noble as my life,

    Bestow a kiss.

ROXANA: A kiss! No more?

STATIRA: *(Aside.)* O gods!

    What shall I say to work her to my end?

    Fain I would see him.— *(Aloud.)* Yes, a little more,

    Embrace you, and forever be your friend.

ROXANA: O, the provoking word! Your friend! Thou di'st.

    Your friend! What, must I bring you then together?

    Adorn your bed and see you softly laid?

    By all my pangs, and labors of my love,

This has thrown off all that was sweet and gentle;
Therefore—

STATIRA: Yet hold thy hand advanced in air.
I see my death is written in thy eyes,
Therefore wreak all thy lust of vengeance on me,
Wash in my blood, and steep thee in my gore,
Feed like a vulture, tear my bleeding heart.
But O Roxana! That there may appear
A glimpse of justice for thy cruelty,
A grain of goodness for a mass of evil,
Give me my death in Alexander's presence.

ROXANA: Not for the rule of heav'n. Are you so cunning?
What, you would have him mourn you as you fall?
Take your farewell, and taste such healing kisses
As might call back your soul? No, thou shalt fall
Now, and when death has seized thy beauteous limbs,
I'll have thy body thrown into a well,
Buried beneath a heap of stones forever.

The Feigned Courtesans
Aphra Behn
1679

Scene: Rome

Two Men

Tickletext (40s) a pompous Englishman traveling abroad and Petro (any age) a barber/pimp.

Here, scheming Petro conspires with lusty Tickletext regarding a certain signorina who has tickled the Brit's fancy.

PETRO: Ah che bella! Bella! I swear by these sparkling eyes and these soft plump dimpled cheeks, there's not a *signiora* in all Rome, could she behold 'em, were able to stand their temptations, and for La Silvianetta, my life on't she's your own.

TICKLETEXT: Tace, tace, speak softly!—But honest Barberacho, do I, do I indeed look plump, and young, and fresh and—hah!

PETRO: Aye sir, as the rosy morn, young as old Time in his infancy, and plump as the pale-faced moon.

TICKLETEXT: Hey—Why this travelling must needs improve a man, *(Aside.)* — why how admirably well-spoken your very barbers are here,—but, Barberacho, did the young gentlewoman say she liked me? Did she, rogue? Did she?

PETRO: A-doated on you signior, doated on you.

TICKLETEXT: *(Aside.)* Why, and that's strange now, in the autumn of my age too, when nature began to be impertinent, as a man may say, that a young lady should fall in love with me.—Why, Barberacho, I do not conceive any great matter of sin only in visiting a lady that loves a man, hah.

PETRO: Sin sir, 'tis a frequent thing nowadays in persons of your complexion.

TICKLETEXT: Especially here at Rome too, where 'tis no scandal.

PETRO: Aye signior, where the ladies are privileged, and fornication licensed.

TICKLETEXT: Right! And when 'tis licensed 'tis lawful, and when 'tis lawful it can be no sin: besides Barberacho, I may chance to turn her, who knows?

PETRO: Turn her signior, alas any way, which way you please.

TICKLETEXT: Hey, hey, hey! There thou wert knavish, I doubt—but I mean convert her—nothing else I profess, Barberacho.

PETRO: True signior, true, she's a lady of an easy nature, and an indifferent argument well handled will do't—ha—here's your head of hair— *(Combing out his hair.)* —here's your natural friz! And such an air it gives the face!—So, signior—now you have the utmost my art can do. *(Takes away the cloth, and bows.)*

TICKLETEXT: Well, signior:—and where's your looking-glass?

PETRO: My looking-glass?

TICKLETEXT: Yes signior, your looking-glass! An English barber would as soon have forgotten to have snapped his fingers, made his leg, or taken his money, as have neglected his looking-glass.

PETRO: Aye, signior, in your country the laity have so little honesty, they are not to be trusted with the taking off your beard unless you see't done,—but here's a glass, sir.

(Gives him the glass. Tickletext sets himself and smirks in the glass. Petro standing behind him, making horns and grimaces, which Tickletext sees in the glass, gravely rises, turns towards Petro.)

TICKLETEXT: Why how now, Barberacho, what monstrous faces are you making there?

PETRO: Ah, my belly, my belly, signior: ah, this wind-colic! this hypocondria does so torment me! Ah—

TICKLETEXT: Alas poor knave; certo, I thought thou hadst been somewhat uncivil with me, I profess I did.

PETRO: Who I sir, uncivil?—I abuse my patrone?—I that have almost made myself a pimp to serve you?

TICKLETEXT: Tace, tace, honest Barberacho! No, no, no, all's well, all's well.

The Fatal Friendship

Catherine Trotter

1698

Scene: France, following a war with Spain

Man and Woman

Bellgard (30s) a protective older brother and Felicia (20s) his sister, secretly married to his best friend, Gramont.

Here, Bellgard unwittingly informs Felicia of Gramont's recent marriage only to discover that she herself married him two years ago and bore him a son.

BELLGARD: So early up, sister?

FELICIA: I was not much disposed for sleep this morning.

BELLGARD: Perhaps my coming home so late disturbed you.

FELICIA: 'Twas late indeed.

BELLGARD: Th'occasion may excuse it.

FELICIA: Am I to know th'occasion?

BELLGARD: Only a friend's marriage. ('Twill be fit
　　To let Felicia know Gramont is married,
　　But not to whom; whilst that is unsuspected,
　　The secret's safe.)

FELICIA: May I ask what friend? Or is't a secret, brother?

BELLGARD: 'Tis indeed a secret, sister, but you
　　Should know it, if I were sure 'twould not disturb you.

FELICIA: That I dare promise you.
　　It is not in the power of any one,
　　To raise the least concern in me that way.

BELLGARD: Then I may safely tell you, but with charge
　　Not to reveal it, Gramont last night was married.

FELICIA: Gramont! You jest with me.

BELLGARD: On my faith, I'm serious.

FELICIA: (What can he mean?) To whom, brother?

BELLGARD: For that you must excuse me, I've given my honour
  Not to disclose it to my dearest friend.
FELICIA: Unless you tell me that, I shall believe
  You said it but to try me.
BELLGARD: Were it not a secret of importance,
  Or if my own, I would not hide it from you,
  None but his father and myself were trusted,
  My faith, my honour, friendship, are engaged.
FELICIA: (With what concern he speaks! And yet it cannot be.)
BELLGARD: I conjure you, sister, not to mention this.
FELICIA: Why such a secret? But you're not in earnest.
BELLGARD: Why should you doubt, when I affirm it thus
  Not from report, but my own certain knowledge?
  Myself was present at the nuptial tie,
  A witness of their vows.
FELICIA: If there is faith in man, this can't be truth.
  I fancy, brother, this is but designed
  To try how I could bear it.
BELLGARD: Those are woman's arts, I understand 'em not.
  Heav'n knows no greater truth than what I've told you.
FELICIA: Swear, by that Heav'n, you're sure Gramont is married,
  And I will doubt no longer.
BELLGARD: Am I not worth your credit? Why all this doubting?
  By every name that's good, Gramont is married.
  I saw him married.
FELICIA: Wretched woman!
BELLGARD: How, Felicia!
FELICIA: Oh, I must not think it,
  He can't be guilty of so base an action.
BELLGARD: What foolish passion's this?
FELICIA: And yet my brother swears it, swears he saw it.
  Oh Gramont! Is all my love and faith rewarded thus?
BELLGARD: For shame at least conceal your folly,
  This fondness for a man, who cares not for you,
  Perhaps scarce thinks of you.
FELICIA: Oh, to be so abused!

BELLGARD: What said you? So abused?

FELICIA: He has wronged me basely.

BELLGARD: Ha! Hast thou not wronged thyself, giv'n up
    Thy honour to him?

FELICIA: Oh, forgive me, brother…

BELLGARD: Dar'st thou own thy infamy, yet hope to be forgiv'n?

FELICIA: I am married.

BELLGARD: No, strumpet, he but served his lust with thee,
    And now has paid thee as thou dost deserve,
    Too wise to marry where he found not virtue.

FELICIA: Can you suspect me of a thing so vile!
    No, by all goodness, I am not dishonest,
    But by all lawful bonds his real wife.

BELLGARD: Oh, curse! What do I hear? What have I done?
    Base dog, so to betray, abuse my friendship,
    Whither does all this lead? Where can it end?
    'Tis misery, dishonour without end,
    And I the instrument of all this ruin.
    Villain, perfidious villain! Ay, trait'ress, weep,
    Weep for thy shame, thy sin, thy disobedience,
    Rebellious girl, pollution of my blood!

FELICIA: Oh, I deserve all this, that could deceive
    And disobey the best of brothers.

BELLGARD: You've met a just return of your ingratitude
    To all my love and tender care of you.

FELICIA: I have indeed. I have no husband now,
    And where, alas, where will my little son
    Now find a father?

BELLGARD: A son! Is then this cursed,
    Unhappy marriage of so long a date?

FELICIA: Two years I've been his wife, and brought in secret
    A wretched infant to partake our sorrows,
    And now they are completed. Oh, my brother,
    Tread me to the earth,
    Double your anger on me, 'tis but just,
    That I may fall a load of miseries,
    And never, never rise.

BELLGARD: Alas, she moves my soul…pr'ythee no more,
　　　　Thy fault was great, but now thy punishment
　　　　Has so exceeded it, I must forgive thee.
　　　　Rise, Felicia, I am still a brother.
　　　　Wipe off these tears, thou shalt have justice done thee,
　　　　Trust me, thou shalt.

PART FOUR:

THE WICKEDLY ELEGANT 18TH CENTURY

The Beau Defeated

Mary Pix
1700

Scene: London

Two Women

Mrs. Rich (30–40) a ridiculously pretentious woman and Betty (20s) her maid.

Here, long-suffering Betty assists Mrs. Rich with her morning routine.

MRS. RICH: Betty.

BETTY: Madam.

MRS. RICH: Prithee what's thy surname?

BETTY: Has your Ladyship forgot?

MRS. RICH: Dost imagine it worth a place in my memory?

BETTY: Cork, madam.

MRS. RICH: Oh, filthy! From henceforth let me call thee *de la Bette;* that has an air French, and agreeable.

BETTY: What you please, madam.

MRS. RICH: De la Bette, whatever bills the mechanical fellows, little trades-people bring ye, let 'em wait, let 'em walk for't, and watch my levee; but if Monsieur comes that brought the prohibited gloves, l'eau de fleur d'orange, and the complexion, you understand me, give him his price, and ready money.

BETTY: Yes, madam.

MRS. RICH: And do ye hear, put a hundred guineas in the embroidered purse for basset.

BETTY: Bless me, madam! Have you lost all that I put in yesterday morning?

MRS. RICH: Impertinence! I am sufficiently recompensed in learning the game, and the honourable company I am admitted into.

BETTY: Indeed, madam, the footmen say, Mrs Trickwell is a perfect female rook, lives upon gaming, nay, and keeps out on't, they say, and they can tell.

MRS. RICH: Hold your tongue, she is a woman of quality, knows everybody at Court, all their intrigues, is as deep in affairs, and keeps as many secrets, as Maintenon, I'll be sworn; ma foi. What a word was there! But, as I was saying, she has told me, and half a dozen ladies more, secrets six hours together; and such secrets *de la Bette,* let me die, were we not women of discretion, might reach the lives, or eternally disgrace, of some that shall be nameless.

BETTY: They are very happy, if they are in her power.

MRS. RICH: Peace, has nobody sent a how-de-ye yet?

BETTY: No.

MRS. RICH: 'Tis my horrid custom of getting up so early in a morning.

BETTY: Madam, 'tis past twelve.

MRS. RICH: And I dressed, and have been abroad, abominable! I charge ye tomorrow don't bring my clothes till past two, if I am so mad to call for 'em.

BETTY: Won't your Ladyship inquire after my Lady Landsworth's health, methinks you neglect her, though she is rich, gay and beautiful, and honours your house with her choice of it whilst she's in town.

MRS. RICH: Honours! Who are thou speaking to, sweetheart? I do not like her, she won't play; nay, will sit ye two hours together and speak ill of nobody; she is not fit for the conversation of quality.

The Tragedy of Jane Shore

Nicholas Rowe

1714

Scene: the court of Lord Hastings

Man and Woman

Lord Hastings (40s) a powerful Lord and Jane Shore (20s) a beautiful young woman in need of protection.

Circumstances have forced Jane to turn to Hastings for protection. When they meet, she unfortunately discovers that his motives towards her are of the basest variety.

LORD HASTINGS: Forgive me, fair one, if officious friendship
Intrudes on your repose, and comes thus late
To greet you with the tidings of success.
The princely Gloster has vouchsaf'd you hearing;
To-morrow he expects you at the court.
There plead your cause with never failing beauty,
Speak all your griefs and find a full redress.
JANE SHORE: *(Kneeling.)* Thus humbly let your lowly servant bend,
Thus let me bow my grateful knee to earth,
And bless your noble nature for this goodness.
LORD HASTINGS: Rise, gentle dame; you wrong my meaning much;
Think me not guilty of a thought so vain,
To sell my courtesy for thanks like these.
JANE SHORE: 'Tis true, your bounty is beyond my speaking;
But though my mouth be dumb, my heart shall thank you;
And when it melts before the throne of mercy,
Mourning and bleeding for my past offences,
My fervent soul shall breathe one prayer for you,
If prayers of such a wretch are heard on high,
That heav'n will pay you back when most you need
The grace and goodness you have shown to me.

LORD HASTINGS: If there be aught of merit in my service,
    Impute it there where most 'tis due, to love;
    Be kind, my gentle mistress, to my wishes,
    And satisfy my panting heart with beauty.
JANE SHORE: Alas! my Lord—
LORD HASTINGS: Why bend thy eyes to earth?
    Wherefore these looks of heaviness and sorrow?
    Why breathes that sigh, my love? And wherefore falls
    This trickling show'r of tears to stain thy sweetness?
JANE SHORE: If pity dwells within your noble breast
    (As sure it does) oh speak not to me thus!
LORD HASTINGS: Can I behold thee and not speak of love!
    Ev'n now, thus sadly as thou stand'st before me,
    Thus desolate, dejected, and forlorn,
    Thy softness steals upon my yielding senses
    Till my soul faints and sickens with desire;
    How canst thou give this motion to my heart,
    And bid my tongue be still?
JANE SHORE: Cast round your eyes
    Upon the highborn beauties of the court;
    Behold, like opening roses, where they bloom,
    Sweet to the sense, unsully'd all, and spotless;
    There choose some worthy partner of your heart,
    To fill your arms and bless your virtuous bed,
    Nor turn your eyes this way, where sin and misery,
    Like loathsome weeds, have overrun the soil,
    And the destroyer shame has laid all waste.
LORD HASTINGS: What means this peevish, this fantastic change?
    Where is thy wonted pleasantness of face?
    Thy wonted graces, and thy dimpled smiles?
    Where hast thou lost thy wit and sportive mirth,
    That cheerful heart, which used to dance forever,
    And cast a day of gladness all around thee?
JANE SHORE: Yes, I will own I merit the reproach,
    And for those foolish days of wanton pride
    My soul is justly humbled to the dust:

All tongues, like yours, are licens'd to upbraid me,
Still to repeat my guilt, to urge my infamy,
And treat me like that abject thing I have been.
Yet let the saints be witness to this truth,
That now, though late, I look with horror back,
That I detest my wretched self, and curse
My past polluted life. All-judging heav'n,
Who knows my crimes, has seen my sorrow for them.

LORD HASTINGS: No more of this dull stuff. 'Tis time enough
To whine and mortify thyself with penance
When the decaying sense is pall'd with pleasure,
And weary nature tires in her last stage.
Then weep and tell thy beads, when alt'ring rheums
Have stain'd the lustre of thy starry eyes,
And failing palsies shake thy wither'd hand.
The present moments claim more generous use;
Thy beauty, night, and solitude reproach me
For having talk'd thus long.—Come, let me press thee, *(Laying
    hold on her.)*
Pant on thy bosom, sink into thy arms,
And lose myself in the luxurious fold.

JANE SHORE: Never! By those chaste lights above, I swear,
My soul shall never know pollution more!
(Kneeling.) Forbear, my Lord! Here let me rather die;
Let quick destruction overtake me here,
And end my sorrows and my shame forever.

LORD HASTINGS: Away with this perverseness—'Tis too much. *(Striving)*
Nay, if you strive—'tis monstrous affectation.

JANE SHORE: Retire! I beg you, leave me—

LORD HASTINGS: Thus to coy it!—
With one who knows you, too.

JANE SHORE: For mercy's sake—

LORD HASTINGS: Ungrateful woman! is it thus you pay
My services?

JANE SHORE: Abandon me to ruin
Rather than urge me—

LORD HASTINGS: *(Pulling her.)* This way to your chamber;
    There if you struggle—
JANE SHORE: *(Crying out.)* Help! O gracious heaven!
    Help! Save me! Help!

The Way of the World
William Congreve
1706

Scene: St. James Park

Two Women

Mrs. Fainall (20s–30s) and Mrs. Marwood (20s–30s) two women with axes to grind.

Here, two married ladies reveal their mutual hatred of men.

MRS. FAINALL: Aye, aye, dear Marwood if we will be happy, we must find the means in ourselves, and among ourselves. Men are ever in extremes, either doting or averse. While they are lovers, if they have fire and sense, their jealousies are insupportable. And when they cease to love, (we ought to think at least) they loath; they look upon us with horror and distaste; they meet us like the ghosts of what we were, and as from such, fly from us.

MRS. MARWOOD: True, 'tis an unhappy circumstance of life that love should ever die before us; and that the man so often should out-live the lover. But say what you will, 'tis better to be left than never to have been loved. To pass our youth in dull indifference, to refuse the sweets of life because they once must leave us, is as preposterous as to wish to have been born old, because we one day must be old. For my part, my youth may wear and waste, but it shall never rust in my possession.

MRS. FAINALL: Then it seems you dissemble an aversion to mankind, only in compliance to my mother's humour?

MRS. MARWOOD: Certainly. To be free, I have no taste of those insipid dry discourses with which our sex of force must entertain themselves, apart from men. We may affect endearments to each other, profess eternal friendships, and seem to dote like lovers; but 'tis not in our natures long to persevere. Love will resume his empire in our breasts; and every heart, or soon or late, receive and readmit him as its lawful tyrant.

MRS. FAINALL: Bless me, how have I been deceived! Why you profess a libertine!

MRS. MARWOOD: You see my friendship by my freedom. Come, be sincere, acknowledge that your sentiments agree with mine.

MRS. FAINALL: Never!

MRS. MARWOOD: You hate mankind?

MRS. FAINALL: Heartily, inveterately.

MRS. MARWOOD: Your husband?

MRS. FAINALL: Most transcendently; aye, though I say it, meritoriously.

MRS. MARWOOD: Give me your hand upon it.

MRS. FAINALL: There.

MRS. MARWOOD: I join with you; what I have said has been to try you.

MRS. FAINALL: Is it possible? Dost thou hate those vipers, men?

MRS. MARWOOD: I have done hating 'em, and am now come to despise 'em; the next thing I have to do, is eternally to forget 'em.

MRS. FAINALL: There spoke the spirit of an Amazon, a Penthesilea!

MRS. MARWOOD: And yet I am thinking sometimes to carry my aversion further.

MRS. FAINALL: How?

MRS. MARWOOD: Faith, by marrying, if I could but find one that loved me very well and would be thoroughly sensible of ill usage, I think I should do myself the violence of undergoing the ceremony.

MRS. FAINALL: You would not make him a cuckold?

MRS. MARWOOD: No, but I'd make him believe I did, and that's as bad.

MRS. FAINALL: Why had not you as good do it?

MRS. MARWOOD: Oh, if he should ever discover it, he would then know the worst, and be out of his pain; but I would have him ever to continue upon the rack of fear and jealousy.

MRS. FAINALL: Ingenious mischief! Would thou wert married to Mirabell.

MRS. MARWOOD: Would I were!

MRS. FAINALL: You change colour.

MRS. MARWOOD: Because I hate him.

MRS. FAINALL: So do I; but I can hear him named. But what reason have you to hate him in particular?

MRS. MARWOOD: I never loved him; he is, and always was, insufferably proud.

MRS. FAINALL: By the reason you give for your aversion, one would think it dissembled; for you have laid a fault to his charge of which his enemies must acquit him.

MRS. MARWOOD: Oh, then it seems you are one of his favourable enemies! Methinks you look a little pale, and now you flush again.

MRS. FAINALL: Do I? I think I am a little sick o' the sudden.

MRS. MARWOOD: What ails you?

MRS. FAINALL: My husband. Don't you see him? He turned short upon me unawares, and has almost overcome me.

The Beaux' Stratagem

George Farquhar

1707

Scene: a country house

Two Men

Aimwell (20s) and Archer (20s) a couple of charming con-men.

> *Aimwell and Archer are philosophical rogues who manage to make a living out of tricking the wealthy out of money. Here, Archer joins Aimwell at a fine home in Lichfield where they hope to live quite nicely until the next opportunity presents itself.*

AIMWELL: The coast's clear, I see.—Now, my dear Archer, welcome to Lichfield.

ARCHER: I thank thee, my dear brother in iniquity.

AIMWELL: Iniquity! prithee, leave canting; you need not change your style with your dress.

ARCHER: Don't mistake me, Aimwell, for 'tis still my maxim, that there is no scandal like rags, nor any crime so shameful as poverty.

AIMWELL: The world confesses it every day in its practice, though men won't own it for their opinion. Who did that worthy lord, my brother, single out of the side-box to sup with him t'other night?

ARCHER: Jack Handycraft, a handsome, well-dressed, mannerly, sharping rogue, who keeps the best company in town.

AIMWELL: Right! And, pray, who married my Lady Manslaughter t'other day, the great fortune?

ARCHER: Why, Nick Marrabone, a professed pickpocket, and a good bowler; but he makes a handsome figure, and rides in his coach, that he formerly used to ride behind.

AIMWELL: But did you observe poor Jack Generous in the Park last week?

ARCHER: Yes, with his autumnal periwig shading his melancholy face, his coat older than anything but its fashion, with one hand idle in his pocket, and with the other picking his useless teeth; and, though the Mall was crowded with company, yet was poor Jack as single and solitary as a lion in a desert.

AIMWELL: And as much avoided, for no crime upon earth but the want of money.

ARCHER: And that's enough. Men must not be poor; idleness is the root of all evil; the world's wide enough, let 'em bustle. Fortune has taken the weak under her protection, but men of sense are left to their industry.

AIMWELL: Upon which topic we proceed, and I think luckily hitherto. Would not any man swear, now, that I am a man of quality, and you my servant; when if our intrinsic value were known—

ARCHER: Come, come, we are the men of intrinsic value, who can strike our fortunes out of ourselves, whose worth is independent of accidents in life, or revolutions in government; we have heads to get money and hearts to spend it.

AIMWELL: As to our hearts, I grant ye, they are as willing tits as any within twenty degrees; but I can have no great opinion of our heads from the service they have done us hitherto, unless it be that they have brought us from London hither to Lichfield, made me a lord, and you my servant.

ARCHER: That's more than you could expect already. But what money have we left?

AIMWELL: But two hundred pound.

ARCHER: And our horses, clothes, rings, &c.—Why, we have very good fortunes now for moderate people; and, let me tell you besides, that this two hundred pound, with the experience that we are now masters of is a better estate than the ten thousand we have spent. Our friends, indeed, began to suspect that our pockets were low; but we came off with flying colors, showed no signs of want either in word or deed—

AIMWELL: Ay, and our going to Brussels was a good pretence enough for our sudden disappearing; and, I warrant you, our friends imagine that we are gone a-volunteering.

ARCHER: Why, faith, if this prospect fails, it must e'en come to that. I am for venturing one of the hundreds, if you will, upon this knight-errantry; but, in case it should fail, we'll reserve the t'other to carry us to some counterscarp, where we may die, as we lived, in a blaze.

AIMWELL: With all my heart; and we have lived justly, Archer; we can't say that we have spent our fortunes, but that we have enjoyed 'em.

ARCHER: Right! So much pleasure for so much money, we have had our pennyworths; and, had I millions, I would go to the same market again.—Oh London! London!—Well, we have had our share, and let us be thankful; past pleasures, for aught I know, are best, such as we are sure of; those to come may disappoint us.

AIMWELL: It has often grieved the heart of me to see how some inhuman wretches murder their kind fortunes; those that, by sacrificing all to one appetite, shall starve all the rest. You shall have some that live only in their palates, and in their sense of tasting shall drown the other four. Others are only epicures in appearances, such who shall starve their nights to make a figure a-days, and famish their own to feed the eyes of others. A contrary sort confine their pleasures to the dark, and contract their spacious acres to the circuit of a muffstring.

ARCHER: Right; but they find the Indies in that spot where they consume 'em. And I think your kind keepers have much the best on't; for they indulge the most senses by one expense. There's the seeing, hearing, and feeling, amply gratified; and some philosophers will tell you that from such a commerce there arises a sixth sense, that gives infinitely more pleasure than the other five put together.

AIMWELL: And to pass to the other extremity, of all keepers I think those the worst that keep their money!

The Busybody
Susanna Centilivre
1709

Scene: London

Two Men

Sir George (20–30) a young man in love and Charles (20s) his best friend.

Here, lovesick George confesses his passion for the fair Miranda to Charles.

CHARLES: Ha! Sir George Airy! A-birding thus early! What forbidden game roused you so soon? For no lawful occasion could invite a person of your figure abroad at such unfashionable hours.

SIR GEORGE: There are some men, Charles, whom Fortune has left free from inquietude, who are diligently studious to find out ways and means to make themselves uneasy.

CHARLES: Is it possible that anything in nature can ruffle the temper of a man whom the four seasons of the year compliment with as many thousand pounds; nay, and a father at rest with his ancestors?

SIR GEORGE: Why there 'tis now! A man that wants money thinks none can be unhappy that has it; but my affairs are in such a whimsical posture, that it will require a calculation of my nativity to find if my gold will relieve me, or not.

CHARLES: Ha, ha, ha! Never consult the stars about that. Gold has a power beyond them; gold unlocks the midnight councils; gold outdoes the wind, becalms the ship, or fills her sails. Gold is omnipotent below: it makes whole armies fight or fly; it buys even souls, and bribes the wretches to betray their country. Then what can the business be, that gold won't serve thee in?

SIR GEORGE: Why, I'm in love.

CHARLES: In love!—Ha, ha, ha, ha! In love, ha, ha, ha, with what, prithee? A cherubim?

SIR GEORGE: No, with a woman.

CHARLES: A woman, good, ha, ha, ha! And gold not help thee?

SIR GEORGE: But suppose I'm in love with two—

CHARLES: Aye, if thou'rt in love with two hundred, gold will fetch 'em, I warrant thee, boy. But who are they! Who are they! Come.

SIR GEORGE: One is a lady whose face I never saw, but witty as an angel; the other beautiful as Venus—

CHARLES: And a fool—

SIR GEORGE: For aught I know, for I never spoke to her, but you can inform me. I am charmed for the wit of one, and die for the beauty of the other.

CHARLES: And pray which are in quest of now?

SIR GEORGE: I prefer the sensual pleasure; I'm for her I've seen who is thy father's ward, Miranda.

CHARLES: Nay then I pity you; for the jew, my father, will no more part with her and 30,000 pounds, than he would with a guinea to keep me from starving.

SIR GEORGE: Now you see gold can't do everything, Charles.

CHARLES: Yes: for 'tis her gold that bars my father's gate against you.

SIR GEORGE: Why, if he is that avaricious wretch, how cam'st thou by such a liberal education?

CHARLES: Not a souse out of his pocket I assure you: I had an uncle who defrayed that charge, but for some little wildnesses of youth, though he made me his heir, left Dad my guardian 'till I came to years of discretion, which I presume the old gentleman will never think I am; and now he has got the estate into his clutches, it does me no more good that if it lay in Prester-John's dominions.

SIR GEORGE: What, can'st thou find no strategem to redeem it?

CHARLES: I have made many essays to no purpose: though want, the mistress of invention still tempts me on, yet still the old fox is too cunning for me—I am upon my last project, which if it fails, then for my last refuge, a brown musket.

Cato

John Addison
1713

Scene: Ancient Rome

Two Men

Cato (40–50) noted Roman statesman and Juba (20s) a young prince
  of the Empire.

*Juba has presented himself to Cato as his late father requested.
Here, the eager young man discusses his thoughts of conquest
and love with the senior statesman.*

CATO: Juba, thy father was a worthy prince,
  And merited, alas! a better fate;
  But heav'n thought otherwise.
JUBA: My father's fate,
  In spite of all the fortitude that shines
  Before my face, in Cato's great example,
  Subdues my soul, and fills my eyes with tears.
CATO: It is an honest sorrow, and becomes thee.
JUBA: My father drew respect from foreign climes:
  The kings of Afric sought him for their friend;
  Kings far remote, that rule, as fame reports,
  Behind the hidden sources of the Nile,
  In distant worlds, on t'other side the sun:
  Oft have their black ambassadors appear'd
  Loaden with gifts, and fill'd the courts of Zama.
CATO: I am no stranger to thy father's greatness.
JUBA: I would not boast the greatness of my father,
  But point out new alliances to Cato.
  Had we not better leave this Utica,
  To arm Numidia in our cause, and court
  Th' assistance of my father's pow'rful friends?

Did they know Cato, our remotest kings
Would pour embattled multitudes about him;
Their swarthy hosts would darken all our plains,
Doubling the native horror of the war,
And making death more grim.

CATO: And canst thou think
Cato will fly before the sword of Caesar?
Reduc'd, like Hannibal, to seek relief
From court to court, and wander up and down,
A vagabond in Afric!

JUBA: Cato, perhaps
I'm too officious, but my forward cares
Would fain preserve a life of so much value.
My heart is wounded, when I see such virtue
Afflicted by the weight of such misfortunes.

CATO: Thy nobleness of soul obliges me.
But know, young Prince, that valour soars above
What the world calls misfortune and affliction.
These are not ills; else would they never fall
On heavn's first fav'rites, and the best of men:
The Gods, in bounty, work up storms about us,
That give mankind occasion to exert
Their hidden strength, and throw out into practice
Virtues that shun the day, and lie conceal'd
In the smooth seasons and the calms of life.

JUBA: I'm charm'd whene'er thou talk'st! I pant for virtue
And all my soul endeavours at perfection.

CATO: Dost thou love watchings, abstinence, and toil,
Laborious virtues all? Learn them from Cato:
Success and fortune must thou learn from Caesar.

JUBA: The best good fortune that can fall on Juba,
The whole success at which my heart aspires,
Depends on Cato.

CATO: What does Juba say?
Thy words confound me.

JUBA: I would fain retract them,

Give 'em back again. They aim'd at nothing.

CATO: Tell me thy wish, young Prince; make not my ear.
 A stranger to thy thoughts.

JUBA: Oh, they're extravagant;
 Still let me hide them.

CATO: What can Juba ask
 That Cato will refuse!

JUBA: I fear to name it.
 Marcia—inherits all her father's virtues.

CATO: What wouldst thou say?

JUBA: Cato, thou hast a daughter.

CATO: Adieu, young Prince: I would not hear a word
 Should lessen thee in my esteem: remember
 The hand of fate is over us, and heav'n
 Exacts severity from all our thoughts:
 It is not now a time to talk of aught
 But chains or conquest, liberty or death.

The Conscious Lovers

Richard Steele

1722

Scene: a flat in 18th century London

Two Women

Indiana (18–20) a young woman in love and Isabella (30s) her overly
sensible aunt.

*Indiana has fallen in love with Mr. Bevil, a young man whose
motives are constantly called into question by her aunt. Here, the
two women argue about the nature of Bevil's feelings for Indiana.*

ISABELLA: This it is to Bevil and all mankind. Trust not those who will
think the worse of you for your confidence in them—serpents
who lie in wait for doves. Won't you be on your guard against
those who would betray you? Won't you doubt those who would
condemn you for believing 'em? Take it from me, fair and natural
dealing is to invite injuries; 'tis bleating to escape wolves who
would devour you! Such is the world— *(Aside.)* and such (since
the behavior of one man to myself) have I believed all the rest of
the sex.

INDIANA: I will not doubt the truth of Bevil, I will not doubt it. He has
not spoken it by an organ that is given to lying. His eyes are all
that have ever told me that he was mine. I know his virtue, I know
his filial piety and ought to trust his management with a father to
whom he has uncommon obligations. What have I to be concerned for? My lesson is very short. If he takes me forever, my
purpose of life is only to please him. If he leaves me (which
Heaven avert) I know he'll do it nobly, and I shall have nothing to
do but to learn to die, after worse than death has happened to
me.

ISABELLA: Ay, do; persist in your credulity! Flatter yourself that a man of his figure and fortune will make himself the jest of the town and marry a handsome beggar for love.

INDIANA: The town! I must tell you, madam, the fools that laugh at Mr. Bevil will but make themselves more ridiculous. His actions are the result of thinking, and he has sense enough to make even virtue fashionable.

ISABELLA: O' my conscience, he has turned her head!—Come, come! If he were the honest fool you take him for, why has he kept you here these three weeks without sending you to Bristol in search of your father, your family, and your relations?

INDIANA: I am convinced he still designs it and that nothing keeps him here but the necessity of not coming to a breach with his father in regard to the match he has proposed him. Beside, has he not writ to Bristol, and has not he advice that my father has not been heard of there almost these twenty years?

ISABELLA: All sham, mere evasion. He is afraid if he should carry you thither your honest relations may take you out of his hands and so blow up all his wicked hopes at once.

INDIANA: Wicked hopes! Did I ever give him any such?

ISABELLA: Has he ever given you any honest ones? Can you say in your conscience he has ever once offered to marry you?

INDIANA: No: but by his behavior I am convinced he will offer it the moment 'tis in his power or consistent with his honor to make such a promise good to me.

ISABELLA: His honor!

INDIANA: I will rely upon it; therefore desire you will not make my life uneasy by these ungrateful jealousies of one to whom I am, and wish to be, obliged, for from his integrity alone I have resolved to hope for happiness.

ISABELLA: Nay! I have done my duty. If you won't see, at your peril be it—

INDIANA: Let it be! This is his hour of visiting me.

ISABELLA: *(Apart.)* Oh, to be sure, keep up your form! Don't see him in a bed chamber. This is pure prudence, when she is liable whenever he meets her to be conveyed where'er he pleases.

INDIANA: All the rest of my life is but waiting till he comes. I only live when I'm with him. *(Exit.)*

The Christmas Party

Ludvig Holberg, Translated by Gerald S. Argetsinger
1724

Scene: a provincial village in Denmark

Man and Woman

Jeronimus (40–50) a stingy burger not in the Christmas spirit and Leonora (30–40) his wife.

On the eve of the annual Christmas party, Jeronimus and Leonora complain about the frivolity of Yuletide festivities.

JERONIMUS: *(To himself.)* If the world is still here at Easter, I'll cut my throat! These ruffles, frills, and curls are nothing more than Lucifer's inventions!

LEONORA: What's the matter, little Husband?

JERONIMUS: We see one sign after another, but we're just as wicked.

LEONORA: Has something bad happened, Little Husband?

JERONIMUS: Listen, Sweetheart, you would be doing me a favor if you wore round hats from now on and have dresses sewn in the same fashion as my old sister Magdelone.

LEONORA: But my sweetest Little Husband, if you compare my dresses with Aunt Magdelone's you'll find that hers are more expensive.

JERONIMUS: That's not the problem, my little doll. Expense neither adds to nor subtracts from it. But these damned new inventions, these ruffles, these frills, these curls that were not known to our honorable forefathers are sinful attire that is the basis for all of the world's misfortunes.

LEONORA: If I'd only known it was a sin, my darling husband, I would have rejected it all.

JERONIMUS: We will not believe the sin before we're warned with signs, and then it's too late. Recently there was a calf born with ruffles, frills, and curls!

LEONORA: How can you be sure that't true?

JERONIMUS: May lightning strike me if it isn't! Pernille and other good people here in Æbeltoft have seen the calf! Listen, Sweetheart, what I want to say is, I'm not at all in the mood to have a Christmas party tonight.

LEONORA: Did that story about the calf frighten you out of it?

JERONIMUS: No, not at all, for that isn't the first such story. But after I thought about it I decided that these Christmas parties and Christmas games bring about nothing good.

LEONORA: To me it doesn't matter one way or the other. You know yourself how little I am of the world. You won't find many young wives like me. I'd be just as happy if there were never any dancing or playing in this world. My joy comes from sitting at home with my work, caring for my Little Husband.

JERONIMUS: I know it, my little doll. You are an example to all young wives in Æbeltoft. The best thing I ever did in this world was to choose such a virtuous soul for my wife.

LEONORA: I simply can't understand how sensible people find pleasure in Christmas games. They may be good enough for children, but they should be disgusting for mature adults.

JERONIMUS: Sometimes these same Christmas games can also have evil consequences.

LEONORA: Christmas games and all other festivities, Sweetheart! I simply don't care for them. If it were not to please my husband I would never go out again.

JERONIMUS: No, my little doll must not completely cut herself off from the world. One must have some enjoyment in life. Otherwise young people will be overcome by melancholy.

LEONORA: I always seem to become melancholic at parties and drive it away again with solitude.

JERONIMUS: Yes, yes, that's fine my Sweetheart, but there is a limit! I am glad, though, that you do not want the Christmas party this evening. I'll go and find out what my sister says about it. *(To himself as he exits.)* Any honorable man who has a wife such as mine should celebrate his anniversary every year like a holiday.

The Beggar's Opera
John Gay
1728

Scene: the Peachum residence, London

Man and Woman

Mr. & Mrs. Peachum (40s–50s) small time thieves and concerned parents.

Here, these two sub-scoundrels discuss their daughter, Polly, and her love for the dread highwayman, Macheath.

PEACHUM: What a dickens is the woman always a-whimp'ring about murder for? No gentleman is ever looked upon the worse for killing a man in his own defence; and if business cannot be carried on without it, what would you have a gentleman do?

MRS. PEACHUM: If I am in the wrong, my dear, you must excuse me, for nobody can help the frailty of an over-scrupulous conscience.

PEACHUM: Murder is as fashionable a crime as a man can be guilty of. How many fine gentlemen have we in Newgate every year, purely upon that article! If they have wherewithal to persuade the jury to bring it in manslaughter, what are they the worse for it? So, my dear, have done upon this subject. Was Captain Macheath here this morning, for the bank-notes he left with you last week?

MRS. PEACHUM: Yes, my dear; and though the bank hath stopped payment, he was so cheerful and so agreeable! Sure there is not a finer gentleman upon the road than the captain! If he comes from Bagshot at any reasonable hour he hath promised to make one with Polly and me, and Bob Booty, at a party of quadrille. Pray, my dear, is the captain rich?

PEACHUM: The captain keeps too good company ever to grow rich. Marybone and the chocolate houses are his undoing. The man that proposes to get money by play should have the education of a fine gentleman, and be trained up to it from his youth.

MRS. PEACHUM: Really, I am sorry upon Polly's account the captain hath not more discretion. What business hath he to keep company with lords and gentlemen? he should leave them to prey upon one another.

PEACHUM: Upon Polly's account! What, a plague, does the woman mean?—Upon Polly's account!

MRS. PEACHUM: Captain Macheath is very fond of the girl.

PEACHUM: And what then?

MRS. PEACHUM: If I have any skill in the ways of women, I am sure Polly thinks him a very pretty man.

PEACHUM: And what then? You would not be so mad to have the wench marry him! Gamesters and highway men are generally very good to their whores, but they are very devils to their wives.

MRS. PEACHUM: But if Polly should be in love, how should we help her, or how can she help herself? Poor girl, I am in the utmost concern about her.

[AIR IV: *Why is your faithful slave disdained? etc.*

If love the virgin's heart invade,

How, like a moth, the simple maid

Still plays about the flame!

If soon she be not made a wife,

Her honor's singed, and then, for life,

She's—what I dare not name.]

PEACHUM: Look ye, wife. A handsome wench in our way of business is as profitable as at the bar of a Temple coffee-house, who looks upon it as her livelihood to grant every liberty but one. You see I would indulge the girl as far as prudently we can—in anything but marriage! After that, my dear, how shall we be safe? Are we not then in her husband's power? For a husband hath the absolute power over all a wife's secrets but her own. If the girl had the discretion of a court lady, who can have a dozen young fellows at her ear without complying with one, I should not matter it; but Polly is tinder, and a spark will at once set her on a flame. Married! If the wench does not know her own profit, sure she knows her own pleasure better than to make herself a property! My daughter to me should be, like a court lady to a minister of state, a key to the whole gang. Married! if the affair is not already done, I'll terrify her from it by the example of our neighbors.

MRS. PEACHUM: Mayhap, my dear, you may injure the girl. She loves to imitate the fine ladies, and she may only allow the captain liberties in the view of interest.

PEACHUM: But 'tis your duty, my dear, to warn the girl against her ruin, and to instruct her how to make the most of her beauty. I'll go to her this moment, and sift her. In the meantime, wife, rip out the coronets, and marks of these dozen of cambric handkerchiefs, for I can dispose of them this afternoon to a chap in the city. *(Exit.)*

The Tragedy of Tragedies

Henry Fielding

1731

Scene: the realm of myth and legend

Man and Woman

Queen (40s) a woman secretly in love with the man her daughter
   loves and intends to marry and Grizzle (any age) her henchman.

*Driven by jealousy, the desperate Queen here orders Grizzle to
prevent the marriage of her daughter to the hero, Tom Thumb.*

QUEEN: Teach me to scold, prodigious-minded Grizzle.
   Mountain of treason, ugly as the devil,
   Teach this confunded hateful mouth of mine
   To spout forth words malicious as thyself,
   Words which might shame all Billingsgate to speak.
GRIZZLE: Far be it from my pride to think my tongue
   Your royal lips can in that art instruct,
   Where in you so excel. But may I ask,
   Without offence, wherefore my queen would scold?
QUEEN: Wherefore? Oh! Blood and thunder! ha'n't you heard
   (What ev'ry corner of the court resounds)
   That little Thumb will be a great man made?
GRIZZLE: I heard it, I confess—for who, alas!
   Can always stop his ears?—but would my teeth,
   By grinding knives, had first been set on edge.
QUEEN: Would I had heard, at the still noon of night,
   The hallaloo of fire in every street!
   Odsbobs! I have a mind to hang myself,
   To think I should a grandmother be made
   By such a rascal!—Sure the king forgets
   When in a pudding, by his mother put,
   The bastard, by a tinker, on a stile
   Was dropp'd—O, good lord Grizzle! can I bear

To see him from a pudding mount the throne?
Or can, oh can! my Huncamunca bear
To take a pudding's offspring to her arms?
GRIZZLE: O horror! horror! horror! cease, my queen;
Thy voice, like twenty screech-owls, wracks my brain.
QUEEN: Then rouse thy spirit—we may yet prevent
This hated match.
GRIZZLE: We will, not fate itself,
Should it conspire with Thomas Thumb, should cause it.
I'll swim through seas; I'll ride upon the clouds;
I'll dig the earth; I'll blow out every fire;
I'll rave; I'll rant; I'll rise; I'll rush; I'll roar;
Fierce as the man whom smiling dolphins bore
From the prosaic to poetic shore.
I'll tear the scoundrel into twenty pieces.
QUEEN: Oh, no! prevent the match but hurt him not;
For, though I would not have him have my daughter,
Yet can we kill the man that kill'd the giants?
GRIZZLE: I tell you, Madam, it was all a trick;
He made the giants first, and then he kill'd them;
As fox-hunters bring foxes to the wood,
And then with hounds they drive them out again.
QUEEN: How! have you seen no giants? Are there not
Now, in the yard, ten thousand proper giants?
GRIZZLE: Indeed I cannot positively tell,
But firmly do believe there is not one.
QUEEN: Hence! from my sight! thou traitor, hie away;
By all my stars! thou enviest Tom Thumb.
Go, Sirrah! go, hie away! hie!—thou art
A setting dog begone!
GRIZZLE: Madam, I go.
Tom Thumb shall feel the vengeance you have rais'd;
So, when two dogs are fighting in the streets,
With a third dog one of the two dogs meets,
With angry teeth he bites him to the bone,
And this dog smarts for what that dog had done.

The London Merchant

George Lillo

1731

Scene: London

Man and Woman

Millwood (30s) an evil manipulator and Barnwell (20s) the gullible young man she drives to ruination.

Millwood has convinced Barnwell to murder his uncle for the money. Following the dark deed, Barnwell arrives at Millwood's apartments; bloody, terrified and full of regret for his impetuous act.

BARNWELL: Where shall I hide me? whither shall I fly to avoid the swift, unerring hand of Justice?

MILLWOOD: Dismiss your fears; though thousands had pursued you to the door, yet being entered here, you are safe as innocence. I have such a cavern, by art so cunningly contrived, that the piercing eyes of Jealousy and Revenge may search in vain, nor find the entrance to the safe retreat. There will I hide you if any danger's near.

BARNWELL: Oh, hide me—from myself if it be possible, for while I bear my conscience in my bosom, though I were hid where man's eye never saw nor light e'er dawned, 'twere all in vain. For oh! that inmate, that impartial judge, will try, convict, and sentence me for murder, and execute me with never-ending torments. Behold these hands all crimsoned o'er with my dear uncle's blood! Here's a sight to make a statue start with horror, or turn a living man into a statue.

MILLWOOD: Ridiculous! Then it seems you are afraid of your own shadow, or, what's less than a shadow, your conscience.

BARNWELL: Though to man unknown I did the accursed act, what can we hide from heaven's all-seeing eye?

MILLWOOD: No more of this stuff! What advantage have you made of his death, or what advantage may yet be made of it? Did you secure the keys of his treasure? those no doubt were about him. What gold, what jewels, or what else of value have you brought me?

BARNWELL: Think you I added sacrilege to murder? Oh! had you seen him as his life flowed from him in a crimson flood, and heard him praying for me by the double name of nephew and of murderer (alas, alas! he knew not then that his nephew was his murderer) how would you have wished, as I did, though you had a thousand years of life to come, to have given them all to have lengthened his one hour! But, being dead, I fled the sight of what my hands had done, nor could I, to have gained the empire of the world, have violated, by theft, his sacred corpse.

MILLWOOD: Whining, preposterous, canting villain, to murder your uncle, rob him of life, nature's first, last, dear prerogative, after which there's no injury; then fear to take what he no longer wanted, and bring to me your penury and guilt! Do you think I'll hazard my reputation—nay, my life, to entertain you?

BARNWELL: O Millwood! this from thee!—but I have done; if you hate me, if you wish me dead, then are you happy—for oh! 'tis sure my grief will quickly end me.

A Matter of Dispute

Marivaux, Translated by John Walters
1744

Scene: the woods

Two Women

Eglea (18–20) and Adina (18–20) two physically perfect yet incredibly naive and self-centered young women.

When these two freakishly perfect gals encounter one another in the woods, the beautiful fur begins to fly.

ADINA: Oh, what's this new creature? *(She comes forward.)*

EGLEA: She's looking at me carefully, but not admiring me. It isn't another Azoro. *(She looks at herself in the mirror.)* Still less is it another Eglea…But I think she's comparing herself with me.

ADINA: I don't know what to think about the way this creature looks. I don't know what's missing from it. There's something insipid about it.

EGLEA: I don't like the look of her sort.

ADINA: Does she have any language? Let's see…Are you a person?

EGLEA: Yes, certainly, and very much a person.

ADINA: Well, have you nothing to say to me?

EGLEA: No. People usually forestall me by speaking to me first.

ADINA: But don't you find me enchanting?

EGLEA: You? I'm the one who enchants people.

ADINA: What! You aren't really delighted to see me?

EGLEA: Sorry, I'm neither delighted nor upset. What does it matter to me?

ADINA: Well, that's very peculiar! You look at me, I show myself, and you don't feel anything! You must be looking somewhere else. Have a good look at me. Now, what do you think of me?

EGLEA: But what's all this about you? Is it you that matters? I tell you, it's me that people see first, me they tell what they're thinking.

That's the way things are done. And you want me to admire you when I'm around!

ADINA: Of course I do. The most beautiful woman must expect to be noticed and admired.

EGLEA: Well, admire then!

ADINA: Don't you know what I'm saying? It's the most beautiful woman who must expect it.

EGLEA: And I tell you she is expecting it.

ADINA: But where is she, if it isn't me? I am the object of admiration for three persons living in the world.

EGLEA: I don't know your persons, but I know there are three that I enchant, and they regard me with wonder.

ADINA: And I know that I am so beautiful, so beautiful, that I bewitch myself every time I look at myself. You see how it is.

EGLEA: What are you saying? I who am talking to you cannot look at myself without swooning with delight.

ADINA: Swooning with delight! It's true you're not bad, and even quite nice. I do you justice, I'm not like you.

EGLEA: (Aside.) I could cheerfully beat her with her justice.

ADINA: But to believe you can compete with me, it's a joke! You only have to look.

EGLEA: But it's precisely by looking that I find you rather ugly.

ADINA: All right! So you feel envious of me, and prevent yourself from finding me beautiful.

EGLEA: It's only your face that prevents me.

ADINA: My face! Oh, that doesn't worry me, I've seen it. Go and ask the flowing waters of the stream, go and ask Mezirion who adores me.

EGLEA: The waters of the stream care nothing for you—they will tell me there is nothing as beautiful as me, and they have already told me so. I don't know what kind of thing a Mezirion is, but he wouldn't look at you if he saw me. I have an Azoto who is worth more than him, an Azoro I love. He is nearly as wonderful as me, and says I am his life. You aren't anybody's life. I also have a mirror, and it finally confirms all that Azoto and the stream have told me. What stronger proof could anyone want?

ADINA: *(Laughing.)* A mirror! You have a mirror too! But what is it to you? For looking at yourself? Ha, ha, ha!

EGLEA: Ha, ha, ha! Didn't I just know that I wouldn't like her?

ADINA: *(Laughing.)* Look, here's a better one. Come and get to know yourself in it. That'll shut you up.

[(Carisa appears in the distance.)]

EGLEA: *(Ironically.)* Cast your eyes on this if you want to know your own mediocrity, and the modesty which is fitting when you're with me.

ADINA: Please go away. Since you refuse to take any pleasure in looking at me, you're no use to me, and I'm not going to speak to you any more.

(They stop looking at each other.)

EGLEA: Well, I don't know you're there.

(They move away from one another.)

ADINA: *(Aside.)* She's crazy!

EGLEA: *(Aside.)* She's out of her mind! Whatever planet is she from?

Miss Sara Sampson

Lessing, Translated by Ernest Bell
1755

Scene: a country inn

Man and Woman

Mellefont (30s) and Marwood (30s), former lovers turned bitter enemies.

Fickle Mellefont has spurned Marwood, with whom he has fathered a daughter, for the beautiful and virtuous young Sara. Here, the former lovers meet and animosity dances in the air.

MARWOOD: No doubt you are little pleased to see me again.

MELLEFONT: I am very pleased, Marwood, to see that your indisposition has had no further consequences. You are better, I hope!

MARWOOD: So, so.

MELLEFONT: You have not done well, then, to trouble to come here again.

MARWOOD: I thank you, Mellefont, if you say this out of kindness to me; and I do not tale it amiss, if you have another meaning in it.

MELLEFONT: I am pleased to see you so calm.

MARWOOD: The storm is over. Forget it. I beg you once more.

MELLEFONT: Only remember your promise, Marwood, and I will forget everything with pleasure. But if I knew that you would not consider it an offence, I should like to ask—

MARWOOD: Ask on, Mellefont! You cannot offend me any more. What were you going to ask?

MELLEFONT: How you liked my Sara?

MARWOOD: The question is natural. My answer will not seem so natural, but it is none the less true for that. I liked her very much.

MELLEFONT: Such impartiality delights me. But would it be possible for him who knew how to appreciate the charms of a Marwood to make a bad choice?

MARWOOD: You ought to have spared me this flattery, Mellefont, if it is flattery. It is not in accordance with our intention to forget each other.

MELLEFONT: You surely do not wish me to facilitate this intention by rudeness? Do not let our separation be of an ordinary nature. Let us break with each other as people of reason who yield to necessity; without bitterness, without anger, and with the preservation of a certain degree of respect, as behoves our former intimacy.

MARWOOD: Former intimacy! I do not wish to be reminded of it. No more of it. What must be, must, and it matters little how. But one word more about Arabella. You will not let me have her?

MELLEFONT: No, Marwood!

MARWOOD: It is cruel, since you can no longer be her father, to take her mother also from her.

MELLEFONT: I can still be her father, and will be so.

MARWOOD: Prove it, then, now!

MELLEFONT: How?

MARWOOD: Permit Arabella to have the riches which I have in keeping for you, as her father's inheritance. As to her mother's inheritance I wish I could leave her a better one than the shame of having been borne by me.

MELLEFONT: Do not speak so! I shall provide for Arabella without embarrassing her mother's property. If she wishes to forget me, she must begin by forgetting that she possesses anything from me. I have obligations towards her, and I shall never forget that really—though against her will—she has promoted my happiness. Yes, Marwood, in all seriousness I thank you for betraying our retreat to a father whose ignorance of it alone prevented him from receiving us again.

MARWOOD: Do not torture me with gratitude which I never wished to deserve. Sir William is too good an old fool; he must think differently from what I should have thought in his place. I should have forgiven my daughter, but as to her seducer I should have—

MELLEFONT: Marwood!

MARWOOD: True; you yourself are the seducer! I am silent.

The School for Scandal

Richard Brinsley Sheridan
1777

Scene: Scandalous London

Man and Woman

Sir Peter (30–40) and Lady Teazle (30s), a bickering married couple.

*Sir Peter is quite exasperated by his wife's extravagance and here
tells her of his displeasure in her wanton spending.*

SIR PETER: Lady Teazle, Lady Teazle, I'll not bear it!

LADY TEAZLE: Sir Peter, Sir Peter, you may bear it or not as you please;
but I ought to have my own way in everything, and, what's more,
I will, too. What! though I was educated in the country, I know
very well that women of fashion in London are accountable to
nobody after they are married.

SIR PETER: Very well, ma'am, very well; so a husband is to have no influence, no authority?

LADY TEAZLE: Authority! No, to be sure! If you wanted authority over
me, you should have adopted me and not married me. I am sure
you were old enough.

SIR PETER: Old enough! Ay, there it is! Well, well, Lady Teazle, though
my life may be made unhappy by your temper, I'll not be ruined
by your extravagance.

LADY TEAZLE: My extravagance! I'm sure I'm not more extravagant than
a woman of fashion ought to be.

SIR PETER: No, no, madam, you shall throw away no more sums on such
unmeaning luxury. 'Slife! to spend as much to furnish your dress-
ing-room with flowers in winter as would suffice to turn the
Pantheon into a greenhouse and give a *fête champêtre* at
Christmas.

LADY TEAZLE: Lord! Sir Peter, am I to blame, because flowers are dear in
cold weather? You should find fault with the climate, and not

with me. For my part, I'm sure I wish it was spring all the year round and that roses grew under one's feet!

SIR PETER: Oons, madam! If you had been born to this, I shouldn't wonder at your talking thus; but you forget what your situation was when I married you.

LADY TEAZLE: No, no, I don't. 'Twas a very disagreeable one, or I should never have married you.

SIR PETER: Yes, yes, madam, you were then in somewhat a humbler style—the daughter of a plain country squire. Recollect, Lady Teazle, when I saw you first, sitting at your tambour in a pretty figured linen gown, with a bunch of keys at your side, your hair combed smooth over a roll, and your apartment hung round with fruits in worsted of your own working.

LADY TEAZLE: Oh, yes! I remember it very well, and a curious life I led. My daily occupation to inspect the dairy, superintend the poultry, make extracts from the family receipt-book, and comb my Aunt Deborah's lap-dog.

SIR PETER: Yes, yes, ma'am, 'twas so indeed.

LADY TEAZLE: And then you know, my evening amusements! To draw patterns for ruffles, which I had not the materials to make up; to play Pope Joan with the curate; to read a sermon to my aunt; or to be stuck down to an old spinet to strum my father to sleep after a fox-chase.

SIR PETER: I am glad you have so good a memory. Yes, madam these were the recreations I took you from; but now you must have your coach,—*vis-à-vis,*—and three powdered footmen before your chair, and in the summer a pair of white cats to draw you to Kensington Gardens. No recollection, I suppose, when you were content to ride double behind the butler on a docked coach-horse.

LADY TEAZLE: No—I swear I never did that. I deny the butler and the coach-horse.

SIR PETER: This, madam, was your situation; and what have I not done for you? I have made you a woman of fashion, of fortune, of rank—in short, I have made you my wife.

LADY TEAZLE: Well, then, and there is but one thing more you can make me to add to the obligation—and that is—

SIR PETER: My widow, I suppose?

LADY TEAZLE: Hem! hem!

SIR PETER: I thank you; madam; but don't flatter yourself; for, though your ill conduct may disturb my peace, it shall never break my heart, I promise you. However, I am equally obliged to you for the hint.

LADY TEAZLE: Then why will you endeavor to make yourself so disagreeable to me and thwart me in every little elegant expense?

SIR PETER: 'Slife, madam, I say, had you any of these little elegant expenses when you married me?

LADY TEAZLE: Lud, Sir Peter, would you have me be out of the fashion?

SIR PETER: The fashion, indeed! What had you to do with the fashion before you married me?

LADY TEAZLE: For my part, I should think you would like to have your wife thought a woman of taste.

SIR PETER: Ay! There again! Taste! Zounds, madam, you had no taste when you married me!

LADY TEAZLE: That's very true, indeed, Sir Peter; and, after having married you, I am sure I should never pretend to taste again.

A Trip To Scarborough

Richard Brinsley Sheridan
1777

Scene: an inn in Scarborough

Man and Woman

Loveless (30s) a husband with a wandering eye and Amanda
(20s–30s) his sharp-witted wife.

*Following an evening out at the theatre, Loveless foolishly gives
voice to his attraction for a young woman in the audience.*

AMANDA: Plays, I must confess, have some small charms, and would
have more, would they restrain that loose encouragement to vice,
which shocks, if not the virtue of some women, at least the modesty of all.

LOVELESS: But, 'till that reformation can be wholly made, 'twould surely
be a pity to exclude the productions of some of our best writers
for want of a little wholesome pruning; which might be effected
by any one who possessed modesty enough to believe that we
should preserve all we can of our deceased authors, at least 'till
they are outdone by the living ones.

AMANDA: What do you think of that you saw last night?

LOVELESS: To say truth, I did not mind it much; my attention was for
some time taken off to admire the workmanship of Nature, in the
face of a young lady who sat some distance from me, she was so
exquisitely handsome!

AMANDA: So exquisitely handsome!

LOVELESS: Why do you repeat my words, my dear?

AMANDA: Because you seem'd to speak them with such pleasure, I
thought I might oblige you with their echo.

LOVELESS: Then you are alarm'd, Amanda?

AMANDA: It is my duty to be so when you are in danger.

LOVELESS: You are too quick in apprehending for me. I view'd her with a world of admiration, but not one glance of love.

AMANDA: Take heed of trusting to such nice distinctions. But were your eyes the only things that were inquisitive? Had I been in your place, my tongue, I fancy, had been curious too. I should have ask'd her, where she liv'd (yet still without design) who was she pray?

LOVELESS: Indeed, I cannot tell.

AMANDA: You will not tell.

LOVELESS: By all that's sacred then, I did not ask.

AMANDA: Nor do you know what company was with her?

LOVELESS: I do not; but why are you so earnest?

AMANDA: I thought I had cause.

LOVELESS: But you thought wrong, Amanda; for turn the case, and let it be your story; should you come home and tell me you had seen a handsome man, should I grow jealous because you had eyes?

AMANDA: But should I tell you he was *exquisitely* so, and that I had gazed on him with admiration, should you not think 'twere possible I might go one step further, and enquire his name?

LOVELESS: *(Aside.)* She has reason on her side, I have talk'd too much; but I must turn off another way. *(To her.)* Will you then make no difference, Amanda, between the language of our sex and yours? There is a modesty restrains your tongues, which makes you speak by halves when you commend, but roving flattery gives a loose to ours, which makes us still speak double what we think. You should not, therefore, in so strict a sense, take what I said to her advantage.

AMANDA: Those flights of flattery, sir, are to our faces only; when women are once out of hearing, you are as modest in your commendations as we are; but I shan't put you to the trouble of farther excuses;—if you please, this business shall rest here, only give me leave to wish, both for your peace and mine, that you may never meet this miracle of beauty more.

LOVELESS: I am content.

Such Things Are

Elizabeth Inchbald

1787

Scene: a British household in 18th Century colonial India

Man and Woman

Sir Luke (30s) a pompous husband and Lady Tremor (32) his wife.

*Here, a well-worn married couple argues about the exact length
of their marriage.*

(Enter Sir Luke, followed by Lady Tremor.)

SIR LUKE: I tell you, madam, you are two and thirty.

LADY: I tell you, sir, you are mistaken.

SIR LUKE: Why, did not you come over from England exactly sixteen
years ago?

LADY: Not so long.

SIR LUKE: Have not we been married, the tenth of next April, sixteen
years?

LADY: Not so long.

SIR LUKE: Did you not come over the year of the great eclipse?—answer
me that.

LADY: I don't remember it.

SIR LUKE: But I do—and shall remember it as long as I live.—The first
time I saw you was in the garden of the Dutch envoy: you were
looking through a glass at the sun—I immediately began to make
love to you, and the whole affair was settled while the eclipse
lasted—just one hour, eleven minutes, and three seconds.

LADY: But what is all this to my age?

SIR LUKE: Because I know you were at that time near seventeen, and
without one qualification except your youth, and your fine clothes.

LADY: Sir Luke, Sir Luke, this is not to be borne!

SIR LUKE: Oh! yes—I forgot—you had two letters of recommendation
from two great families in England.

LADY: Letters of recommendation!

SIR LUKE: Yes; your character—that you know, is all the fortune we poor Englishmen, situated in India, expect with a wife, who crosses the sea at the hazard of her life, to make us happy.

LADY: And what but our characters would you have us bring?—Do you suppose any lady ever came to India, who brought along with her friends or fortune?

SIR LUKE: No, my dear: and what is worse, she seldom leaves them behind.

LADY: No matter, Sir Luke: but if I delivered to you a good character—

SIR LUKE: Yes, my dear, you did: and if you were to ask me for it again, I can't say I could give it to you.

Slaves In Algiers

Susana Haswell Rowson

1794

Scene: a harem in Algiers

Two Women

Fetnah (18–20) an unhappy slave and Selima (18–20) her complacent companion.

Fetnah desires her freedom above all things. Here, she reveals the source of her thirst for liberty and equality to her sister slave.

FETNAH: Well, it's all vastly pretty—the gardens, the house and these fine clothes. I like them very well, but I don't like to be confined.

SELIMA: Yet, surely, you have no reason to complain. Chosen favorite of the Dey, what can you wish for more?

FETNAH: Oh, a great many things. In the first place, I wish for liberty. Why do you talk of my being a favorite? Is the poor bird that is confined in a cage (because a favorite with its enslaver) consoled for the loss of freedom? No! Though its prison is of golden wire, its little heart still pants for liberty. Gladly would it seek the fields of air, and even perched upon a naked bough, exulting carol forth its song, nor once regret the splendid house of bondage.

SELIMA: Ah! But then our master loves you.

FETNAH: What of that? I don't love him.

SELIMA: Not love him?

FETNAH: No. He is old and ugly; then he wears such tremendous whiskers. And when he makes love, he looks so grave and stately that, I declare, if it was not for fear of his huge scimitar, I should burst out a-laughing in his face.

SELIMA: Take care you don't provoke him too far.

FETNAH: I don't care how I provoke him, if I can but make him keep his distance. You know I was brought here only a few days since. Well, yesterday, as I was amusing myself, looking at the fine things I saw everywhere about me, who should bolt into the room, but that great, ugly thing Mustapha. "What do you want?" said I! "Most beautiful Fetnah," said he, bowing till the tip of his long, hooked nose almost touched the toe of his slipper, "Most beautiful Fetnah, our powerful and gracious master, Muley Moloc, sends me, the humblest of his slaves, to tell you he will condescend to stop in your apartment tonight, and commands you to receive the high honor with proper humility."

SELIMA: Well—and what answer did you return?

FETNAH: Lord, I was so frightened, and so provoked, I hardly know what I said; but finding the horrid-looking creature didn't move, at last I told him that if the Dey was determined to come, I supposed he must, for I could not hinder him.

SELIMA: And did he come?

FETNAH: No, but he made me go to him; and when I went trembling into the room, he twisted his whiskers and knit his great beetle brows. "Fetnah," said he, "You abuse my goodness; I have condescended to request you to love me." And then he gave me such a fierce look, as if he would say, and if you don't love me, I'll cut your head off.

SELIMA: I dare say you were finely frightened.

FETNAH: Frightened! I was provoked beyond all patience, and thinking he would certainly kill me one day or other, I thought I might as well speak my mind, and be dispatched out of the way at once.

SELIMA: You make me tremble.

FETNAH: So, mustering up as much courage as I could: "Great and powerful Muley," said I, "I am sensible I am your slave. You took me from an humble state, placed me in this fine palace, and gave me these rich clothes. You bought my person of my parents, who loved gold better than they did their child; but my affections you could not buy. I can't love you." "How!" cried he, starting from his seat, "How, can't love me?" And he laid his hand upon his scimitar.

SELIMA: Oh, dear! Fetnah!

FETNAH: When I saw the scimitar half drawn, I caught hold of his arm. "Oh, good my lord," said I, "Pray do not kill a poor little girl like me! Send me home again, and bestow your favor on some other, who may think splendor a compensation for the loss of liberty."

"Take her away," said he. "She is beneath my anger."

SELIMA: But how is it, Fetnah, that you have conceived such an aversion to the manners of a country where you were born?

FETNAH: You are mistaken. I was not born in Algiers. I drew my first breath in England. My father, Ben Hassan, as he is now called, was a Jew. I can scarcely remember our arrival here, and have been educated in the Moorish religion, though I always had a natural antipathy to their manners.

SELIMA: Perhaps imbibed from your mother.

FETNAH: No. She has no objection to any of their customs, except that of their having a great many wives at a time. But some few months since, my father, who sends out many corsairs, brought home a female captive to whom I became greatly attached. It was she who nourished in my mind the love of liberty and taught me woman was never formed to be the abject slave of man. Nature made us equal with them and gave us the power to render ourselves superior.

SELIMA: Of what nation was she?

FETNAH: She came from that land where virtue in either sex is the only mark of superiority. She was an American.

SELIMA: Where is she now?

FETNAH: She is still at my father's, waiting the arrival of her ransom, for she is a woman of fortune. And though I can no longer listen to her instructions, her precepts are engraven on my heart. I feel that I was born free, and while I have life, I will struggle to remain so.

PART FIVE:

PASSION AND FANTASY IN THE 19TH CENTURY

The Female Enthusiast

Sarah Pogson
1807

Scene: a country estate in France during the Reign of Terror

Man and Woman

Belcour (20s) a man suffering from a broken heart and Estelle (18–20)
the object of his unrequited affection.

*Here, Estelle confesses to Belcour that she has married his best
friend, Henry.*

BELCOUR: Still a prisoner to this apartment?
ESTELLE: Liberty, to me, is not desirable.
　　Had I permission to go where I pleased,
　　This room would still retain its prisoner.
　　When real sorrow doth afflict the heart,
　　It will naturally seek solitude.
BELCOUR: Sorrow is relieved when participated.
　　Let me, then, bear away thy every grief,
　　So double anguish shall consume me quite.
　　But far hence be every selfish thought,
　　Till brighter prospects for thy friends arise!
ESTELLE: And are they not thy friends also, Belcour?
　　(Belcour looks earnestly at her. She appears confused.)
BELCOUR: These unconscious looks are daggers to my heart.
　　Henry's not unfortunate—not hopeless.
　　Estelle, dost thou not love Henry Corday?
　　(Belcour turns away his head, as if afraid to hear the reply.)
ESTELLE: I will never deceive thee. I do love—
BELCOUR: Ha! Beware, I cannot bear to hear it.
　　What would I not give to obtain that love?
　　The world's wide range would be a paltry step;
　　Its farthest verge my willing feet should find

To serve thee—blessed pilgrimage to me
If, when I returned, thy welcome smile,
Thy dear loved hand the rich, too rich reward.
And must I never hope again?

ESTELLE: Never!

BELCOUR: I must. It is my sole existence.
I cannot part with hope! No, Estelle!
No, never—till thou art another's.

ESTELLE: Not...if my happiness required it?
Oh, let me prove the generosity
Which once declared that thou would'st sacrifice
Thy heart's best interest to secure my peace!

BELCOUR: Name the sacrifice. Behold me ready.
Oh, bid me say—do—think—live or expire—
And, though it would be torture to resign thee,
Bid me again despair! I will say adieu! *(Looks anxiously at Estelle.)*

ESTELLE: Ah! Wilt thou, then, receive my confidence?
And, though I create a pang in that heart
Where I would ever fix content and peace,
Yet there is an act of duty which I owe
Both to myself and thee. It is to impart
A secret most important—

BELCOUR: Oh, proceed—

ESTELLE: I am married—

BELCOUR: Married! Married, Estelle?

ESTELLE: Heaven knows I am the wife of Henry.
Soften that angry look. He is thy friend!

BELCOUR: Thou'rt not married. I dare not believe it.

ESTELLE: Would I impose a falsehood on thee?
Good Belcour, be our friend—our brother.

BELCOUR: Thy friend? Thy brother?

ESTELLE: Alas! Our Henry,
Too, too soon he may be taken from us.
How critical his present situation!
If his father was not spared even here—
So distant from the fatal scenes at Paris—

How very poor the hope of his escape
From the fury of Marat's associates.
Oh, could'st thou behold the upraised arm
Preparing cruel execution—
The blow impending, that would bear away
A precious friend forever from thy sight—
No, no, Belcour, thy nature is more kind.
Thou could'st not endure the heart-rending scene,
Much less thine own arm raise against the youth,
Who was—who is thy friend!
(Belcour stands as if motionless for a time. At length, he approaches Estelle and respectfully takes her hand.)

BELCOUR: And still shall be.
Great was the effort, but 'tis conqueror now.
Surely thou wilt forgive, and Henry too.
I could not bear to see him lead thee off.
Then, the mean supposition that Le Brun
Was stationed there to watch me stung my soul;
And mad with rage, revenge, jealousy,
I sunk the prey of stormy passions.
But no more. All my endeavors shall be
To promote thy happiness. Allow me
Still to visit here, till by slow degrees
Thy father is weaned from his present plans.
Oh, farewell! *(Exit Belcour.)*

ESTELLE: Heaven give thee full reward!
(Curtain falls.)

Smiles and Tears

Marie-Thérèse De Camp

1815

Scene: a garden at night

Man and Woman

Cecil (20s) a homeless young mother and Fitzharding (50s) her emotionally distraught father.

The ruination of his beloved daughter, Cecil, by the cruel Delaval has driven Fitzharding to madness. Cecil, on the other hand, wanders the night with her baby despairing of ever finding shelter. Here the two tortured souls are unexpectedly reunited.

MR. FITZHARDING: *(Without.)* Ha, ha! have I escaped you, ruffians? here I shall be safe from their pursuit.
(He is seen climbing the wall, and with the assistance of the arm of a tree, lets himself down upon the stage; in this effort he breaks one of the smaller branches, and uses it as a weapon of defence.)
MR. FITZHARDING: —Here will I lie concealed—they shall not again imprison me!
CECIL: Some miscreant escaped from justice! What will become of us?
MR. FITZHARDING: There, there they go!—One, two, three, four!—So, so; lie close; they are gone, they are gone, and now I breathe again.
CECIL: Alas! a maniac! what's to be done? shall I conceal myself? No I'll make for the gate, and endeavour to regain the public road.
(Fitzharding turns suddenly round.)
MR. FITZHARDING: What are you? one lying in ambush to entrap me Wretch! advance one hair's breadth, and I'll fell you to the ground! *(Raising the broken branch.)* —Ah! a woman!
CECIL: Yes; one without the power or wish to harm you.

MR. FITZHARDING: That's false—you are a woman, born only to betray—I know you are leagued against me—but thus— *(Threateningly.)*

CECIL: O! for my child's sake, do not harm me.

MR. FITZHARDING: A child!—have you a child? give it me—let me strangle it, before the little serpent turns to sting the breast that nourished it—pity is folly—if she live, she lives to blast your comfort. I had a child, a child more precious to me than my own heart's blood—but she betrayed me—made a gay festival to welcome me upon my return from a long, tedious journey—invited guests too—three hideous guests! Seduction, Penury, and Despair—With the first she fled, and left me victim to the other two.

CECIL: What do I hear? what horrid vision darts across my brain! Can it be? No, no! and yet, although destruction follow, I must, I will be satisfied. *(She throws off Fitzharding's hat, recognises, and falls at his feet.)* —Great God! my father!

MR. FITZHARDING: *(Raising her, looks wistfully in her face and laughs wildly—pause.)* They are coming—you will not give me up to my pursuers—you will have more compassion than my unnatural daughter.

CECIL: Can I hear this, and yet not curse thee, Delaval?

MR. FITZHARDING: Ha! does that damned name again assail my ears. Does *he* pursue me still? What new torment can he inflict upon me? Yes, yes, I see him now—where is my daughter, villain? Give her back—restore her to me, polluted as she is, and I will bless you—but you have murdered her—your barbarous hand has nipped my pretty rose-bud ere it was blown, and now she lies, scorned, pale, and lifeless—monster! no longer shall your poisonous breath infect the air—an injured father strikes this poniard to your faithless heart—no struggling—down—down—Oh, oh!
(Cecil supports him.)

CECIL: *(Weeping.)* O, sight of horror! will all the agony I feel restore your peace, beloved, much injured father!

MR. FITZHARDING: *(Recovering—feels her cheeks.)* How! weeping! tears, real tears! poor thing, poor thing! don't cry—I cannot be a partner in your grief—since my poor Cecil died (For she is dead, is she not?) I have not shed a tear.

CECIL: Oh, Heaven! too much, too much to bear!

MR. FITZHARDING: Poor thing! poor thing! *(Pause.)* You will not leave me, will you? *(Draws her close to his bosom.)*

CECIL: Leave you! O never, never; I will serve you, live for you, die for you.

MR. FITZHARDING: Come then, come with me; and I will shew you Cecil's grave; and we will strew fresh yew and cypress over it—Come, come!

(As he is leading her away, voices of the Keepers are heard without—

[1ST KEEPER: This way, this way; I'll follow him over the wall—do you secure the gate.'—He leaps from the wall, two more come on at the gate.]

MR. FITZHARDING: I hear them, they are coming—don't let them tear me from you—save, O, save me!

Manfred

Lord Byron
1817

Scene: a remote cottage high in the Alps

Two Men

A Chamois Hunter (any age) a simple man of the mountains and
Manfred (30s) a man tortured by his past.

*Manfred has escaped to the Alps where he hopes to find either
salvation or permanent damnation for sins he has committed
against those who loved him. Here, he encounters a well-meaning peasant.*

CHAMOIS HUNTER: What is it
That thou dost see, or think thou look'st upon?
MANFRED: Myself, and thee—a peasant of the Alps,
Thy humble virtues, hospitable home,
And spirit patient, pious, proud and free;
Thy self-respect, grafted on innocent thoughts;
Thy days of health, and nights of sleep; thy toils,
By danger dignified, yet guiltless; hopes
Of cheerful old age and a quiet grave,
With cross and garland over its green turf,
And thy grandchildren's love for epitaph;
This do I see—and then I look within—
It matters not—my soul was scorch'd already!
CHAMOIS HUNTER: And wouldst thou then exchange thy lot for mine?
MANFRED: No, friend! I would not wrong thee nor exchange
My lot with living being: I can bear—
However wretchedly, 't is still to bear—
In life what others could not brook to dream,
But perish in their slumber.
CHAMOIS HUNTER: And with this—

This cautions feeling for another's pain,
Canst thou be black with evil?—say not so.
Can one of gentle thoughts have wreak'd revenge
Upon his enemies?
MANFRED: Oh! no no, no!
My injuries came down on those who loved me—
On those whom I best loved: I never quell'd
An enemy, save in my just defence—
But my embrace was fatal.
CHAMOIS HUNTER: Heaven give thee rest!
And penitence restore thee to thyself;
My prayers shall be for thee.
MANFRED: I need them not,
But can endure thy pity. I depart—
'T is time—farewell!—Here's gold, and thanks for thee;
No words—it is thy due. Follow me not;
I know my path—the mountain peril's past:
And once again, I charge thee, follow not! *(Exit Manfred.)*

Black-Ey'd Susan

Douglas Jerrold
1829

Scene: a harbor town

Two Men

Doggrass (50s) a selfish and cruel man and Gnatbrain (any age) his critic.

Here, intrepid Gnatbrain attempts to take Doggrass to task for having wronged his beautiful young niece, Susan.

DOGGRASS: Tut! if you are inclined to preach, here is a milestone—I'll leave you in its company.

GNATBRAIN: Ay, it's all very well—very well; but you have broken poor Susan's heart, and as for William—

DOGGRASS: What of him?

GNATBRAIN: The sharks of him, for what you care. Didn't you make him turn a sailor, and leave his young wife, the little delicate black-ey'd Susan, that pretty piece of soft-speaking womanhood, your niece? Now say, haven't you qualms? On a winter's night, now, when the snow is drifting at your door, what do you do?

DOGGRASS: Shut it.

GNATBRAIN: And what, when you hear the wind blowing at your chimney corner?

DOGGRASS: Get closer to the fire.

GNATBRAIN: What, when in your bed, you turn up one side at the thunder?

DOGGRASS: Turn round on the other. Will you go on with your catechism?

GNATBRAIN: No, I'd rather go and talk to the echoes. A fair day to you, Master Doggrass. If your conscience—

DOGGRASS: Conscience! Phoo! my conscience sleeps well enough.

GNATBRAIN: Sleeps! Don't wake it then—it might alarm you.

DOGGRASS: One word with you—no more of your advice: I go about like a surly bull, and you a gadfly buzzing around me. From this moment throw off the part of counsellor.

GNATBRAIN: But, don't you see?—

DOGGRASS: Don't you see these trees growing about us?

GNATBRAIN: Very well.

DOGGRASS: If a cudgel was cut from them for every knave who busies himself in the business of others—don't you think it would mightily open the prospect?

GNATBRAIN: Perhaps it might: and don't you think that if every hard-hearted, selfish rascal that destroys the happiness of others, were strung up to the boughs before they were cut for cudgels, it would, instead of opening the prospect, mightily darken it?

DOGGRASS: I have given you warning—take heed! take heed! and with this counsel, I give you a good day. *(Exit, left.)*

GNATBRAIN: Ay, it's the only thing good you can give: and that, only good, because it's not your own.

Francis The First

Fanny Kemble

1832

Scene: the royal court of France

Man and Woman

De Bourbon (30s) a proud knight and statesman and Princess
Margaret (20s) the object of his affection.

*Weary of the queen's love of tournaments and play, De Bourbon
here steals a moment with Margaret.*

*(An apartment of the Princess Margaret's. Enter De Bourbon, fol-
lowed by Margaret.)*

BOURBON: A plague upon their tournaments, I say!

MARGARET: Nay then, de Bourbon, by my woman's word,
This must not be; oh, say it shall not be!
Say, thou wilt rein this hot, impatient mood,
For thy sake—no, for mine, for mine I meant:
Are we not twined together in our love?
What wonder then, if, speaking of myself,
Thy name was on my lips?—for my sake, Bourbon.

BOURBON: If thou wilt bid me journey to the moon
Upon a moth's wing, or wilt send me forth,
Belted and spurred, to fight some score of devils—
Or worse, wilt bid me with some twenty men
Turn out Colonna from the Milanese,
Say so; and by this light I'll *do* it too!
But, to submit to *this*—to bear all this—
To let a woman tear my laurels off—
And trample them—Hell! when I think on it!
Pshaw! never fix those dangerous eyes on me,
And clasp thy hands—I say—

MARGARET: She is my mother!

BOURBON: I'faith I've often doubted of that truth;
    Thou art not like her, for the which thank heaven!
MARGARET: I *can* be like her though, my lord, in this:
    Not to endure the licence of your tongue.
    If headlong passion urge you, sir, beyond
    The bounds of prudence, look that you control it,
    Nor vent bold thoughts in bolder words to me;
    Else you may chance to find—
BOURBON: She *is* thy mother?
    Nay, smooth that brow, thou art too like the Queen;
    And in those soft blue eyes, whose orbs reflect
    Heaven's light with heaven's own purity, let not
    The stormy gleam of anger e'er flash forth!
    I had thought, Margaret, that love forgot
    All ranks and all distinctions?
MARGARET: Ay, so it doth.
    All ties, the world, its wealth, its fame, or fortune,
    Can twine; but never those of nature, Bourbon.
    So mine can give up all, save the first bond
    My heart e'er knew—the love of those who gave
    Life, and the power to love; those early links
    Lie wreathed like close-knit fibres round my heart,
    Never to sever thence till my heart break.
BOURBON: Lo! at thy feet I sue for pardon, sweet!
    By thine own purity, thou virgin lily!
    Thou flower of France! forgive the word that broke
    Too hastily from my rash lips; which thus,
    Having offended, will do penance now
    Upon this marble shrine, my lady-love. *(Kisses her hand.)*
MARGARET: A goodly penitent! Nay, never kneel,
    And look so pitiful—there, I forgive thee.
    But, Bourbon, by the faith of our sworn love,
    I do implore thee to bear with my mother.
BOURBON: Pshaw!—
MARGARET: Why, look now, there's your brow dark and contracted—

I see the passion flashing in your eyes;
You will *not* think of me, and bear with her?

BOURBON: If I could think of thee, and not see her—
Or think of thee, and not hear her, why, then—
Well, patience, and kind thoughts of thee befriend me!
And I will do my best to second them.

MARGARET: Go you to meet my mother now?

BOURBON: This hour
Love stole from duty to bestow on thee;
And now I must attend upon the Queen.

MARGARET: See you observe my lesson.

BOURBON: Fear me not;
Oh! I'll be wonderfully calm and patient.

MARGARET: *(Aside.)* Methinks I'll try thee. *(Aloud.)* —How if she should ask
Some question of your late left government?
I see you're very calm already! How
If she should speak of a fit successor?
Most patient! Lautrec now, or Bonnivet?

BOURBON: Confusion light upon them! Bonnivet?
And Lautrec? Beardless boys! whose maiden swords
Have not yet blushed with one red drop of blood;
Whose only march hath been a midnight measure,
Whose only field hath been a midnight masque;
Is it for these, and their advancement, I
Have watched, have toiled, have fought, have bled, have conquered;
Rushed over fields strewed with the dead and dying,
Swam streams that ran all curdled with the blood
Of friend and foe, stood in the bristling breach,
And in the hour of death and desolation
Won never fading victories for France?
Shall the Queen's minions—by this living light—

MARGARET: Oh, patient gentleman! how calm he is!
Now in those flaming eyes, and scornful lips,
I read how well my lesson profits thee.
Thou shalt not to the Queen in this hot mood.

BOURBON: I'faith I must; the storm is over now;

And having burst, why, I shall be the calmer.
Farewell, sweet monitress! I'll not forget.

MARGARET: Oh, but I fear—

BOURBON: Fear not—she is thy mother!

Ernest Maltreavers

Louise Medina

1838

Scene: a poor country cottage during a storm

Man and Woman

Ferrers (20–40) a man of evil and lecherous intent and Alice (18–20) an innocent young woman trying to fend off his unwanted advances.

When Ferrers threatens to take Alice by force, she has no choice but to defend herself with her father's gun.

FERRERS: Alice Darvil!

ALICE: Ha! You here again?

FERRERS: Undo the door and let me speak with you. The rain is pouring.

ALICE: I shall not. Pray, be gone. I have no dealings with you. You shall not enter here.

(Ferrers leaps in at the window.)

FERRERS: There go two words to that, my pretty one. All this dignity is very becoming, but very much out of place. I am a man of fortune and birth, in love with you. You are the daughter of the most notorious thief, vagabond, poacher that—

ALICE: Silence, sir! Whatever may be my father's failings, his daughter's ear is not the one to listen to their detail!

FERRERS: Then I'll speak of yourself. Here you live in a wretched hovel without even the necessaries of life—you, whose budding youth and excelling beauty might well become a coronet.

ALICE: Truly, sir, I am often cold, thinly clad, and hungry. Where's the remedy?

FERRERS: In my love, my sweet little cowslip of the common. Trust yourself to me, and I will wreathe that perfect brow with pearl and fold those graceful limbs in silk. Thou shalt sleep on down, eat off gold, and have no care save to vary pleasure.

ALICE: And when that pleasure surfeits, to be turned forth to suffer bitterer poverty without that best of antidotes—an honest heart! Oh, sir, sir! poor and ignorant as I am, I can confound your rhetoric. You talk of *love!* I know that love exalts, not debases, its object. You despise the peasant Alice too much to call her *wife;* she scorns you too much to be your wanton!

FERRERS: *(Aside.)* Humph! A very pretty sermon. I look damned silly here. *(To her.)* All this is very fine, Alice, but in two words take my reply. I love you; you are necessary to me. If you do not listen to reason, you shall be mine by force. *(Approaches her.)*

ALICE: Attempt no violence here. I am not alone.

FERRERS: The devil you're not. Why, who protects you?

ALICE: *(Takes up gun.)* Myself and this. You called my father "poacher." A poacher needs a gun, and his child knows how to use it.

FERRERS: *(Aside.)* What a virago! *(To her.)* Well, Alice, I see you have a spice of the devil in you, and that will fit you the better for me. Farewell, this time. The next time I come for you, it will not be alone.

Fashion
Anna Cora Mowatt
1845

Scene: the drawing room of a wealthy New Yorker

Two Women

Mrs. Tiffany (30–40) a pretentious society wannabe, and Millinette (20s) her obliging maid.

Here, we can see that foolish Mrs. Tiffany is obsessed with all things French to the point of absurdity.

MRS. TIFFANY: Is everything in order, Millinette? Ah! very elegant, very elegant, indeed! There is a *jenny-says-quoi* look about this furniture—an air of fashion and gentility perfectly bewitching. Is there not, Millinette?

MILLINETTE: Oh, *oui,* Madame!

MRS. TIFFANY: But where is Miss Seraphina? It is twelve o'clock; our visitors will be pouring in, and she has not made her appearance. But I hear that nothing is more fashionable than to keep people waiting.—None but vulgar persons pay any attention to punctuality. Is it not so, Millinette?

MILLINETTE: Quite *comme il faut.*—Great personnes always do make little personnes wait, Madame.

MRS. TIFFANY: This mode of receiving visitors only upon one specified day of the week is a most convenient custom! It saves the trouble of keeping the house continually in order and of being always dressed. I flatter myself that *I* was the first to introduce it amongst the New York *ee-light.* You are quite sure that it is strictly a Parisian mode, Millinette?

MILLINETTE: Oh, *oui,* Madame; entirely *mode de Paris.*

MRS. TIFFANY: *(Aside.)* This girl is worth her weight in gold. Millinette, how do you say *armchair* in French?

MILLINETTE: *Fauteuil,* Madame.

MRS. TIFFANY: *Fo-tool!* That has a foreign—an out-of-the-wayish sound that is perfectly charming—and so genteel! There is something about our American words decidedly vulgar. *Fowtool!* how refined. *Fowtool! Arm-chair!* what a difference!

MILLINETTE: Madame have one charmante pronunciation. *Fowtool (Mimicking aside.)* charmante, Madame!

MRS. TIFFANY: Do you think so, Millinette? Well, I believe I have. But a woman of refinement and of fashion can always accommodate herself to everything foreign! And a week's study of that invaluable work—*French without a Master,* has made me quite at home in the court language of Europe! But where is the new valet? I'm rather sorry that he is black, but to obtain a white American for a domestic is almost impossible; and they call this a free country! What did you say was the name of this new servant, Millinette?

MILLINETTE: He do say his name is Monsieur Zeke.

MRS. TIFFANY: Ezekiel, I suppose. Zeke! Dear me, such a vulgar name will compromise the dignity of the whole family. Can you not suggest something more aristocratic, Millinette? Something *French!*

MILLINETTE: *Oh, oui,* Madame; *Adolph* is one very fine name.

MRS. TIFFANY: A-dolph! Charming! Ring the bell, Millinette!
(Millinette rings the bell.)

MRS. TIFFANY: I will change his name immediately, besides giving him a few directions.

A Live Woman In The Mines

Alonzo Delano

1850

Scene: California during the gold rush

Two Men

Cash (20–40) and Dice (20–40) two unscrupulous con-men.

Here, Dice brags to Cash of how he bilked his latest victim out of five thousand dollars.

CASH: How much did you pluck that goose?

DICE: A cool five-thousand.

CASH: Five-thousand! you are in capital luck. How did you come it over the greenhorn so nicely?

DICE: Why, the moment he came in I had my eye on him. I saw he was a green 'un, just from the Mines, and therefore proper game. I carelessly began talking with him and found out that he was on his way home; told me a long yarn about his father and mother; old man was crippled, and the old woman supported the family by washing and all that nonsense, and how he should surprise them when he got home, and that they shouldn't work any more, and all that sort of thing; let out that he had dug a pile by hard labor, and had the money in his belt. Well, of course I rejoiced with him, commended him as a dutiful son, and to show him my appreciation of so much virtue, insisted on his drinking with me.

CASH: Ha! ha! ha! You're a perfect philanthropist—well—

DICE: At first he rather backed water, but I would take no denial, and I finally succeeded in getting the first dose down him. A little while after, not to be mean, he offered to treat me.

CASH: Of course you was dry.

DICE: Dry as a contribution box. I winked at Tom, so he made Sluice

Forks smash good and strong and somehow forgot to put any liquor in mine.

CASH: What monstrous partiality!

DICE: Directly he began to feel the second dose and grew friendly and confidential. Well, I offered to show him around among the girls, in the evening, with all the sights in town, and at the same time cautioned him against falling into bad hands, for he might be swindled or robbed by strangers.

CASH: Good fatherly adviser—ha! ha! ha!

DICE: Yes, and he grew grateful fast, for he insisted on my drinking with him.

CASH: Ah! that hurt your feelings.

DICE: I told him I seldom drank anything—

CASH: Only when you could get it, I s'pose?

DICE: As he would take no denial I—hem!—reluctantly consented and nodded to Tom, who flavored his glass with morphine and mine, particularly, with cold water.

CASH: You're a practical illustration of a California temperance society.

DICE: It wasn't long before he was the richest man in California, and a damned sight the smartest. Of course he was, so I invited him up to the table to see the boys play. He asked me if I ever played. I told him I seldom staked anything, but what I did I was sure to win, so I threw a dollar on the red.

CASH: And won, of course.

DICE: Of course. And then I proposed that he should try it. He demurred some, but I told him a dollar was nothing—if he lost I would share the loss—so he finally let a dollar slip on the red.

CASH: And won, of course.

DICE: To be sure; our Jake knows what he's about. Sluice Box was absolutely surprised when two dollars were pushed back to him. He then doubled his stakes and went on winning till he thought he had Fortune by the wings, when suddenly his luck changed. and he began to lose and became excited. It was my treat now, and that settled the matter, for he swore he would not leave the table till he had won the money back. So he staked his pile, and we fleeced him out of every dime, and a happier man than Sluice Box is at this moment does not exist.

CASH: How, at being robbed?

DICE: Not that exactly, but, by the time his money was gone he was so beastly drunk that Tim kicked him out of the Round Tent into the gutter. where he now lays fast asleep, getting ready for another trip to the Mines, instead of helping his mother wash at home, and plastering up his father's sore shins.

CASH: Ha! ha! ha! the fools are not all dead. We'll go it while we're young. *(Sings.)* "O, Californy, the land for me."

Masks and Faces

Taylor & Reade
1854

Scene: a modest apartment

Man and Woman

Vane (30s) a man in love with Woffington (30s) an actress from the
wrong side of the tracks.

Here, Vane and Woffington declare their love for one another.

WOFFINGTON: At last! I have been here so long.

VANE: Alone?

WOFFINGTON: In company and solitude. What has annoyed you?

VANE: Nothing.

WOFFINGTON: Never try to conceal anything from me, I know the map
of your face. These fourteen days you have been subject to some
adverse influence; and today I have discovered whose it is

VANE: No influence can ever shake yours.

WOFFINGTON: Dear friend, for your own sake, not mine; trust your own
heart, eyes, and judgement.

VANE: I do. I love you; your face is the shrine of sincerity, truth, and
candour. I alone know you: your flatterers do not—your detrac-
tors—oh! curse them!

WOFFINGTON: You see what men are! Have I done ill to hide the riches
of my heart from the heartless, and keep them all for one honest
man, who will be my friend, I hope, as well as my lover?

VANE: Ah, that is my ambition.

WOFFINGTON: We actresses make good the old proverb, 'Many lovers,
but few friends.' And oh! it is we who need a friend. Will you be
mine?

VANE: I will. Then tell me the way for me, unequal in wit and address
to many of your admirers, to win your esteem.

WOFFINGTON: I will tell you a sure way; never act in my presence, never try to be very clever or eloquent. Remember! I am the goddess of tricks: I can only love my superior. Be honest and frank as the day, and you will be my superior; and I shall love you, and bless the hour you shone on my artificial life.

VANE: Oh! thanks, thanks, for this, I trust, is in my power!

WOFFINGTON: Mind—it is no easy task: to be my friend is to respect me, that I may respect myself the more; to be my friend is to come between me and the temptations of an unprotected life—the recklessness of a vacant heart.

VANE: I will place all that is good about me at your feet. I will sympathize with you when you are sad; I will rejoice when you are gay.

WOFFINGTON: Will you scold me when I do wrong?

VANE: Scold you?

WOFFINGTON: Nobody scolds me now—a sure sign nobody loves me. Will you scold me?

VANE: *(Tenderly.)* I will try! and I will be loyal and frank. You will not hate me for a confession I make myself?
(Agitated.)

WOFFINGTON: I shall like you better—oh! so much better.

VANE: Then I will own to you—

WOFFINGTON: Oh! do not tell me you have loved others before me; I could not bear to hear it.

VANE: No—no—I never loved till now.

WOFFINGTON: Let me hear that only. I am jealous even of the past. Say you never loved but me—never mind whether it is true—say so;—but it is true, for you do not yet know love. Ernest, shall I make you love me, as none of your sex ever loved? with heart, and brain, and breath, and life, and soul?

VANE: Teach me so to love, and I am yours for ever.

Lady Audley's Secret

C. H. Hazlewood
1863

Scene: a garden at night

Man and Woman

Lady Audley (30s) a scheming murderess and George (30–40) her unlucky first husband.

Mrs. Talboys deserted her first husband and married the elderly and wealthy Sir Michael Audley. Everything seems to be coming up roses for the duplicitous Lady Audley until the unexpected arrival of George. Here, the desperate charlatan commits murder to protect her awful secret.

LADY AUDLEY: *(Turning with a shriek.)* George Talboys!
GEORGE: Aye, your husband!—the husband of her who now calls herself Lady Audley! Really, for a woman who has been dead and buried, you look remarkably well, my dear.
LADY AUDLEY: I am lost!
GEORGE: You turn away; this is but a cold welcome from a wife to her husband, after a three years' separation. You are a traitress, madam!
LADY AUDLEY: One word before we proceed further. Is it to be peace or war between us?
GEORGE: War! war to the last! war till I see thee placed in a felon's dock and sentenced by the judge.
LADY AUDLEY: Be prudent; remember, I am now rich.
GEORGE: But your reign will soon be over. What will be your position, do you think, when the world knows all? What will your noble husband think, when he finds you are the wife of another man?
LADY AUDLEY: Oh, spare me, spare me!
GEORGE: Spare you, no! I will expose you, woman—you whom—

LADY AUDLEY: Whom you left here in poverty and dependence—whom you promised to write to from India.

GEORGE: And to whom I did write.

LADY AUDLEY: Never!

GEORGE: I say, yes!

LADY AUDLEY: And I say, no! I tell you, not one letter reached my hands; I thought myself deserted, and determined to make reprisals on you; I changed my name: I entered the family of a gentleman as governess to his daughters; became the patient drudge for a miserable stipend, that I might carry my point—that point was to gain Sir Michael Audley's affections; I did so, I devoted all my energies, all my cunning, to that end! and now I have gained the summit of my ambition, do you think I will be cast down by you, George Talboys? No, I will conquer you or I will die!

GEORGE: And what means will you take to conquer me? What power will you employ to silence me?

LADY AUDLEY: The power of gold.

GEORGE: Gold! gold purchased by your falsehood—gold in my hand that has polluted yours, for which you have sold yourself to a man old enough to be your grandsire. No, false woman, I seek not a bribe, but for justice!

LADY AUDLEY: Listen to me. I have fought too hard for my position to yield it up tamely. Take every jewel, every penny I have and leave me! henceforth I can be nothing to you, nor you to me. Our first meeting was a mistake. it was the ardent passion of a boy and girl, which time has proved to have been ill advised on either side—I am no longer the weak confiding girl you first knew me—no, I am a resolute woman—and where I cannot remove an obstacle I will crush it.

GEORGE: Or be crushed.

LADY AUDLEY: You will turn informer then?

GEORGE: No, avenger—the avenger of my wrongs—the punisher of a heartless deceitful wife.

LADY AUDLEY: (With a sardonic smile.) Then you will war with a woman?

GEORGE: To the death!

LADY AUDLEY: *(Starting—aside.)* 'Death! death!' Aye that is the word—that is the only way of escape. *(Aloud.)* Then you are as merciless—

GEORGE: As you are crafty. Last night the luxurious mansion of Audley Court sheltered you—tonight a prison's roof will cover your head.

LADY AUDLEY: I defy you—scorn you—spurn you for a vindictive fool. Go to Sir Michael, if you will—denounce me, do—and I will swear to him that you are a liar—a madman—he will believe me before you. I gained his heart, his soul, his unbounded confidence, and before there is the felon's dock for me, there shall be the maniac's cell for you. Ah, ha! What think you now?

GEORGE: That you are a fool, that passion blinds your judgement and your sense. You forget, madam, that I have a friend here, his name is Robert Audley, he is devoted to me, and to serve me would sacrifice himself. I am not so helpless as you imagine, did any harm befall me, woe, woe, to the guilty one!

LADY AUDLEY: *(Aside.)* Robert Audley, his friend!

GEORGE: You see I am not so easily got rid of.

LADY AUDLEY: *(Aside.)* We shall see. I have offer'd a bribe, I have used threats. I must now employ cunning.

GEORGE: *(Seizing her by the wrist.)* Come

LADY AUDLEY: One moment. I will accompany you if you will let me be a few seconds to myself, so that I may send a few lines in my tablets to Sir Michael, saying I shall never see him more.

GEORGE: Well, be quick then.

(Music, piano, to end of act.)

LADY AUDLEY: I will.

(George goes up, and as his back is turned she goes to the well, takes off the iron handle, and conceals it in her right hand behind her.)

LADY AUDLEY: *(Aside.)* It is mine! that is one point gained—now for the second. *(Aloud, pretending faintness.)* Water, water, for mercy's sake!

(George comes down.)

LADY AUDLEY: My head burns like fire!

GEORGE: This is some trick to escape me; but I will not leave you.

LADY AUDLEY: I do not wish you. Stoop down and dip this in the well, *(Gives him her white handkerchief.)* that I may bathe my throbbing temples.

(George takes handkerchief and goes to well.)

LADY AUDLEY: Quick, quick!

GEORGE: *(Stooping down to well.)* It is the last service I shall render you. *(Lady Audley creeps up behind him unperceived.)*

LADY AUDLEY: *(Striking him with the iron handle.)* It is indeed—die! *(Pushes him down the well, the ruined stones fall with him.)*

LADY AUDLEY: He is gone—gone! and no one was a witness to the deed!

[LUKE: *(Looking on, R.U.E.)* Except me!]

LADY AUDLEY: *(Exulting.)* Dead men tell no tales! I am free! I am free! I am free!—Ha, ha, ha!

Caste

T. W. Robertson
1867

Scene: a drawing room in a modest apartment in London

Man and Woman

George (20–30) a man of rank and privilege and Esther (20–30) a
hardworking dancer and seamstress.

*Esther has decided to take a job in Manchester, forcing George to
propose.*

GEORGE: Who is that from?

ESTHER: Why do you wish to know?

GEORGE: Because I love you, and I don't think you love me, and I fear
a rival.

ESTHER: You have none.

GEORGE: I know you have so many admirers.

ESTHER: They're nothing to me.

GEORGE: Not one?

ESTHER: No. They're admirers, but there's not a husband among them.

GEORGE: Not the writer of that letter?

ESTHER: Oh, I like him very much. *(Coquettishly sighing.)*

GEORGE: Ah!

ESTHER: And I'm very fond of this letter.

GEORGE: Then, Esther, you don't care for me.

ESTHER: Don't I! How do you know?

GEORGE: Because you won't let me read that letter.

ESTHER: It won't please you if you see it.

GEORGE: I dare say not. That's just the reason that I want to. You
won't?

ESTHER: *(Hesitates.)* I will. There! *(Giving it to him.)*

GEORGE: *(Reads.)* 'Dear Madam.'

ESTHER: That's tender, isn't it?

GEORGE: 'The terms are four pounds—your dresses to be found. For eight weeks certain, and longer if you should suit. *(George L., in astonishment.)* I cannot close the engagement until the return of my partner. I expect him back today, and will write you as soon as I have seen him.—Yours very,' &c. Four pounds—find dresses. What does this mean?

ESTHER: It means that they want a Columbine for the pantomime at Manchester, and I think I shall get the engagement.

GEORGE: Manchester; then you'll leave London!

ESTHER: I must. *(Pathetically.)* You see this little house is on my shoulders. Polly only earns eighteen shillings a week, and father has been out of work a long, long time. I make the bread here, and it's hard to make sometimes. I've been mistress of this place, and forced to think ever since my mother died, and I was eight years old. Four pounds a week is a large sum, and I can save out of it. *(This speech is not to be spoken in a tone implying hardship.)*

GEORGE: But you'll go away, and I shan't see you.

ESTHER: P'raps it will be for the best. *(Rises and crosses left.)* What future is there for us? You're a man of rank, and I am a poor girl who gets her living by dancing. It would have been better that we had never met.

GEORGE: No.

ESTHER: Yes, it would, for I'm afraid that—

GEORGE: You love me?

ESTHER: I don't know. I'm not sure; but I think I do. *(Stops left, and turns half-face to George.)*

GEORGE: *(Trying to seize her hand.)* Esther!

ESTHER: No. Think of the difference of our stations.

GEORGE: That's what Hawtree says. Caste! caste! curse caste!

ESTHER: If I go to Manchester it will be for the best. We must both try to forget each other.

GEORGE: *(Comes down left, and left of table.)* Forget you! no.

Peer Gynt

Henrick Ibsen, Translated by Paul Green
1867

Scene: high in the rugged mountains

Two Men

Peer Gynt (50–60) a wandering fool and The Buttonmolder (any age)
a divine entity.

*At the end of his life, Peer finally realizes that he stupidly aban-
doned everything that was worthwhile many years ago in his
youth. When the Buttonmolder appears to escort Peer to the
afterlife, he resists.*

PEER: Your time is running out, Peer Gynt, no doubt of that. And the
shoe is beginning to pinch—to blister in fact *(Grimly as he blinks
about him.)* I'm no Napoleon, that's certain. He didn't need witnesses to prove he existed. He left his mark on the world.

BUTTONMOLDER: *(Comes in at the left front. Calling out.)* Where are the
affidavits of your sins, Peer Gynt?

(Without turning around, Peer shakes his head.)

BUTTONMOLDER: I see you haven't got them, let's get started.

PEER: I'd like to ask you a simple question.

BUTTONMOLDER: Proceed.

PEER: I'll come straight to the point. What is it to be one's self, actually?

BUTTONMOLDER: To be one's self is to destroy the worser self.

PEER: Still the wretched moralist.

BUTTONMOLDER: Man must always strive to learn what the Master
means—him to be.

PEER: *(Dully.)* But suppose a man never found out what he was meant
to be?

BUTTONMOLDER: He must feel it by intuition.

PEER: *(Frustrated.)* Intuition!

BUTTONMOLDER: But we waste time. You missed your calling, so come along.

PEER: What was my calling?

BUTTONMOLDER: A man must first conquer himself before he finds out. You didn't, so you failed to exist. Come.

PEER: But I've had existence, I tell you. I have been a dreadful sinner.

BUTTONMOLDER: Don't start that all over again.

PEER: *(Volubly.)* I mean a really great sinner. Not just in deeds, but in desires and words. I've lived a damnable life.

BUTTONMOLDER: A trifling matter.

PEER: Remember, I sold Negro slaves.

BUTTONMOLDER: Others sell minds and hearts.

PEER: I sent Hindu idols to China.

BUTTONMOLDER: Effort wasted.

PEER: *(Vehemently.)* I played at being prophet.

BUTTONMOLDER: Prophets usually end up in the casting ladle.

PEER: And I believed in fate, not God.

BUTTONMOLDER: Fate is only God in the past tense. *(Sharply.)* Time's up.

PEER: *(Ragingly.)* Everything is up. The owl smells the daylight. Don't you hear him hooting?

(In the distance the church bells begin ringing, followed by faraway singing. Peer shrinks away from the sound as if his ears were sensitive and hurt by it and draws closer to the Buttonmolder. The Buttonmolder takes him by the arm.)

BUTTONMOLDER: The people are going to church. You and I go another way.

PEER: *(Pointing.)* Look, what's shining there.

BUTTONMOLDER: Only a light in a house.

PEER: *(Quaveringly.)* Who is that singing?

(Solveig's voice is heard in the background tender, lyric and ethereal.)

BUTTONMOLDER: Only the song of some woman.

(The singing of the people continues in the distance. The outlines of the little house now come clearer to view. Peer stands there listening to Solveig's voice, thoughts beating in his fermenting

mind. His eyes light on an axe leaning against the steps to the little house. He pulls loose from the Buttonmolder.)

PEER: My axe! My little house! Solveig's kept them for me. Listen, she's singing. *(He runs over and picks up the axe. He stares at it, feels it with his hand and turns to the Buttonmolder in angry jubilance, pointing the helve at the little house.)* Fool that I have been! There is the witness I wanted. Solveig. She can swear to my sins. *(The little hut at the rear becomes still clearer.)*

BUTTONMOLDER: *(Loudly.)* Too late, the summons is served.

PEER: It is not too late. Get away. If your ladle were as big as a coffin, it still couldn't hold me and all of my sins. She will prove it to you. *(He draws closer to the house as the Buttonmolder remains suddenly silent watching him.)*

PEER: Go around said the Voice, but I can't do that now. Straight through all these wishes and appetites to her. And so let her damn me to salvation. *(He shudders and then turns sharply away from the steps of the little house, feeling the axe with his hand as if for comfort.)* But what right have I to ask her to judge me!

BUTTONMOLDER. True. What right?

(He chuckles grimly and sardonically. The song in the house rises audibly again, Peer pulls off his old hat, lifts his bearded and time scarred visage and straightens his shoulders, holding the axe tight in his grasp.)

PEER: Tighten your belt, Peer. Face the music.

Arms and the Man

George Bernard Shaw
1894

Scene: a country estate in Bulgaria

Two Women

Raina (18–20) a headstrong young lady and Catherine (40s) her
    mother.

> *During a war with Serbia, the women of the house delight in
> news from the battlefield, particularly if it details the exploits of
> handsome young Sergius, the soldier who has captured Raina's
> heart—for the moment.*

CATHERINE: *(Entering hastily, full of good news.)* Raina! *(She pro-
    nounces it Rah-eena, with the stress on the ee.)* Raina! *(She goes
    to the bed, expecting to find Raina there.)* Why, where—?
    (Raina looks into the room.)

CATHERINE: Heavens, child! are you out in the night air instead of in
    your bed? You'll catch your death. Louka told me you were
    asleep.

RAINA: *(Dreamily.)* I sent her away. I wanted to be alone. The stars are
    so beautiful! What is the matter?

CATHERINE: Such news! There has been a battle.

RAINA: *(Her eyes dilating.)* Ah! *(She comes eagerly to Catherine.)*

CATHERINE: A great battle at Slivnitza! A victory! And it was won by
    Sergius.

RAINA: *(With a cry of delight.)* Ah!
    (They embrace rapturously.)

RAINA: Oh, mother! *(Then, with sudden anxiety.)* Is Father safe?

CATHERINE: Of course: he sends me the news. Sergius is the hero of the
    hour, the idol of the regiment.

RAINA: *(Up center.)* Tell me. tell me. How was it? *(Ecstatically.)* Oh,

Mother! Mother! Mother! *(She pulls her Mother down on the ottoman; and they kiss one another frantically.)*

CATHERINE: *(With surging enthusiasm.)* You cant guess how splendid it is. A cavalry charge! think of that! He defied our Russian commanders—acted without orders—led a charge on his own responsibility—headed it himself—was the first man to sweep through their guns. Can't you see it, Raina: our gallant splendid Bulgarians with their swords and eyes flashing thundering down like an avalanche and scattering the wretched Serbs and their dandified Austrian officers like chaff. And you! *(Slaps her playfully on hand.)* you kept Sergius waiting a year before you would be betrothed to him. Oh, if you have a drop of Bulgarian blood in your veins, you will worship him when he comes back.

RAINA: What will he care for my poor little worship after the acclamations of a whole army of heroes? But no matter: I am so happy! so proud! *(She rises and walks about excitedly.)* It proves that all our ideas were real after all.

CATHERINE: *(Indignantly.)* Our ideas real! What do you mean?

RAINA: Our ideas of what Sergius would do. Our patriotism. Our heroic ideals. I sometimes used to doubt whether they were anything but dreams. Oh, what faithless little creatures girls are! When I buckled on Sergius's sword he looked so noble: it was treason to think of disillusion or humiliation or failure. And yet—and yet— *(She sits down again suddenly.)* Promise me you'll never tell him.

CATHERINE: Don't ask me for promises until I know what I'm promising.

RAINA: Well, it came into my head just as he was holding me in his arms and looking into my eyes, that perhaps we only had our heroic ideas because we are so fond of reading Byron and Pushkin, and because we were so delighted with the opera that season at Bucharest. Real life is so seldom like that! indeed never, as far as I knew it then. *(Remorsefully.)* Only think, Mother: I doubted him: I wondered whether all his heroic qualities and his soldiership might not prove mere imagination when he went into a real battle. I had an uneasy fear that he might cut a poor figure there beside all those clever officers from the Tsar's court.

CATHERINE: A poor figure! Shame on you! The Serbs have Austrian officers who are just as clever as the Russians; but we have beaten them in every battle for all that.

RAINA: *(Laughing and snuggling against her Mother.)* Yes: I was only a prosaic little coward. Oh, to think that it was all true! that Sergius is just as splendid and noble as he looks! that the world is really a glorious world for women who can see its glory and men who can act its romance! What happiness! what unspeakable fulfillment!

The Ambassador

Pearl Craigie
1898

Scene: Lady Beauvedere's in the Champs Elysees, Paris

Two Women

Juliet (18) an unhappily engaged young woman and Alice (20s) her sympathetic sister, a nun.

Juliet has accepted Sir William's proposal of marriage despite the fact that she doesn't love him. Here, she confesses her misery to Alice.

ALICE: Oh, Juliet! how you have changed since you came out!

JULIET: *(Stifling a sob.)* No, dear; I haven't changed, But, from the Convent window, we used to watch the sea. And the sea—no matter how rough it may be—always reflects the sky. Now, I have left school…I am watching the *earth* and that… *(Crosses.)*

ALICE: Well?…

JULIET: That, so far, seems to reflect…the other place! *(Covers her face with her hands.)* Oh, I am disillusioned!

ALICE: Ah no! *(Rises.)* Disillusions all come from within…from the failure of some dear and secret hope. The *world* makes no promises; we only dream it does; and when we wake, we cry!…Is Lady Beauvedere kind to you? *(Puts letters on piano.)*

JULIET: All kindness. She gave me this frock; her maid does my hair; her newest genius is painting my portrait; her dearest friends will soon be mine. But…

ALICE: What?

JULIET: In her soul she cannot bear me.

ALICE: *(Moving towards Juliet.)* Juliet!

JULIET: She thinks I am mercenary—I am not. She thinks I am frivolous—I am not. She thinks me vain, heartless, selfish—I am not…I am not! *(She bursts into tears.)*

ALICE: *(Seating herself.)* She cannot be so unjust! Consider—she has invited you here to this beautiful place.

JULIET: It isn't hers. It all belongs to Bill. That's why I feel an intruder. I am turning her out of her own home. As though I wanted it! I'd rather be a sparrow alone on a housetop than lead the life of these women of the world!

ALICE: Are you so miserable?

JULIET: Can't you see that I am utterly wretched!

ALICE: Juliet, do you…do you love him?

JULIET: No! no! no! I don't. But what shall I do? He has been so good to me. I must love him in time…Yet, that's not all…There's more.

ALICE: What else?

JULIET: There *is* a girl…who *does* love him.

ALICE: Who's that?

JULIET: Gwen Marleaze. I have just made this discovery. She's not kind; she's proud, suspicious and cold; she's cruel, she's worldly, but…she loves him. She would sell her soul for him. She's suffering…she's breaking her heart…she's dying, I believe, of love.

ALICE: Poor girl!

JULIET: Then what…is to be done?

ALICE: *(Rising.)* Dearest, this engagement must be broken off. Misery…piercing misery will come of it. You will repent it—Oh, with what anguish! what desolation of heart!

JULIET: Of course! Who ever heard of a pleasant, easy, enjoyable repentance!

ALICE: Where is Sir William now?

JULIET: At Berlin.

ALICE: Then write to him. Write to him now, and let me post the letter. Tell him, that in your attempt to make him happy, you have made two people miserable already, and the third will be himself! Tell him it is impossible, and again impossible, and yet again, impossible!

JULIET: *(With a cry of relief.)* Oh, Alice, that is just what I have been writing to him.

ALICE: You don't mean it?

JULIET: *(Drawing letter from pocket.)* See, I wrote this this morning.

(Gives letter to Alice.) I daren't tell you at first, till I knew what you thought. *(With emotion.)* I felt such a burden at home, and I knew it was my duty to feel grateful for Sir William's kindness! But I can't marry him—I cannot!

When We Dead Awaken

Henrick Ibsen, Translated by Brian Johnson and Rick Davis
1899

Scene: a snowfield in Norway

Man and Woman

Irene (40s) a woman driven to madness and suicide by despair and
   Rubek (40–50) the man she loves.

> *Irene's life was destroyed when Rubek left her for another. Years
> later the unstable woman returns to their village with the intent
> of confronting Rubek. Here, the two former lovers resolve all that
> is past, present and future.*

RUBEK: *(Grabbing for the knife.)* You've a knife!

IRENE: Always, always. Both day and night. In bed, too.

RUBEK: Give me the knife, Irene!

IRENE: *(Hiding it.)* You're not having it. I may well find a use for it.

RUBEK: What would you want to use it for here?

IRENE: *(Looking fixedly at him.)* It was meant for you, Arnold.

RUBEK: For *me!*

IRENE: When we sat by Lake Taunitz last night.

RUBEK: By Lake Taunitz—?

IRENE: In front of the farmhouse. And we played with swans and water
   lilies—

RUBEK: And then? And then?

IRENE: And I heard you say, in a voice cold as ice, out of the grave, that
   I was nothing more than an episode in your life—

RUBEK: It was you who said that, Irene! Not I.

IRENE: *(Continuing.)* I had the knife out ready. I wanted to plunge it
   into your back.

RUBEK: *(Darkly.)* Then why didn't you?

IRENE: Because it became horribly apparent to me you were already
   dead—had been dead a long time.

RUBEK: Dead?

IRENE: Dead. Dead. You as well as I. There we sat, by Lake Taunitz, we two clammy corpses, playing games with each other.

RUBEK: I don't call that dead. But you don't understand me.

IRENE: Where is that burning desire for me that you strove and fought against when I stood freely before you as the woman risen from the dead?

RUBEK: Our love is not dead, Irene.

IRENE: That love that belongs to the life of earth—that beautiful, miraculous earthlife, so full of mysteries—*that* is dead in both of us.

RUBEK: *(Ardently.)* I tell you, that same love seethes and burns in me now as fiercely as ever it did before.

IRENE: And I? Have you forgotten what I am now?

RUBEK: You can choose to be whoever and whatever you want with me. For me, you're the woman I dream of you being.

IRENE: I've stood on the stage—naked—And showed myself before hundreds of men—after you.

RUBEK: It was I who drove you onto that stage—blind as I was at the time! I set that dead image of clay above the joy of life and of love.

IRENE: *(Eyes downcast.)* Too late. Too late.

RUBEK: Everything that lies between then and now has not lowered you a hair's breadth in my eyes.

IRENE: *(Her head raised.)* Nor in mine, either.

RUBEK: Well then! So we are free. And there's still time for us to live our lives, Irene!

IRENE: *(Regarding him sadly.)* The desire for life died in me, Arnold. Now I am risen. And I search for you and find you. And then discover that both you and life lie dead—just as I lay dead.

RUBEK: Oh, you are deluded! Life within us and around us still seethes and surges as it ever did!

IRENE: *(Smiling and shaking her head.)* Your young woman risen from the dead sees the whole of life as laid out in a morgue.

RUBEK: *(Throws his arms ardently around her.)* Then let us two dead souls live life to the full for once—before we go down into our graves again!

IRENE: *(With a cry.)* Arnold!

RUBEK: But not here in this half light. Not here with this hideous, wet grave cloth flapping about us—

IRENE: *(In mounting passion.)* No, no—up into the light glittering in all its glory. Up to the promised mountain peaks.

RUBEK: And up there we'll celebrate our marriage feast, Irene—my beloved.

IRENE: *(Proudly.)* The sun will look gladly on us, Arnold.

RUBEK: All the powers of light may look gladly on us. And those of darkness, too. *(Grasping her hands.)* Will you now follow me, my bride, redeemed and blest?

IRENE: *(As if transfigured.)* Gladly and willingly, I follow my lord and master.

RUBEK: *(Leading her.)* First we must go through the mist, Irene, and then—

IRENE: Yes, through all the mists. And then right up to the top of the tower that gleams in the sunrise.

PART SIX:

THE EARLY
20TH CENTURY...
SEX AND POLITICS

The Three Sisters

Anton Chekhov, Translated by Carol Rocamora
1901

Scene: a provincial Russian town

Man and Woman

Masha (30s) the daughter of a military officer and Vershinin (30s–50s)
a lieutenant colonel battery commander.

*Despite the fact that they are each married, Masha and Vershinin
have been spending a great deal of time together. Here, Vershinin
finally breaks down and confesses his feelings.*

MASHA: I don't know. *(Pause.)* Really, I don't know. Of course, it all
depends on what you're used to. After father died, for example,
it took us forever to get used to the fact that there weren't so
many military orderlies around any more. But apart from that, I
think it's fair to say, it may not be so in other places, but in our
town, the most decent, the most honorable, the most cultivated
people are the military.

VERSHININ: I'm thirsty. I wouldn't mind some tea.

MASHA: *(Glances at the clock.)* They'll bring it in, soon. They married
me off when I was eighteen, and, oh, was I terrified of my husband then, well, after all, he was a teacher, and I'd only just finished school myself. He seemed so terribly learned, so brilliant. so
important. Not any more. I'm sorry to say.

VERSHININ: Yes...I see.

MASHA: But, it's not my husband I'm talking about, I've gotten used to
him. It's just that among the civilian population in general there
are so many rude, ill-bred, uneducated people. Rudeness offends
me, it upsets me, I suffer when I see people who lack sensitivity,
gentility, refinement. And when I'm in the company of the other
faculty, my husband's colleagues, oh, how I suffer...

VERSHININ: Yes, indeed...But, it seems to me, it make no difference whatsoever whether they're civilian or whether they're military, they're all dull, at least they are in this town. No difference at all! If you listen to a member of the local intelligentsia, civilian or military, why, he's bored to tears, he's fed up with his wife, he's fed up with his house, he's fed up with his estate, he's fed up with his horses...A Russian prides himself on nobility of mind, loftiness of thought, he seeks the higher ground, so then tell me, why in real life does he sink so low? Why?

MASHA: Why?

VERSHININ: Why is he fed up with his children, why is he fed up with his wife? And why are his wife and children fed up with him?

MASHA: You're in a funny mood tonight.

VERSHININ: Perhaps. I haven't had any dinner yet, I've had nothing to eat since this morning. My daughter's ill, and when my little girls aren't well, I'm tormented by anxiety, tortured by my conscience, by the fact that they have such a mother! Oh, if only you could have seen her today! What a wretched creature she is! We started quarreling at seven this morning, and at nine I walked out and slammed the door. *(Pause.)* I never talk about this, isn't it strange, not to anyone but you, you alone. *(Kisses her hand.)* Don't be angry with me. Without you, I have no one, no one... *(Pause.)*

MASHA: What a strange noise there is, coming from the stove...Shortly before Father died, there was a moaning in the chimney. It sounded just like that.

VERSHININ: Are you superstitious?

MASHA: Yes.

VERSHININ: Strange. *(Kisses her hand.)* What a dazzling, ravishing woman you are. Dazzling, ravishing! It's dark in here, but I can see your eyes shining.

MASHA: *(Sits in another chair.)* It's lighter over here.

VERSHININ: I love you, I love you, I love you...I love your eyes, your every movement, you come to me in my dreams...A dazzling, ravishing woman!

MASHA: *(Laughs softly.)* You speak to me like that, and I can't help laughing, even though it petrifies me. Don't say it again, I beg of you… *(In a lower voice.)* Oh. go ahead, say it anyway, I don't care… *(Covers her face with her hands.)* I don't care. They're coming, talk about something else…

The Playboy of the Western World

John Millington Synge
1907

Scene: a small village in Ireland

Man and Woman

Widow Quin (30–40) an earthy woman looking for love and Mahon
(50s) a man tracking down his wayward son.

*Young Christy has appeared in the village and is soon declared
the playboy of the western world by all for his self-proclaimed
feats of bravery and panache. Here, Christy's dad arrives at the
widow's door and she soon learns the truth about the so-called
playboy.*

WIDOW QUIN: *(In great amusement.)* God save you, my poor man.

MAHON: *(Gruffly.)* Did you see a young lad passing this way in the early
morning or the fall of night?

WIDOW QUIN: You're a queer kind to walk in not saluting at all.

MAHON: Did you see the young lad?

WIDOW QUIN: *(Stiffly.)* What kind was he?

MAHON: An ugly young streeler with a murderous gob on him, and a
little switch in his hand. I met a tramper seen him coming this
way at the fall of night.

WIDOW QUIN: There's harvest hundreds do be passing these days for the
Sligo boat For what is it you're wanting him, my poor man?

MAHON: I want to destroy him for breaking the head on me with the
clout of a loy. *(He takes off a big hat, and shows his head in a
mass of bandages and plaster, with some pride.)* It was he did
that, and amn't I a great wonder to think I've traced him ten days
with that rent in my crown?

WIDOW QUIN: *(Taking his head in both hands and examining it with
extreme delight.)* That was a great blow. And who hit you? A robber maybe?

MAHON: It was my own son hit me, and he the divil a robber, or anything else, but a dirty, stuttering lout.

WIDOW QUIN: *(Letting go his skull and wiping her hands in her apron.)*
You'd best be wary of a mortified scalp, I think they call it, lep-
ping around with that wound in the splendor of the sun. It was
a bad blow surely, and you should have vexed him fearful to
make him strike that gash in his da.

MAHON: Is it me?

WIDOW QUIN: *(Amusing herself.)* Aye. And isn't it a great shame when
the old and hardened do torment the young?

MAHON: *(Raging.)* Torment him is it? And I after holding out with the
patience of a martyred saint till there's nothing but destruction
on, and I'm driven out in my old age with none to aid me.

WIDOW QUIN: *(Greatly amused.)* It's a sacred wonder the way that
wickedness will spoil a man.

MAHON: My wickedness, is it? Amn't I after saying it is himself has me
destroyed, and he a liar on walls, a talker of folly, a man you'd see
stretched the half of the day in the brown ferns with his belly to
the sun.

WIDOW QUIN: Not working at all?

MAHON: The divil a work, or if he did itself, you'd see him raising up a
haystack like the stalk of a rush, or driving our last cow till he
broke her leg at the hip, and when he wasn't at that he'd be fool-
ing over little birds he had—finches and felts—or making mugs
at his own self in the bit of a glass he had hung on the wall.

WIDOW QUIN: *(Looking at Christy.)* What way was he so foolish? It was
running wild after the girls maybe?

MAHON: *(With a shout of derision.)* Running wild, is it? If he seen a red
petticoat coming swinging over the hill, he'd be off to hide in the
sticks, and you'd see him shooting out his sheep's eyes between
the little twigs and the leaves, and his two ears rising like a hare
looking out through a gap. Girls, indeed!

WIDOW QUIN: It was drink maybe?

MAHON: And he a poor fellow would get drunk on the smell of a pint.
He'd a queer rotten stomach, I'm telling you, and when I gave
him three pulls from my pipe a while since, he was taken with

contortions till I had to send him in the ass cart to the females' nurse.

WIDOW QUIN: *(Clasping her hands.)* Well, I never till this day heard tell of a man the like of that!

MAHON: I'd take a mighty oath you didn't surely, and wasn't he the laughing joke of every female woman where four baronies meet, the way the girls would stop their weeding if they seen him coming the road to let a roar at him, and call him the looney of Mahon's.

WIDOW QUIN: I'd give the world and all to see the like of him. What kind was he?

MAHON: A small low fellow.

WIDOW QUIN: And dark?

MAHON: Dark and dirty.

WIDOW QUIN: *(Considering.)* I'm thinking I seen him.

MAHON: *(Eagerly.)* An ugly young blackguard.

WIDOW QUIN: A hideous, fearful villain, and the spit of you.

MAHON: What way is he fled?

WIDOW QUIN: Gone over the hills to catch a coasting steamer to the north or south.

MAHON: Could I pull up on him now?

WIDOW QUIN: If you'll cross the sands below where the tide is out, you'll be in it as soon as himself, for he had to go round ten miles by the top of the bay. *(She points to the door.)* Strike down by the head beyond and then follow on the roadway to the north and east.

(Mahon goes abruptly.)

WIDOW QUIN: *(Shouting after him.)* Let you give him a good vengeance when you come up with him, but don't put yourself in the power of the law, for it'd be a poor thing to see a judge in his black cap reading out his sentence on a civil warrior the like of you.

A Man's World

Rachel Crothers
1909

Scene: an old house in lower New York City

Man and Woman

Fritz (20s) a young German musician and Lione (20s) a singer.

> *Fritz and Lione live in the same apartment house as Frank, a beautiful writer with whom Fritz is infatuated. Frank is the guardian of Kiddie, a little boy that she brought to New York with her from Paris. Here, jealous Lione gives Fritz her opinion of Kiddie's true parentage.*

LIONE: What I don't understand about you is—how can you let a woman flirt with you when you know she is crazy about another man.

FRITZ: You mean Frank? She does not flirt with me. She iss a friend.

LIONE: Will you admit that she's in love with Gaskell?

FRITZ: She don't want to love any man.

LIONE: Oh, is that what she tells you?

FRITZ: No—no—she tells me nodding. Dat iss what I tink.

LIONE: You do? Well, you're about as wise as a kitten. I know she's in love with Gaskell and I think she always has been—that is—long before she came here.

FRITZ: Ach! Why? Why you tink dot? She never know him.

LIONE: *(Lifting the miniature.)* Whom does Kiddie look like?

FRITZ: What do you mean?

LIONE: Look.

FRITZ: No, no—I will not look.

LIONE: *(Catching his arm.)* Why won't you look? Are you afraid to?

FRITZ: No—no—I am not afraid. Why should I be?

LIONE: Why you are so excited?

FRITZ: I am not excited.

LIONE: You are. Oh! You see the resemblance too, do you?

FRITZ: What resemblance? I don't know what you are talking about.

LIONE: Don't you? Who is he like through the eyes?

FRITZ: Who? He iss like himself.

LIONE: *(Holding the picture before him.)* It's Malcolm Gaskell!

FRITZ: *(Closing his eyes.)* Ach Gott! What do you mean?

LIONE: You know what it means. Frank came here alone with this child. There is a mystery about her—then Gaskell comes—they're in love with each other and pretend not to be. I'll bet anything you like, Gaskell is this boy's father.

FRITZ: You have made it all up.

LIONE: You either know it's the truth or you're *afraid* it is. I'll tell her that I know.

FRITZ: No.

LIONE: I will—I will—I will. There's no reason why I shouldn't and there's every reason why I should.

FRITZ: Listen to me. If you will promise to keep still—if you will promise to say nodding to anybody about it, I will tell you what I tink.

LIONE: *(Looking at him keenly.)* What's that?

FRITZ: Frank has told us he is de child of a woman who died.

LIONE: Yes—but who is the father?

FRITZ: *She* don't know who de fadder was. But when Gaskell first came here *I* see dis resemblance and *I* believe he is de boy's fadder. Maybe he don't know it—maybe he do—but Frank don't know it. I am as sure of dat as I am standing here.

LIONE: Fritz, you must think I'm an awful fool. Of all the cock and bull stories I ever heard—that's the worst.

FRITZ: It might—it might be. Dis iss a strange und funny old world.

LIONE: But it isn't as funny as that. Oh Fritz, I want to save you from this woman, from her influence.

FRITZ: She iss de best influence dot efer came into my life.

LIONE: What's going to come of it?

FRITZ: Nodding.

LIONE: You love her?

FRITZ: You are two women, Lione. You and I used to haf such good times togedder. I lof your voice, Lione, you haf someding great in it. I like to play for you when you sing. You are so jolly and so sweet when you—when you are nice. Why can't it always be so? Why can't we always be friends?

LIONE: She's changed everything. She's spoiled everything. She's ruining your life—and I'm trying to save you.

FRITZ: No—Lione—you don't—

LIONE: I've wasted my friendship on you—wasted it—wasted it—!

Recklessness

Eugene O'Neill

1913

Scene: a well-appointed home

Man and Woman

Baldwin (40s) an unsuspecting husband and Gene (20s) his angry
maid.

> *Fred, the chauffeur, has broken up with Gene and begun an
> affair with Mrs. Baldwin. Here, fury propels the woman scorned
> to reveal all to her employer.*

BALDWIN: But what is it that's troubling you?

GENE: I hardly dare to tell you, sir.

BALDWIN: I love to comfort beauty in distress.

GENE: I know you'll be awful angry at me when you hear it.

BALDWIN: You are foolish to think so. It's a love affair, of course.

GENE: Yes, sir.

BALDWIN: Well, who is the fortunate party and what has he done or not
done?

GENE: Oh no, you're mistaken, sir. It isn't my love affair. It's someone
else's.

BALDWIN: *(Impatiently.)* You're very mysterious. Whose is it then?

GENE: It's Fred's, sir.

BALDWIN: But—I had rather an idea that you and Fred were not altogether indifferent to each other. *(Sarcastically.)* You don't mean to
tell me the handsome young devil has jilted you?

GENE: *(Her voice harsh with anger.)* He does not love me any more.

BALDWIN: *(Mockingly.)* I shall have to chide him. His morals are really
too corrupt for his station in life. My only advice to you is to find
another sweetheart. There is nothing that consoles one so much
for the loss of a lover as—another lover.

GENE: *(Trembling with rage at his banter.)* I am well through with him.

It's you and not me who ought to be concerned the most this time.

BALDWIN: *(Frowning.)* I? And pray tell me why I should be interested in the amours of my chauffeur?

GENE: *(A bit frightened.)* There's lots of things happened since you've been away.

BALDWIN: *(Irritably.)* I am waiting for you to reveal in what way all this concerns me.

GENE: They've been together all the time you've been away—every day and *(Hesitating for a moment at the changed look on his face—then resolutely.)* every night too. *(Vindictively.)* I've watched them when they thought no one was around. I've heard their "I love yous" and their kisses. Oh, they thought they were so safe! But I'll teach him to throw me over the way he did. I'll pay her for all her looking down on me and stealing him away. She's a bad woman, is what I say! Let her keep to her husband like she ought to and not go meddling with other people—

BALDWIN: *(Interrupting her in a cold, hard voice and holding himself in control by a mighty effort.)* It isn't one of the servants?

(Gene shakes her head.)

BALDWIN: No. I forget you said she was married. One of the summer people near here?

(Gene shakes her head.)

BALDWIN: Someone in this house?

(Gene nods. Baldwin's body grows tense. His heavy lids droop over his eyes, his mouth twitches. He speaks slowly as if the words came with difficulty.)

BALDWIN: Be careful! Think what you are saying! There is only one other person in this house. Do—you—mean to—say it is that person?

(Gene is too terrified to reply.)

BALDWIN: Answer me, do you hear? Answer me! Is that the person you refer to?

GENE: *(In a frightened whisper.)* Yes.

BALDWIN: *(Springing at her and clutching her by the throat with both hands.)* You lie! You lie!

(He forces her back over the edge of the table. She frantically tries to tear his hands away.)

BALDWIN: Tell me you lie, damn you, or I'll choke you to hell!

(She gasps for breath and her face becomes a dark crimson. Baldwin suddenly realizes what he is doing and takes his hands away. Gene falls half across the table, her breath coming in great shuddering sobs. Baldwin stands silently beside her waiting until she can speak again. Finally he leads her to one of the Morris chairs and pushes her into it. He stands directly in front of her.)

BALDWIN: You can speak again?

GENE: *(Weakly.)* Yes—no thanks to you.

BALDWIN: You understand, don't you, that what you have said requires more proof than the mere statement of a jealous servant. *(He pronounces the "servant" with a sneer of contempt.)*

GENE: I've got proof, don't you worry, but I don't know whether I'll show it to you or not. A man that chokes women deserves to be made a fool of.

Miss Lulu Bett

Zona Gale
1920

Scene: a general store in a small town

Man and Woman

Cornish (30s) a kind-hearted store clerk in love with Lulu (30s) a
woman on the verge of being truly free for the first time in her
life.

*Lulu unwittingly married a duplicitous bigamist. When the truth
about his first marriage was revealed, Lulu returned to her family
home in disgrace where she has been regarded as little more
than an unappreciated servant for years. When her husband's
first wife is finally located and the false marriage annulled, Lulu
decides to set out on her own. Here, she stops by the general
store to say good-bye to Cornish and receives an unexpectes proposal of marriage.*

CORNISH: And you're free now.
LULU: That's so—I am. I hadn't thought of that…It's late. Now I'm
really going. Good-by.
CORNISH: Don't say good-by.
LULU: It's nearly train time.
CORNISH: Don't you go…Do you think you could possibly stay here
with me?
LULU: Oh!…
CORNISH: I haven't got anything. I guess maybe you've heard something about a little something I'm supposed to inherit. Well, it's
only five hundred dollars…That little Warden house—it don't cost
much—you'd be surprised. Rent, I mean. I can get it now. I went
and looked at it the other day but then I didn't think…well, I
mean, it don't cost near as much as this store. We could furnish

up the parlor with pianos…that is; if you could ever think of such a thing as marrying me.

LULU: But—you *know!* Why, don't the disgrace—

CORNISH: What disgrace?

LULU: Oh, you—you—

CORNISH: There's only this about that. Of course, if you loved him very much then I ought not to be talking this way to you. But I didn't think—

LULU: You didn't think what?

CORNISH: That you did care so very much about him. I don't know why.

LULU: I wanted somebody of my own. That's the reason I done what I done. I know that now.

CORNISH: I figured that way…Look here, I ought to tell you. I'm not— I'm awful lonesome myself. This is no place to live. Look—look here. *(He draws the green curtain revealing the mean little cot and washstand.)* I guess living so is one reason why I want to get married. I want some kind of a home.

LULU: Of course.

CORNISH: I ain't never lived what you might say private.

LULU: I've lived too private.

(Pause.)

CORNISH: Then there's another thing. I—I don't believe I'm ever going to be able to do anything with the law.

LULU: I don't see how anybody does.

CORNISH: And I'm not much good in a business way. Sometimes I think that I may never be able to make any money.

LULU: Lots of men don't.

CORNISH: Well, there it is. I'm no good at business. I'll never be a lawyer. And—and everything I say sounds wrong to me. And yet I do believe that I'd know enough not to bully a woman. Not to make her unhappy. Maybe even, I could make her a little happy.

LULU: Lots of men do.

Color Struck

Zora Neale Hurston
1924

Scene: a southern city

Man and Woman

John (42) a man searching for his lost love and Emmaline (30s) his lost love.

Here, John returns to the south to find Emma, the woman he once loved, with the intent of bringing her back north to his home in Philadelphia.

WOMAN: Who's that?

VOICE OUTSIDE: Does Emma Beasely live here?

EMMA: Yeah— *(Pause.)* —who is it?

VOICE: It's me—John Turner.

EMMA: *(Puts hands eagerly on the fastening.)* John? did you say John Turner?

VOICE: Yes, Emma, it's me.

(The door is opened and the man steps inside.)

EMMA: John! Your hand *(She feels for it and touches it.)* John flesh and blood.

JOHN: *(Laughing awkwardly.)* It's me all right, old girl. Just as bright as a basket of chips. Make a light quick so I can see how you look. I'm crazy to see you. Twenty years is a long time to wait, Emma.

EMMA: *(Nervously.)* Oh, let's we all just sit in the dark awhile. *(Apologetically.)* I wasn't expecting nobody and my house aint picked up. Sit down. *(She draws up the chair. She sits in rocker.)*

JOHN: Just to think! Emma! Me and Emma sitting down side by each. Know how I found you?

EMMA: *(Dully.)* Naw. How?

JOHN: *(Brightly.)* Soon's I got in town I hunted up Wesley and he told me how to find you. That's who I come to see, you!

Sex

Mae West
1926

Scene: a lavish hotel room in NYC, the Roaring 20s

Two Women

Margy (20s–30s) a woman with a shady past in love with a guy from the right side of the tracks and Agnes (30s) her friend; a prostitute down on her luck.

On the eve of a cruise, Margy is paid a visit by her old friend, Agnes. When Agnes discovers that Margy and the wealthy Stanton are in love, she begs her friend to take advantage of the opportunity to live a good life.

AGNES: *(Enters.)* Margy, Margy.

MARGY: Agnes, Agnes— You poor kid, I thought you went home

AGNES: I did, but you were right. They wouldn't let me come back.

MARGY: What? Your folks?

AGNES: When I got back home, Mother was dead. If she had lived it might have been different. But the others—

MARGY: They forgive you but they won't let you forget—Oh what's the difference? *(Pats Agnes on the back.)*

AGNES: And when I got back to Montreal, Curley was—

MARGY: What, another jane?

AGNES: No, an overdose of morphine.

MARGY: You poor kid. But what brought you here?

AGNES: I heard you were following the fleet and doing well—And I thought travelling around would help me to forget.

MARGY: But you didn't—

AGNES: No, it's all too much—My—Mother— *(Cough. Agnes is crying.)*

MARGY: You poor kid—Come on over here and have a drink. Pull yourself together. *(Offers her a drink.)*

AGNES: Thanks. *(Drinks.)* I been trying to get a chance to talk to you, but the gobs said you were ritzing it.

MARGY: So that's what they think?

AGNES: I wanted to tell you that I saw Rocky before I left and I'm afraid that he—

MARGY: I don't want to hear anything about that rat.

AGNES: Gee, you must have caught that rich guy you were talking about in Montreal!

MARGY: Kid, I could have caught a dozen had I been so inclined.

AGNES: And you didn't?

MARGY: No, I did not. I guess I've been saved up to try and forget.

AGNES: Margy, you're in love with someone.

MARGY: How did you guess?

AGNES: Who?

MARGY: A clean boy, Agnes, and he loves me and wants me to marry him. A boy that believes I'm straight.

AGNES: My Gawd, that's wonderful. What are you going to do?

MARGY: I'm sending him back to his folks. Sometimes I feel that I should tell him the truth.

AGNES: Don't do that—don't do that—What he don't know won't hurt him.

MARGY: You mean I should marry this boy and pretend—No, I can't. That's what's worrying me.

AGNES: Margy, this is your chance! Suppose you tell him, what good would it do? If he really loves you it won't matter to him what you've been, but for God's sake get out of this life—just look at me—I'm a wreck—my health is all gone—and I'm nothing— *(She coughs.)*

MARGY: Come on, pull yourself together, you're all to pieces.

AGNES: Sometimes I wish I were out of it all.

MARGY: Come, Aggie, brace up, I've never seen you as bad as this before.

AGNES: Marge, promise me you'll do it, promise me you'll marry him, you must! God, if I had your chance nothing in the world would keep me from it. Don't be a fool, it don't matter what you were—it's the kind of a wife you make that counts.

MARGY: Maybe you're right.

AGNES: I *am* right! *(Coughs.)*

MARGY: Come on, I can't let you get away like this. Let me get you a room and some clothes, and get these rags off of you.

AGNES: No Marge, what would they think of you if they saw me here—

MARGY: The whole hotel is down at the ball on the flagship.

AGNES: No Marge, I got to go—I got to walk—I got to think—I may see you later—But I got to go—I got to go— *(Exits sobbing.)*

The Drag

Mae West

1927

Scene: a suburban home

Two Men

Rolly (30–40) a closeted homosexual married to Clair and Grayson
(20s–30s) his employee.

*Here, Rolly tries unsuccessfully to seduce Grayson, who happens
to be secretly in love with Clair.*

ROLLY: Cigarette, Allen?
   *(Grayson takes cigarette—doesn't pay any attention—keeps
   looking at blueprint.)*
ROLLY: *(Watching Grayson intently.)* Light? *(Lights his own and
   Grayson's cigarettes.)*
   *(Grayson feels uncomfortable. Sits left of table, but interests self
   in blueprint.)*
ROLLY: *(Crosses to divan and sits.)* Well, what did you think of my
   friends?
GRAYSON: I didn't see very much of them. I felt I was rushing them out.
ROLLY: Great boys, great boys, I am going on a weekend party and I'd
   love to have you join us. You'll find the boys rather interesting, I
   think.
GRAYSON: You think so?
ROLLY: You've never met that particular type before?
GRAYSON: I can't say that I have.
ROLLY: Perhaps you have and you didn't know it.
   (Grayson looks up.)
ROLLY: Why do you suppose I've had you come here so often? Haven't
   you noticed the friendship I've had for you since the day you
   stepped into the office? All I could do was eat, drink, sleep, think
   of Allen Grayson.

GRAYSON: Why, Rolly, I'd hate to have you think of me in just that way. *(Rises.)* I've always looked at you as a he-man. God, this is— *(Crosses over to left of center, faces left.)*

ROLLY: I *(Rises. Crosses toward him and over to table. Hums song.)* I thought you had some idea of how I felt toward you—my great interest in you.

GRAYSON: Yes, I did think it extraordinary. *(Crosses center, turns and looks at him.)* But what about your wife?

ROLLY: You mean why I married?

GRAYSON: Yes.

ROLLY: That is very easy to explain. Clair's dad and mine were very good friends, it was their one ambition that we should marry. It was practically arranged ever since we were children together and Clair is the same today as the day I married her, if you know what I mean.

GRAYSON: Why, I think that's the most contemptible thing you could do—marry a woman and use her as a cloak to cover up what you are.

ROLLY: I don't see why you should feel this way about it. She's perfectly contented.

GRAYSON: You don't mean to tell me she knows what you are.

ROLLY: No. Clair is just the type of woman that wouldn't understand if she did know.

GRAYSON: How could you play on a woman's innocence like that?

ROLLY: Just why should you take such an interest in my wife? *(Takes step to center.)*

GRAYSON: I just can't stand to see a sweet innocent girl like Clair treated that way.

ROLLY: Oh, I see. *(Takes step toward him.)* I think I understand where your interest lies. After I've given you the hospitality of my home, trusted you with my wife.

GRAYSON: Yes, I am interested in your wife. As for your hospitality, your plans and the great Kingsbury works, they can go to hell. I think you're a rotter. God! *(He throws the plans on the table—starts to go.)*

ROLLY: *(Tries to stop him.)* Just a minute, Allen.

GRAYSON: Please...

ROLLY: Now you can't go like this. You're taking the wrong attitude. Now, let's forget all about it.

GRAYSON: Forget about it.

Waiting for Lefty

Clifford Odets
1935

Scene: an office

Two Men

Miller (30–40) a man facing a moral dilemma and Fayette (any age) a
   ruthless businessman.

*When Fayette offers Miller a substantial sum of money to become
an industrial spy, it only takes a moment for Miller to make up his
mind.*

MILLER: May I ask the nature of the new work?
FAYETTE: *(Looking around first.)* Poison gas…
MILLER: Poison!
FAYETTE: Orders from above. I don't have to tell you from where. New
   type poison gas for modern warfare.
MILLER: I see.
FAYETTE: You didn't know a new war was that close, did you?
MILLER: I guess I didn't.
FAYETTE: I don't have to stress the importance of absolute secrecy.
MILLER: I understand!
FAYETTE: The world is an armed camp today. One match sets the whole
   world blazing in forty-eight hours. Uncle Sam won't be caught
   napping!
MILLER: *(Addressing his pencil.)* They say twelve million men were killed
   in that last one and twenty million more wounded or missing.
FAYETTE: That's not our worry. If big business went sentimental over
   human life there wouldn't be big business of any sort!
MILLER: My brother and two cousins went in the last one.
FAYETTE: They died in a good cause.
MILLER: My mother says "no!"

FAYETTE: She won't worry about you this time. You're too valuable behind the front.

MILLER: That's right.

FAYETTE: All right, Miller. See Siegfried for further orders.

MILLER: You should have seen my brother—he could ride a bike without hands…

FAYETTE: You'd better move some clothes and shaving tools in tomorrow. Remember what I said—you're with a growing organization.

MILLER: He could run the hundred yards in 9:8 flat…

FAYETTE: Who?

MILLER: My brother. He's in the Meuse-Argonne Cemetery. Mama went there in 1926…

FAYETTE: Yes, those things stick. How's your handwriting Miller, fairly legible?

MILLER: Fairly so.

FAYETTE: Once a week I'd like a little report from you.

MILLER: What sort of report?

FAYETTE: Just a few hundred words once a week on Dr. Brenner's progress.

MILLER: Don't you think it might be better coming from the Doctor?

FAYETTE: I didn't ask you that.

MILLER: Sorry.

FAYETTE: I want to know what progress he's making, the reports to be purely confidential—between you and me.

MILLER: You mean I'm to watch him?

FAYETTE: Yes!

MILLER: I guess I can't do that…

FAYETTE: Thirty a month raise…

MILLER: You said twenty…

FAYETTE: Thirty!

MILLER: Guess I'm not built that way.

FAYETTE: Forty…

MILLER: Spying's not in my line, Mr. Fayette!

FAYETTE: You use ugly words, Mr. Miller!

MILLER: For ugly activity? Yes!

FAYETTE: Think about it, Miller. Your chances are excellent…

MILLER: No...

FAYETTE: You're doing something for your country. Assuring the United States that when those goddamn Japs start a ruckus we'll have offensive weapons to back us up! Don't you read your newspapers, Miller?

MILLER: Nothing but Andy Gump.

FAYETTE: If you were on the inside you'd know I'm talking cold sober truth! Now, I'm not asking you to make up your mind on the spot. Think about it over your lunch period.

MILLER: No.

FAYETTE: Made up your mind already?

MILLER: Afraid so.

FAYETTE: You understand consequences?

MILLER: I lose my raise—And my job!

FAYETTE: *(Simultaneously.)* And your job!

MILLER: *(Simultaneously.)* You misunderstand—Rather dig ditches first!

FAYETTE: That's a big job for foreigners

MILLER: But sneaking—and making poison gas—that's for Americans?

FAYETTE: It's up to you.

MILLER: My mind's made up.

FAYETTE: No hard feelings?

MILLER: Sure hard feelings! I'm not the civilized type, Mr. Fayette. Nothing suave or sophisticated about me. Plenty of hard feelings! Enough to want to bust you and all your kind square in the mouth! *(Does exactly that.)*

The Little Foxes

Lillian Hellman
1939

Scene: the home of a squabbling and scheming extended family

Man and Woman

Regina (30s) a woman trying to exploit her estranged husband,
    Horace (40s)

> *Horace has returned to the family home from Baltimore where he
> has been treated for a serious heart condition only to find every-
> one waging war over an upcoming inheritance. Here, he and
> Regina agree not to fight, if they can help it.*

HORACE: *(There is silence for a minute.)* Regina.
    (She turns to him.)
HORACE: Why did you send Zan to Baltimore?
REGINA: Why? Because I wanted you home. You can't make anything
    suspicious out of that, can you?
HORACE: I didn't mean to make anything suspicious about it.
    (Hesitantly, taking her hand.) Zan said you wanted me to come
    home. I was so pleased at that and touched. It made me feel
    good.
REGINA: *(Taking away her hand.)* Touched that I should want you
    home?
HORACE: I'm saying all the wrong things as usual. Let's try to get along
    better. There isn't so much more time. Regina, what's all this crazy
    talk I've been hearing about Zan and Leo? Zan and Leo marrying?
REGINA: *(Turning to him, sharply.)* Who gossips so much around here?
HORACE: *(Shocked.)* Regina!
REGINA: *(Anxious to quiet him.)* It's some foolishness that Oscar
    thought up. I'll explain later. I have no intention of allowing any
    such arrangement. It was simply a way of keeping Oscar quiet in
    all this business I've been writing you about—

HORACE: *(Carefully.)* What has Zan to do with any business of Oscar's? Whatever it is, you had better put it out of Oscar's head immediately. You know what I think of Leo.

REGINA: But there's no need to talk about it now.

HORACE: There is no need to talk about it ever. Not as long as I live. *(Horace stops, slowly turns to look at her.)* As long as I live. I've been in a hospital for five months. Yet since I've been here you have not once asked me about—about my health. *(Then gently.)* Well, I suppose they've written you. I can't live very long.

REGINA: I've never understood why people have to talk about this kind of thing.

HORACE: *(There is a silence. Then he looks up at her, his face cold.)* You misunderstand. I don't intend to gossip about my sickness. I thought it was only fair to tell you. I was not asking for your sympathy.

REGINA: *(Sharply, turns to him.)* What do the doctors think caused your bad heart?

HORACE: What do you mean?

REGINA: They didn't think it possible, did they, that your fancy women may have—

HORACE: *(Smiles unpleasantly.)* Caused my heart to be bad? I don't think that's the best scientific theory. You don't catch heart trouble in bed.

REGINA: *(Angrily.)* I thought you might catch a bad conscience—in bed, as you say.

HORACE: I didn't tell them about my bad conscience. Or about my fancy women. Nor did I tell them that my wife has not wanted me in bed with her for— *(Sharply.)* How long is it, Regina? Ten years? Did you bring me home for this, to make me feel guilty again? That means you want something. But you'll not make me feel guilty anymore. My "thinking" has made a difference.

REGINA: I see that it has. *(She look toward dining-room door. Then comes to him, her manner warm and friendly.)* It's foolish for us to fight this way. I didn't mean to be unpleasant. I was stupid.

HORACE: *(Wearily.)* God knows I didn't either. I came home wanting so much not to fight, and then all of a sudden there we were.

REGINA: *(Hastily.)* It's all my fault. I didn't ask about—about your illness because I didn't want to remind you of it. Anyway, I never believe doctors when they talk about— *(Brightly.)* when they talk like that.

HORACE: I understand. Well, we'll try our best with each other.

The Man Who Came To Dinner

George S. Kaufman and Moss Hart
1939

Scene: a middle-class home in the Midwest at Christmas

Man and Woman

Maggie (30s) personal secretary to Sheridan Whiteside (50–60) a popular radio personality.

> *An accident has landed the famed curmudgeon in a wheelchair in the home of the Stanley family where he must remain until his leg heals. Whiteside's presence in the small town has turned life in the Stanley household into a circus. To make matters worse, loyal Maggie has fallen in love and intends to leave her employer.*

MAGGIE: *(Crossing to back of sofa with box of debris.)* Oh, stop behaving like a spoiled child, Sherry.

WHITESIDE: Don't take that patronizing tone with me, you flea-bitten Cleopatra. I am sick and tired of your sneaking out like some love-sick high-school girl every time my back is turned.

MAGGIE: Well, Sherry—I'm afraid you've hit the nail on the head. *(Taking off hat and putting it on table back of couch.)*

WHITESIDE: Stop acting like Zazu Pitts and explain yourself.

MAGGIE: *(To center.)* I'll make it quick, Sherry. I'm in love.

WHITESIDE: Nonsense. This is merely delayed puberty.

MAGGIE: No, Sherry, I'm afraid this is it. You're going to lose a very excellent secretary.

WHITESIDE: You are out of your mind.

MAGGIE: Yes, I think I am, a little. But I'm a girl who's waited a long time for this to happen, and now it has. Mr. Jefferson doesn't know it yet, but I'm going to try my darnedest to marry him. *(Ease left.)*

WHITESIDE: *(As she pauses.)* Is that all?

MAGGIE: Yes, except that—well—I suppose this is what might be called my resignation, as soon as you've got someone else.

WHITESIDE: *(A slight pause.)* Now listen to me, Maggie. We have been together for a long time. You are indispensable to me, but I think I am unselfish enough not to let that stand in the way where your happiness is concerned. Because whether you know it or not, I have a deep affection for you.

MAGGIE: *(Ease right.)* I know that, Sherry.

WHITESIDE: That being the case, I will not stand by and allow you to make a fool of yourself.

MAGGIE: I'm not, Sherry.

WHITESIDE: You are, my dear. You are behaving like a Booth Tarkington heroine. It's—it's incredible. I cannot believe that a girl who for the past ten years has had the great of the world served up on a platter before her, I cannot believe that it is anything but a kind of temporary insanity when you are swept off your feet in seven days by a second-rate, small-town newspaper man.

MAGGIE: *(To him.)* Sherry, I can't explain what's happened. I can only tell you that it's so. It's hard for me to believe, too, Sherry. Here I am, a hard-bitten old cynic, behaving like True Story Magazine, and liking it. Discovering the moon, and ice-skating—I keep laughing to myself all the time, but there it is. What can I do about it, Sherry? I'm in love.

WHITESIDE: *(With sudden decision.)* We're leaving tomorrow. Hip or no hip, we're leaving here tomorrow. I don't care if I fracture the other one. Get me a train schedule and start packing. I'll pull you out of this, Miss Stardust. I'll get the ants out of those moonlit pants.

MAGGIE: *(Crosses left.)* It's no good, Sherry. It's no good. I'd be back on the next streamlined train.

WHITESIDE: It's completely unbelievable. Can you see yourself, the wife of the editor of the Mesalia Journal, having an evening at home for Mr. and Mrs. Stanley, Mr. and Mrs. Poop-Face, and the members of the Book-of-the-Month Club?

MAGGIE: *(Crosses right.)* Sherry, I've had ten years of the great figures of our time, and don't think I'm not grateful to you for it. I've loved every minute of it. They've been wonderful years, Sherry. Gay, and stimulating—I don't think anyone has ever had the fun we've had. But a girl can't laugh all the time, Sherry. There comes a time when she wants—Bert Jefferson. You don't know Bert, Sherry. He's gentle and he's unassuming, and—well, I love him, that's all. *(Ease left.)*

WHITESIDE: I see. Well, I remain completely unconvinced. You are drugging yourself into this Joan Crawford fantasy, and before you become completely anesthetized I shall do everything in my power to bring you to your senses.

MAGGIE: *(Wheeling on him.)* Now listen to me, Whiteside. I know you. Lay off. I know what a devil you can be. I've seen you do it to other people, but don't you dare do it to me. Don't drug *yourself* into the idea that all you're thinking of is my happiness. You're thinking of yourself a little bit, too, and all those months of breaking in somebody new. I've seen you in a passion before when your life has been disrupted, and you couldn't dine in Calcutta on July twelfth with Boo-Boo. Well, that's too bad, but there it is. *(Crosses to stairs.)* I'm going to marry Bert if he'll have me, and don't you dare try any of your tricks. I'm on to every one of them. So lay off. That's my message to you, Big Lord Fauntleroy.

PART SEVEN:

THE LATE 20TH CENTURY... MILLENNIUM'S EDGE

The Autumn Garden

Lillian Hellman
1951

Scene: a living room

Man and Woman

Nick (30–40) a failed portrait artist and Nina (30–40) the woman who
loves him.

Here, longtime lovers finally go their separate ways.

NINA: *(Carefully.)* What are you talking about?

NICK: Rose fixed it for me. I'm going to do a portrait of her niece, the
heiress to the fortune. The girl is balding and has braces. *(Looks
at her.)* Five thousand dollars.

NINA: Are you crazy?

NICK: Not a bit.

NINA: It's all right to kid around here—

NICK: *(Gets up.)* I *don't* know what you mean.

NINA: *(Violently.)* Please don't let's talk this way. Just tell Mrs. Griggs
that you've changed your mind—

NICK: I demand that you tell me what you mean.

NINA: *(Angrily.)* How many years have we avoided saying it? Why must
you walk into it now? *(Pauses, looks at him.)* All right. Maybe it's
time: You haven't finished a portrait in twelve years. And money
isn't your reason for wanting to do this portrait. You're setting up
a silly flirtation with Mrs. Griggs. I'm not going to New Orleans,
Nick. I am not going to watch it all again. I can't go on this way
with myself— *(Then softly.)* Don't go. Call it off. You know how
it will end. Please let's don't this time—We're not young any
more, Nick. Somewhere we must have learned something.

NICK: *(Softly, carefully.)* If I haven't finished every picture I started it's
because I'm good enough to know they weren't good enough.

All these years you never understood that? I think I will never for-give you for talking that way.

NINA: Your trouble is that you're an amateur, a gifted amateur. And like all amateurs you have very handsome reasons for what you do not finish—between trains and boats.

NICK: You have thought that about me, all these years?

NINA: Yes.

NICK: Then it was good of you and loyal to pretend you believed in me.

NINA: Good? Loyal? What do they mean? I loved you.

NICK: Yes, good and loyal. But I, too, have a little vanity—

(She laughs; he comes to her.)

NICK: And no man can bear to live with a woman who feels that way about his work. I think you ought to leave tomorrow, Nina. For good and forever.

NINA: *(Softly.)* Yes. *(She turns.)* Yes, of course—

(She starts to exit. He follows behind her, talking.).

NICK: But it must be different this time. Remember I said years ago— "Ten times of threatening is out, Nina," I said—the tenth time you stay gone.

NINA: All right. Ten times is out. *(Quietly, desperately.)* I promise for good and forever.

NICK: *(She is climbing the staircase.)* This time, spare yourself the return. And the begging and the self-humiliation and the self-hate. And the disgusting self-contempt. This time they won't do any good. *(He is following her but we cannot see him.)* Let's write it down, darling. And have a drink to seal it.

The Lottery

Shirley Jackson, Adapted by Brainerd Duffield
1953

Scene: a town square

Man and Woman

Hutchison (30s) and Tessie (20–30) a married couple facing up to their civic responsibilities.

> *It is the custom in their town to hold an annual lottery in which the "winner" is stoned to death. Everyone must participate; there are no exceptions. This year Tess, who is the mother of a young boy, has had second thoughts as she here reveals to her husband.*

HUTCHISON: What ever kept you?

TESSIE: I don't know, Bill. I just wasn't thinkin', I guess.

HUTCHISON: That story's all right for the women. I know better. You knew the Lottery was today.

TESSIE: Well, it don't matter now. So long as I'm here.

HUTCHISON: What about Davy? Why'd you try to hide him?

TESSIE: Hide him? I didn't hide him. What makes you say that?

HUTCHISON: I found him in the stable loft. He said you told him to wait there—

TESSIE: Yes, but I was goin' to get him, Bill. I was goin' to bring him— honest.

HUTCHISON: What reason did you have to put him there?

TESSIE: Oh, Bill, he's such a little boy! And his birthday just last month. I hate to see the children takin' part in grownup ructions before they've even put aside their toys.

HUTCHISON: I went through it when I was little.

TESSIE: I know, Bill. I guess I was born and brought up with it, same as yourself.

HUTCHISON: Then how did you think you could get away with such a thing? You know Davy's name has to be there along with ours.

And you know how careful Joe Summers is. Why, we'd have been a laughin'stock in front of everbody.

TESSIE: But I told you I intended to bring him. You got to believe me, Bill.

HUTCHISON: Talkin' a lot of sentimental tommyrot. I always gave you credit for more sense than some of these other females. What's come over you lately, anyway?

TESSIE: I told you—nothin'.

HUTCHISON: Next thing you'll be sayin' we ought to give up Lotteries altogether—like poor Joe Summers' sister.

TESSIE: Well, I've not come to that yet. But some places have given them up. Lots of little towns up to the north—

HUTCHISON: No good'll come of it, either. You wait and see.

TESSIE: I don't say it will. No, I reckon the Lottery serves its useful purpose. When a custom's been handed down from generation to generation, there must be good in it.

HUTCHISON: *(Wagging head, grinning.)* Then you shouldn't be so cussed busy, findin' fault.

Look Back In Anger

John Osborne
1956

Scene: a flat in England

Man and Woman

Alison (20s–30s) an abused and neglected wife and Cliff (30s) her
husband's best friend.

*Following a scuffle, Alison is accidentally burned by an iron. Here,
kindly Cliff does his best to soothe both her physical and spiritual
pain.*

ALISON: I don't think I want anything more to do with love. Any more.
I can't take it on.

CLIFF: You're too young to start giving up. Too young, and too lovely.
Perhaps I'd better put a bandage on that—do you think so?

ALISON: There's some on my dressing table.

(Cliff crosses to the dressing table right.)

ALISON: I keep looking back, as far as I remember, and I can't think
what it was to feel young, really young. Jimmy said the same
thing to me the other day. I pretended not to be listening—
because I knew that would hurt him, I suppose. And—of
course—he got savage, like tonight. But I knew just what he
meant. I suppose it would have been so easy to say 'Yes, darling,
I know just what you mean. I know what you're feeling.' *(Shrugs.)*
It's those easy things that seem to be so impossible with us.

(Cliff stands down right, holding the bandage, his back to her.)

CLIFF: I'm wondering how much longer I can go on watching you two
tearing the insides out of each other. It looks pretty ugly sometimes.

ALISON: You wouldn't seriously think of leaving us, would you?

CLIFF: I suppose not. *(Crosses to her.)*

ALISON: I think I'm frightened. If only I knew what was going to happen.

CLIFF: *(Kneeling on the arm of her chair.)* Give it here.
   (She holds out her arm.)
CLIFF: Yell out if I hurt you. *(He bandages it for her.)*
ALISON: *(Staring at her outstretched arm.)* Cliff—
CLIFF: Um? *(Slight pause.)* What is it, lovely?
ALISON: Nothing.
CLIFF: I said: what is it?
ALISON: You see— *(Hesitates.)* I'm pregnant.
CLIFF: *(After a few moments.)* I'll need some scissors.
ALISON: They're over there.
CLIFF: *(Crossing to the dressing table.)* That is something, isn't it? When did you find this out?
ALISON: Few days ago. It was a bit of a shock.
CLIFF: Yes, I dare say.
ALISON: After three years of married life, I have to get caught out now.
CLIFF: None of us infallible, I suppose. *(Crosses to her.)* Must say I'm surprised though
ALISON: It's always been out of the question. What with—this place, and no money, and oh—everything. He's resented it, I know. What can you do?
CLIFF: You haven't told him yet.
ALISON: Not yet.
CLIFF: What are you going to do?
ALISON: I've no idea.
CLIFF: *(Having cut her bandage, he starts tying it.)* That too tight?
ALISON: Fine, thank you. *(She rises, goes to the ironing board, folds it up, and leans it against the food cupboard right.)*
CLIFF: Is it...Is it...?
ALISON: Too late to avert the situation? *(Places the iron on the rack of the stove.)* I'm not certain yet. Maybe not. If not, there won't be any problem, will there?
CLIFF: And if it is too late?
   (Her face is turned away from him. She simply shakes her head.)
CLIFF: Why don't you tell him now?
   (She kneels down to pick up the clothes on the floor, and folds them up.)

CLIFF: After all, he does love you. You don't need me to tell you that.

ALISON: Can't you see? He'll suspect my motives at once. He never stops telling himself that I know how vulnerable he is. Tonight it might be all right—we'd make love. But later, we'd both lie awake, watching for the light to come through that little window, and dreading it. In the morning, he'd feel hoaxed, as if I were trying to kill him in the worst way of all. He'd watch me growing bigger every day, and I wouldn't dare to look at him.

CLIFF: You may have to face it, lovely.

ALISON: Jimmy's got his own private morality, as you know. What my mother calls 'loose.' It is pretty free, of course, but it's very harsh too. You know, it's funny, but we never slept together before we were married.

CLIFF: It certainly is—knowing him!

ALISON: We knew each other such a short time, everything moved at such a pace, we didn't have much opportunity. And, afterwards, he actually taunted me with my virginity. He was quite angry about it, as if I had deceived him in some strange way. He seemed to think an untouched woman would defile him.

CLIFF: I've never heard you talking like this about him. He'd be quite pleased.

ALISON: Yes, he would. *(She gets up, the clothes folded over her arm.)* Do you think he's right?

CLIFF: What about?

ALISON: Oh—everything.

CLIFF: Well, I suppose he and I think the same about a lot of things, because we're alike in some ways. We both come from working people, if you like. Oh I know some of his mother's relatives are pretty posh, but he hates them as much as he hates yours. Don't quite know why. Anyway, he gets on with me because I'm common. *(Grins.)* Common as dirt, that's me.

(She puts her hand on his head, and strokes it thoughtfully.)

ALISON: You think I should tell him about the baby?

(He gets up, and puts his arm round her.)

CLIFF: It'll be all right—you see. Tell him.

The Visit

Friederich Dürrenmatt, Translated by Patrick Bowles
1956

Scene: a provincial town

Man and Woman

Claire (50–60) a vengeful woman and Alfred (50–60) the man who wronged her.

> *Now wealthy and famous, Claire has returned to the village of her youth in order to exact revenge from Alfred, the man who seduced her and then abandoned her for another. To this end Claire has offered the town an enormous sum of money in exchange for Alfred's execution. The people of the town eagerly accept Claire's terms and here, two former lovers bid a final adieu.*

CLAIRE ZACHANASSIAN: We often smoked together in this wood; do you remember? You used to buy the cigarettes from little Matilda. Or steal them.

[*(Man One taps key on pipe.)*]

CLAIRE ZACHANASSIAN: That woodpecker again.

[(MAN FOUR: Cuckoo! Cuckoo!)]

CLAIRE ZACHANASSIAN: Would you like Roby to play for you on his guitar?

ILL: Please.

CLAIRE ZACHANASSIAN: My amnestied killer plays well. I need him for meditative moments. I hate gramophones. And radios.

ILL: There's an army marching in an African valley.

CLAIRE ZACHANASSIAN: Your favourite song. I taught it to him.

(Silence. They smoke. Cuckoo call, forest sounds, etc. Roby plays ballad.)

ILL: You had—I mean, we had a child.

CLAIRE ZACHANASSIAN: True.

ILL: Was it a boy or a girl?

CLAIRE ZACHANASSIAN: A girl.

ILL: And what name did you give it?

CLAIRE ZACHANASSIAN: Genevieve.

ILL: Pretty name.

CLAIRE ZACHANASSIAN: I only saw the thing once. At birth. Then they took it away. The Salvation Army.

ILL: Eyes?

CLAIRE ZACHANASSIAN: Not yet open.

ILL: Hair?

CLAIRE ZACHANASSIAN: I think it had black hair. But then new-born babies often have black hair.

ILL: Yes, they often do.

(Silence. They smoke. Guitar plays.)

ILL: Where did it die?

CLAIRE ZACHANASSIAN: With some people. I've forgotten their name.

ILL: What of?

CLAIRE ZACHANASSIAN: Meningitis. Perhaps it was something else. I did receive a card from the authorities.

ILL: In cases of death you can rely on them.

(Silence.)

CLAIRE ZACHANASSIAN: I've talked about our little girl. Now you talk about me.

ILL: About you?

CLAIRE ZACHANASSIAN: The way I was, when I was seventeen, when you loved me.

ILL: I had to look for you a long while once in Petersens' Barn; I found you in the old carriage with nothing on but a blouse and a long straw between your lips.

CLAIRE ZACHANASSIAN: You were strong and brave. You fought that railwayman when he tried to paw me. I wiped the blood off your face with my red petticoat.

(Guitar stops playing.)

CLAIRE ZACHANASSIAN: The ballad has ended.

ILL: One more: "Home Sweet Home."

CLAIRE ZACHANASSIAN: Yes, Roby can play that.

(Guitar resumes play.)

ILL: Thank you for the wreaths, and for the chrysanthemums and roses. They'll look fine on the coffin in the Golden Apostle. Distinguished. They fill two rooms already. Now the time has come. It is the last time we shall sit in our old wood and hear the cuckoo calling and the sound of the wind. They are meeting this evening. They will sentence me to death, and one of them will kill me. I don't know who it will be, and I don't know where it will happen, I only know that my meaningless life will end.

CLAIRE ZACHANASSIAN: I shall take you in your coffin to Capri. I have had a mausoleum built, in my Palace Park. It is surrounded by cypress-trees. Overlooking the Mediterranean.

ILL: I only know it from pictures.

CLAIRE ZACHANASSIAN: Deep blue. A grandiose panorama. You will remain there. A dead man beside a stone idol. Your love died many years ago. But my love could not die. Neither could it live. It grew into an evil thing, like me, like the pallid mushrooms in this wood, and the blind, twisted features of the roots, all over-grown by my golden millions. Their tentacles sought you out, to take your life, because your life belonged to me, for ever. You are in their toils now, and you are lost. You will soon be no more than a dead love in my memory, a gentle ghost haunting the wreckage of a house.

ILL: "Home Sweet Home" has ended now as well.

[*(Husband IX returns.)*]

CLAIRE ZACHANASSIAN: Here's the Nobel Prize-winner. Back from his ruins. Well, Zoby?

[(HUSBAND IX: Early Christian. Sacked by the Huns.)]

CLAIRE ZACHANASSIAN: What a pity. Give me your arm. Roby, Toby, the sedan. *(Gets into sedan-chair.)* Goodbye, Alfred.

ILL: Goodbye, Clara.

A Slight Ache
Harold Pinter
1959

Scene: a kitchen

Man and Woman

Edward (30s–40s) and Flora (30s–40s) a married couple facing an unusual challenge.

When an unfortunate wasp becomes trapped in the marmalade jar, Edward and Flora find themselves facing a possible insect catastrophe.

FLORA: Can you hear him?
EDWARD: Hear him?
FLORA: Buzzing.
EDWARD: Nonsense. How can you hear him? It's an earthenware lid.
FLORA: He's becoming frantic.
EDWARD: Rubbish. Take it away from the table.
FLORA: What shall I do with it?
EDWARD: Put it in the sink and drown it.
FLORA: It'll fly out and bite me.
EDWARD: It will not bite you! Wasps don't bite. Anyway, it won't fly out. It's stuck. It'll drown where it is, in the marmalade.
FLORA: What a horrible death.
EDWARD: On the contrary.
    (*Pause.*)
FLORA: Have you got something in your eyes?
EDWARD: No. Why do you ask?
FLORA: You keep clenching them, blinking them.
EDWARD: I have a slight ache in them.
FLORA: Oh, dear.
EDWARD: Yes, a slight ache. As if I hadn't slept.
FLORA: Did you sleep, Edward?

EDWARD: Of course I slept. Uninterrupted. As always.

FLORA: And yet you feel tired.

EDWARD: I didn't say I felt tired. I merely said I had a slight ache in my eyes.

FLORA: Why is that, then?

EDWARD: I really don't know.

(Pause.)

FLORA: Oh goodness!

EDWARD: What is it?

FLORA: I can see it. It's trying to come out.

EDWARD: How can it?

FLORA: Through the hole. It's trying to crawl out, through the spoon-hole.

EDWARD: Mmmnn, yes. Can't do it, of course. (Silent pause.) Well, let's kill it, for goodness' sake.

FLORA: Yes, let's. But how?

EDWARD: Bring it out on the spoon and squash it on a plate

FLORA: It'll fly away. It'll bite.

EDWARD: If you don't stop saying that word I shall leave this table.

FLORA: But wasps do bite.

EDWARD: They don't bite. They sting. It's snakes…that bite.

FLORA: What about horseflies?

(Pause.)

EDWARD: (To himself.) Horseflies suck.

(Pause.)

FLORA: (Tentatively.) If we…if we wait long enough, I suppose it'll choke to death. It'll suffocate in the marmalade.

EDWARD: (Briskly.) You do know I've got work to do this morning, don't you? I can't spend the whole day worrying about a wasp.

FLORA: Well, kill it.

EDWARD: You want to kill it?

FLORA: Yes.

EDWARD: Very well. Pass me the hot water jug.

FLORA: What are you going to do?

EDWARD: Scald it. Give it to me.

(She hands him the jug. Pause.)

EDWARD: Now...

FLORA: *(Whispering.)* Do you want me to lift the lid?

EDWARD: No, no, no. I'll pour down the spoon hole. Right...down the spoon-hole.

FLORA: Listen!

EDWARD: What?

FLORA: It's buzzing.

EDWARD: Vicious creatures. *(Pause.)* Curious, but I don't remember seeing any wasps at all, all summer, until now. I'm sure I don't know why. I mean, there must have been wasps.

FLORA: Please.

EDWARD: This couldn't be the first wasp, could it?

FLORA: Please.

EDWARD: The first wasp of summer? No. It's not possible.

FLORA: Edward.

EDWARD: Mmmmnnn?

FLORA: Kill it.

EDWARD: Ah, yes. Tilt the pot. Tilt. Aah...down here...right down... blinding him...that's...it.

FLORA: Is it?

EDWARD: Lift the lid. All right, I will. There he is! Dead. What a monster. *(He squashes it on a plate.)*

FLORA: What an awful experience.

Phedre

Jean Racine, Translated by William Packard
1966

Scene: ancient Greece

Man and Woman

Theseus (50s) the king and Aricie (20s) in love with his son, Hippolyte.

> *Unknown to Theseus, his wife, Phedre has made romantic over-tures to handsome young Hippolyte. To avoid a scandal, Hippolyte has decided to leave his father's court with Aricie, whom he intends to marry. Here. Theseus angrily confronts Aricie, thinking that she has unfairly lured Hippolyte away from his responsibilities at court and from his father's love.*

THESEUS: You color now, Madam, and you are seized with fright;
   now why did Hippolyte leave here so secretly?
ARICIE: My Lord, he came to say his last farewells to me.
THESEUS: Your eyes have overcome the high pride of his heart;
   and his first secret sighs are those you made him start.
ARICIE: My Lord, I cannot lie and hide the truth from you:
   nothing could make him take your hateful point of view;
   he never treated me like some lost criminal.
THESEUS: I know: he swore his love would be perpetual.
   But do not put your trust in his inconstant mind;
   for he swore other loves with vows of the same kind.
ARICIE: My Lord?
THESEUS: You should have trained this Prince to be less vain:
   how could you bear to share his love without great pain?
ARICIE: How can you bear to say such evil of his ways,
   maligning this fair man and darkening his days?
   Have you so little wit to understand his heart?
   Or can you not keep crime and innocence apart?
   Must you see his virtue in some grotesque disguise,

when it so brightly shines before all other eyes?
You damn him to slander and scandal everywhere.
Stop it: you should repent of your relentless prayer;
O you should fear, my Lord, that heaven will fulfill
its own great hate for you and execute your will.
Its fatal rage may take away our prey sometimes.
Sometimes its benefits repay us for our crimes.

THESEUS: No, now you cannot hide how he has been so lewd:
your love has made you blind to his ingratitude.
But I have witnesses who testified right here:
and I myself have seen fierce tears which are sincere.

ARICIE: Take care, my Lord, take care: for your heroic hands
have slain the numberless monsters of many lands;
but all are not destroyed, because you did not seek
one…But your son, my Lord, forbids me now to speak.
Informed of the respect which he still holds for you,
I would grieve him too much if I said what I knew.
So I shall be discreet, and leave your presence now;
if I stayed I might say more than I should somehow.

Rosencrantz and Guildenstern are Dead

Tom Stoppard
1966

Scene: a castle in Denmark

Two Men

Rosencrantz (20–40) and Guildenstern (20–40) hapless courtiers.

Following a confusing encounter with a certainly melancholy prince of Denmark, these easily confused attendants try to figure out what is wrong with their liege.

ROSENCRANTZ: Who was that?
GUILDENSTERN: Didn't you know him?
ROSENCRANTZ: He didn't know me.
GUILDENSTERN: He didn't see you.
ROSENCRANTZ: I didn't see him.
GUILDENSTERN: We shall see. I *hardly* knew him, he's changed.
ROSENCRANTZ: You could see that?
GUILDENSTERN: Transformed.
ROSENCRANTZ: How do you know?
GUILDENSTERN: Inside and out.
ROSENCRANTZ: I see.
GUILDENSTERN: He's not himself.
ROSENCRANTZ: He's changed.
GUILDENSTERN: I could see that. *(Beat.)* Glean what afflicts him.
ROSENCRANTZ: Me?
GUILDENSTERN: Him.
ROSENCRANTZ: How?
GUILDENSTERN: Question and answer. Old ways are the best ways.
ROSENCRANTZ: He's afflicted.
GUILDENSTERN: You question, I'll answer.

ROSENCRANTZ: He's not himself, you know.

GUILDENSTERN: I'm him, you see.

(Beat.)

ROSENCRANTZ: Who am I then?

GUILDENSTERN: You're yourself.

ROSENCRANTZ: And he's you?

GUILDENSTERN: Not a bit of it.

ROSENCRANTZ: Are you afflicted?

GUILDENSTERN: That's the idea. Are you ready?

ROSENCRANTZ: Let's go back a bit.

GUILDENSTERN: I'm afflicted.

ROSENCRANTZ: I see.

GUILDENSTERN: Glean what afflicts me.

ROSENCRANTZ: Right.

GUILDENSTERN: Question and answer.

ROSENCRANTZ: How should I begin?

GUILDENSTERN: Address me.

ROSENCRANTZ: My dear Guildenstern!

GUILDENSTERN: (Quietly.) You've forgotten—haven't you?

ROSENCRANTZ: My dear Rosencrantz!

GUILDENSTERN: (Great control.) I don't think you quite understand. What we are attempting is a hypothesis in which *I* answer for *him*, while *you* ask me questions.

ROSENCRANTZ: Ah! Ready?

GUILDENSTERN: You know what to do?

ROSENCRANTZ: What?

GUILDENSTERN: Are you stupid?

ROSENCRANTZ: Pardon?

GUILDENSTERN: Are you deaf?

ROSENCRANTZ: Did you speak?

GUILDENSTERN: (Admonishing.) Not now—

ROSENCRANTZ: Statement.

GUILDENSTERN: (Shouts.) Not now! (Pause.) If I had any doubts, or rather hopes, they are dispelled. What could we possibly have in common except our situation?

(They separate and sit.)

GUILDENSTERN: Perhaps he'll come back this way.

ROSENCRANTZ: Should we go?

GUILDENSTERN: Why?

(Pause.)

ROSENCRANTZ: (Starts up. Snaps fingers.) Oh! You mean—you pretend to be him, and I ask you questions!

GUILDENSTERN: (Dry.) Very good.

ROSENCRANTZ: You had me confused.

GUILDENSTERN: I could see I had.

ROSENCRANTZ: How should I begin?

GUILDENSTERN: Address me.

(They stand and face each other posing.)

ROSENCRANTZ: My honoured Lord!

GUILDENSTERN: My dear Rosencrantz!

(Pause.)

ROSENCRANTZ: Am I pretending to be you, then?

GUILDENSTERN: Certainly not. If you like. Shall we continue?

ROSENCRANTZ: Question and answer.

GUILDENSTERN: Right.

ROSENCRANTZ: Right. My honoured lord!

GUILDENSTERN: My dear fellow!

ROSENCRANTZ: How are you?

GUILDENSTERN: Afflicted!

ROSENCRANTZ: Really? In what way?

GUILDENSTERN: Transformed.

ROSENCRANTZ: Inside or out?

GUILDENSTERN: Both.

ROSENCRANTZ: I see. (Pause.) Not much new there.

GUILDENSTERN: Go into details. Delve. Probe the background, establish the situation.

ROSENCRANTZ: So—So your uncle is the king of Denmark?!

GUILDENSTERN: And my father before him.

ROSENCRANTZ: His father before him?

GUILDENSTERN: No, my father before him.

ROSENCRANTZ: But surely—

GUILDENSTERN: You might well ask.

ROSENCRANTZ: Let me get it straight. Your father was king. You were his only son. Your father dies. You are of age. Your uncle becomes king.

GUILDENSTERN: Yes.

ROSENCRANTZ: Unorthodox.

GUILDENSTERN: Undid me.

ROSENCRANTZ: Undeniable. Where were you?

GUILDENSTERN: In Germany.

ROSENCRANTZ: Usurpation, then.

GUILDENSTERN: He slipped in.

ROSENCRANTZ: Which reminds me.

GUILDENSTERN: Well, it would.

ROSENCRANTZ: I don't want to be personal.

GUILDENSTERN: It's common knowledge.

ROSENCRANTZ: Your mother's marriage.

GUILDENSTERN: He slipped in.

(Beat.)

ROSENCRANTZ: *(Lugubriously.)* His body was still warm.

GUILDENSTERN: So was hers.

ROSENCRANTZ: Extraordinary.

GUILDENSTERN: Indecent.

ROSENCRANTZ: Hasty.

GUILDENSTERN: Suspicious.

ROSENCRANTZ: It makes you think.

GUILDENSTERN: Don't think I haven't thought of it.

ROSENCRANTZ: And with her husband's brother.

GUILDENSTERN: They were close.

ROSENCRANTZ: She went to him—

GUILDENSTERN: —Too close—

ROSENCRANTZ: —for comfort.

GUILDENSTERN: It looks bad.

ROSENCRANTZ: It adds up.

GUILDENSTERN: Incest to adultery.

ROSENCRANTZ: Would you go so far?

GUILDENSTERN: Never.

ROSENCRANTZ: To sum up: your father, whom you love, dies, you are his heir, you come back to find that hardly was the corpse cold before his young brother popped onto his throne and into his sheets, thereby offending both legal and natural practice. Now why exactly are you behaving in this extraordinary manner?

GUILDENSTERN: I can't imagine! *(Pause.)* But all that is well known, common property. Yet he sent for us. And we did come.

Tango

Slawomir Mrozek, Translated by Ralph Manheim
and Teresa Dzieduscycka
1968

Scene: eastern Europe during the cold war

Man and Woman

Arthur (20–30) an idealistic adherent to current trends in political philosophy and Ala (20s) the a-political woman he loves.

*Here, Ala fields a decidedly unromantic proposal of marriage
from Arthur.*

ARTHUR: Well, what do you say? Have you thought it over?

ALA: You mean will I marry you? But I've already told you. I don't see
the point.

ARTHUR: You mean the answer is no?

ALA: Why do you get so worked up about it? I mean—I don't care—
if it means so much to you, we can get married tomorrow. We're
already cousins.

ARTHUR: But I *want* you to care! I want you to realize that marriage is
something very important.

ALA: Important? Why? I don't get it. If I'm going to have a baby it'll be
with you, not with the minister. So what's the problem?

ARTHUR: Well, if it's not important in itself, then we've got to make it
important.

ALA: What for?

ARTHUR: Nothing is important in itself. Things in themselves are meaningless. Unless we give them character, we drown in a sea of
indifference. We have to create meanings, because they don't
exist in nature.

ALA: But what for? What for?

ARTHUR: Well if you must have a reason, let's say: for our own pleasure
and profit.

ALA: Pleasure?

ARTHUR: Yes. We derive pleasure from profit and we only profit from doing things we attach importance to—difficult things, the unusual things that seem rare and precious. And that's why we have to create a system of values.

ALA: Philosophy bores me. I think I prefer Stomil. *(She sticks her leg out from under the nightgown.)*

ARTHUR: You only think that. Kindly remove that leg.

ALA: You don't like it?

ARTHUR: That has nothing whatsoever to do with the subject.

ALA: *(Obstinately.)* You really don't like it?

ARTHUR: *(With difficulty takes his eyes off her leg.)* Oh, all right, show your leg if you want to. Anyway, it only proves my point.

ALA: My leg? *(She examines her leg closely.)*

ARTHUR: Yes. Do you know why you're showing your leg? Because I don't leap all over you like my artist father and everybody else does. That worries you. You were pretty bewildered this morning when we were all alone. You thought you knew what I wanted from you.

ALA: That's not true.

ARTHUR: Not true? Ha. You think I didn't see how upset you were when I proposed marriage instead of just picking you up and throwing you down on the bed?

ALA: I had a headache.

ARTHUR: Headache? Go on. You just couldn't figure out what was going on. You thought I wasn't attracted, that you must be losing your charms. If I suddenly started acting like my father, it would be a relief, wouldn't it? Yes. Except you'd run away, just to get even with me.

ALA: *(Stands up with dignity.)* I'm running all right.

ARTHUR: *(Takes her by the hand and pulls her down into the chair.)* Sit down. I haven't finished yet. All you care about is your sex appeal. You're so primitive! You can't think about anything else. You don't know anything else!

ALA: Are you suggesting that I'm backward? *(She tries again to stand up.)*

ARTHUR: *(Holding her down.)* You stay right here. You've confirmed my theory. My behavior was atypical; that baffled you. The unusual is a value in itself. See? I have given meaning to an encounter that would otherwise have meant nothing. I!

ALA: Well, if you're so terribly clever, what do you need me for? If you're so awfully superior, why don't you just live all by yourself?

ARTHUR: You don't have to be so touchy.

ALA: We'll see how far you get alone. Or with Uncle Eugene. *(She resolutely draws her nightgown over her knees, buttons it up to the neck, and wraps herself in a steamer rug. She puts on the bowler and draws it down deep over her forehead.)*

ARTHUR: *(Shyly.)* Don't be angry.

ALA: What do you care?

Where Has Tommy Flowers Gone?

Terrence McNally

1971

Scene: a street in New York City

Man and Woman

Tommy (30) a wanderer and Bunny (16) right off the bus from Tarzana and full of spunk.

Here, laconic Tommy encounters an enormous ball of energy and opinions named Bunny.

BUNNY BARNUM: Hello. My name is Bunny Barnum from Tarzana, California, outside of Los Angeles? It's where Edgar Rice Burroughs is from, he wrote *Tarzan,* that's why it's called Tarzana and I'm here for five days with my high school civics class on our annual "Know America" trip, the Tarzana Kiwanis Club and American Legion post are sponsoring us, and everyone else is taking that Circle Line boat trip around the island right now except me: I snuck off, and I believe that people should really try to talk to one another and I'd like to talk to you. *(She's already taken Tommy's picture with her Instamatic camera.)* You're a hippie, aren't you?

TOMMY: *(Dazzled.)* Oh wow!

BUNNY: That's okay. We have hippies in Tarzana, too. Mildred Miller's taken LSD three whole times.

TOMMY: She has?

BUNNY: It made all her hair fall out. I bet you smoke marijuana, too.

TOMMY: I do, miss, I most surely do.

BUNNY: I don't. I think people who smoke marijuana should be electrocuted.

TOMMY: You do?

BUNNY: Oh yes. My parents started turning on—my daddy's a nuclear physicist, he was born in Mannheim, that's in Germany, but I was born in Tarzana and he's a naturalized American now; my mother's a real Okie. ugh!—anyway, they were stoned half the time, real heads, the two of them, and they were growing their own stuff right in the backyard and so I turned them in. Citizen's arrest. Here. You look poor. How old are you?

TOMMY: Your parents were electrocuted for growing pot?

BUNNY: No! They were just busted! What's the matter? Wax in your ears? How old are you?

TOMMY: Thirty.

BUNNY: Thirty? You're thirty? Yikes!

TOMMY: (Pleased.) I know.

BUNNY: Drugs, hunh? You should see what Cubby Dodge looks like. A real wreck. I have her. Do you mind if I say something? You're too pale. It's against the law practically to be that pale in California. Why don't you go to California? Too poor, hunh? I'd hate to be poor. I couldn't stand it. I'd probably have another nervous break-down.

TOMMY: How many have you had?

BUNNY: (Dismissing this.) Just one! How many does it look like?

TOMMY: Oh, no more than that certainly.

BUNNY: I was Student Council recording secretary, head cheerleader and going steady with Rusty Winkler all in one semester! No wonder I flipped. Boy, I'd have to live in New York City. Do you know how to surf?

TOMMY: Oh sure.

BUNNY: Randy Nelson is from Tarzana.

TOMMY: He is?

BUNNY: You don't know who Randy Nelson is? From what rock are you under? He's the world champion seventeen-year-old surfer. I'm supposed to be going with him. He's on the boat, looking for me probably. But I just had to ditch him today, you know? He's got fantastic knobs on both knees. He may even need surgery.

TOMMY: Knobs?

BUNNY: From surfing, dolt! We're reading Shakespeare on the bus and dolt's a very big word with everybody right now. Dolt, varlet, and bared bodkin. Have you ever taken a bus from California to New

York? It's a drag. I told Mrs. Burmeinster, our chaperone, do you believe it? that if she didn't make them do something about the restroom I was going to call my father collect.

TOMMY: What would you like Mrs. Burmeister to do?

BUNNY: Bur*mein*ster. It's filthy in there. Please, can we change the subject? Thirty years old! I can't believe it. Yikes, that girl looks like Connie Nugent when she had both legs! Talk about resemblances! *(Calling off.)* Connie! Connie Nugent! *(Shrugs.)* You never know. Boy, I'd love some tacos and a chocolate milk shake right now. Mmmmmm! With French fries. I used to have pimples. Acne practically. I couldn't go anywhere. Ecch! What's the matter?

TOMMY: Connie Nugent when she had both legs.

BUNNY: Oh that! She was my brother Fritz's fiancée and they were driving home from somewhere, Disneyland, I think, and they had this terrible accident and they cut off Connie's leg. That girl looked just like her. Listen, stranger things have happened, right? Donna Barr lost the tip of her nose in a refrigerator door and they sewed it back on and all she has is a teen-tiny bump right there. Granted, it was a freak accident but *still*. Big Sur! They were coming back from group encounter in Big Sur.

TOMMY: Connie and Fritz?

BUNNY: Right. I almost lost my faith in God when that happened. But then I realized Fritz would have had to marry her and who wants a one-legged sister-in-law? I don't mean that cruelly, believe me, that is not a vicious remark. I'm just being realistic.

TOMMY: Then he didn't marry her?

BUNNY: Of course not! He was killed! That's why I almost lost my faith in God! It's true, people *don't* listen to one another.

TOMMY: I'm listening to you, all right, only I'm having trouble following you.

BUNNY: Drugs again, hunh? Boy, I'd love to see your chromosomes under a microscope! I bet they're really bent.

TOMMY: That's the most erotic thing anybody's ever said to me.

BUNNY: Erotic! Don't get me started on that!

TOMMY: On what?

BUNNY: Smut. I'll talk your ear off. There was a man in Tarzana we found out was making pornographic movies.

TOMMY: Let me guess: citizens arrest.

BUNNY: We burned his house down.

TOMMY: We...?

BUNNY: The Hi-Y's. This stupid girls' club my mother made me join. Coke parties, slumber parties, swimming parties, the whole schmear.

TOMMY: I don't suppose there's any chance we could continue this conversation somewhere else?

BUNNY: There's a very big one.

The Actor's Nightmare

Christopher Durang
1981

Scene: on stage during the performance of a play

Man and Woman

George (30–40) and Sarah (20–40) understudies enjoying a momentary spotlight.

George and Sarah finally have an opportunity to take over the roles they understudy. Too bad George has never bothered reading the script.

SARAH: Extraordinary how potent cheap music is.
GEORGE: What?
SARAH: Extraordinary how potent cheap music is.
GEORGE: Yes, that's true. Am I supposed to be Hamlet?
SARAH: *(Alarmed; then going on.)* Whose yacht do you think that is?
GEORGE: Where?
SARAH: The duke of Westminster, I expect. It always is.
GEORGE: Ah, well, perhaps. To be or not to be. I don't know any more of it.
    (She looks irritated at him; then she coughs three times. He remembers and unzips her dress; she slaps him.)
SARAH: Elyot, please. We are on our honeymoons.
GEORGE: Are we?
SARAH: Yes. *(Irritated being over-explicit.)* Me with Victor and you with Sibyl.
GEORGE: Ah.
SARAH: Tell me about Sibyl.
GEORGE: I've never met her.
SARAH: Ah, Elyot, you're so amusing. You're married to Sybyl. Tell me about her.
GEORGE: Nothing much to tell really. She's sort of nondescript I'd say.

SARAH: I bet you were going to say that she's just like Lady Bundle, and that she has several chins, and one blue eye and one brown eye, and a third eye in the center of her forehead. Weren't you?

GEORGE: Yes. I think so.

SARAH: Victor's like that too. *(Long pause.)* I bet you were just about to tell me that you traveled around the world.

GEORGE: Yes I was. I traveled around the world.

SARAH: How was it?

GEORGE: The world?

SARAH: Yes.

GEORGE: Oh, very nice.

SARAH: I always feared the Taj Mahal would look like a biscuit box. Did it?

GEORGE: Not really.

SARAH: *(She's going to give him the cue again.)* I always feared the Taj Mahal would look like a biscuit box. Did it?

GEORGE: I guess it did.

SARAH: *(Again.)* I always feared the Taj Mahal would look like a biscuit box. Did it?

GEORGE: Hard to say. What brand biscuit box?

SARAH: I always feared the Taj Mahal would look like a biscuit box. Did it? *(Pause.)* Did it? Did it?

GEORGE: I wonder whose yacht that is out there.

SARAH: Did it? Did it? Did it? Did it?

[*(Enter Meg. She's put on an apron and maid's hat and carries a duster but is otherwise still in her stage manager's garb.)*]

[MEG: My, this balcony looks dusty. I think I'll just clean it up a little. *(Dusts and goes to George and whispers in his ear; exits.)*]

GEORGE: Not only did the Taj Mahal look like a biscuit box, but women should be struck regularly like gongs. *(Applause.)*

SARAH: Extraordinary how potent cheap music is.

GEORGE: Yes. Quite extraordinary.

SARAH: How was China?

GEORGE: China?

SARAH: You traveled around the world. How was China?

GEORGE: I liked it, but I felt homesick.

SARAH: *(Again this is happening; gives him cue again.)* How was China?

GEORGE: Lots of rice. The women bind their feet.

SARAH: How was China?

GEORGE: I hated it. I missed...Sibyl.

SARAH: How was China?

GEORGE: I...miss the maid. Oh, maid!

SARAH: *How was China?*

GEORGE: Just wait a moment please. Oh, maid!

[*(Enter Meg.)*]

GEORGE: Ah, there you are. I think you missed a spot here.

[*(She crosses dusts and whispers in his ear; exits.)*]

SARAH: How was China?

GEORGE: *(With authority.)* Very large, China.

SARAH: And Japan?

GEORGE: *(Doesn't know, but he makes a guess.)* Very...small, Japan.

SARAH: And Ireland?

GEORGE: Very...green.

SARAH: And Iceland?

GEORGE: Very white.

SARAH: And Italy?

GEORGE: Very...Neapolitan.

SARAH: And Copenhagen?

GEORGE: Very...cosmopolitan.

SARAH: And Florida?

GEORGE: Very...condominium.

SARAH: And Perth Amboy?

GEORGE: Very...mobile home, I don't know.

SARAH: And Sibyl?

GEORGE: What?

SARAH: Do you love Sibyl?

GEORGE: Who's Sibyl?

SARAH: Your new wife, who you married after you and I got our divorce.

GEORGE: Oh were we married? Oh yes, I forgot that part.

SARAH: Elyot, you re so amusing. You make me laugh all the time. *(Laughs.)* So, do you love Sibyl?

GEORGE: Probably. I married her.

(Pause. She coughs three times, he unzips her dress, she slaps him.)

SARAH: Oh, Elyot, darling, I'm sorry. We were mad to have left each other. Kiss me.

Am I Blue

Beth Henley
1982

Scene: a bar

Man and Woman

John Polk (18–20) a college frat boy en route to a brothel and Ashbe
(15–16) the plucky young girl who has latched on to him for the
evening.

Ashbe has followed John Polk into a bar and here the two
engage in a frank discussion of John's plans for the evening.

ASHBE: I was just looking at your pin. What fraternity are you in?
JOHN POLK: SAE.
ASHBE: Is it a good fraternity?
JOHN POLK: Sure, it's the greatest.
ASHBE: I bet you have lots of friends.
JOHN POLK: Tons.
ASHBE: Are you being serious?
JOHN POLK: Yes.
ASHBE: Hmm. Do they have parties and all that?
JOHN POLK: Yeah, lots of parties, booze, honking horns; it's exactly what
    you would expect.
ASHBE: I wouldn't expect anything. Why did you join?
JOHN POLK: I don't know. Well, my brother—I guess it was my
    brother—he told me how great it was, how the fraternity was
    supposed to get you dates, make you study, solve all your prob-
    lems.
ASHBE: Gee, does it?
JOHN POLK: Doesn't help you study.
ASHBE: How about dates? Do they get you a lot of dates?
JOHN POLK: Some.
ASHBE: What were the girls like?

JOHN POLK: I don't know—they were like girls.

ASHBE: Did you have a good time?

JOHN POLK: I had a pretty good time.

ASHBE: Did you make love to any of them?

JOHN POLK: *(To self.)* Oh, Christ—

ASHBE: I'm sorry—I just figured that's why you had the appointment with the whore—'cause you didn't have anyone else—to make love to.

JOHN POLK: How did you know I had the, ah, the appointment?

ASHBE: I saw you put the red card in your pocket when I came up. Those red cards are pretty familiar around here. The house is only about a block or so away. It's one of the best, though, really very plush. Only two murders and a knifing in its whole history. Do you go there often?

JOHN POLK: Yeah, I like to give myself a treat.

ASHBE: Who do you have?

JOHN POLK: What do you mean?

ASHBE: I mean which girl.

(John Polk gazes into his drink.)

ASHBE: Look, I just thought I might know her is all.

JOHN POLK: Know her, ah, how would you know her?

ASHBE: Well, some of the girls from my high school go there to work when they get out.

JOHN POLK: G.G., her name is G.G.

ASHBE: G.G.—Hmm, well, how does she look?

JOHN POLK: I don't know.

ASHBE: Oh, you've never been with her before?

JOHN POLK: No.

ASHBE: *(Confidentially.)* Are you one of those kinds that likes a lot of variety?

JOHN POLK: Variety? Sure, I guess I like variety.

ASHBE: Oh, yes, now I remember.

JOHN POLK: What?

ASHBE: G.G., that's just her working name. Her real name is Myrtle Reims; she's Kay Reims's older sister. Kay is in my grade at school.

JOHN POLK: Myrtle? Her name is Myrtle?

ASHBE: I never liked the name, either.

JOHN POLK: Myrtle, oh, Christ. Is she pretty?

ASHBE: *(Matter-of-fact.)* Pretty, no she's not real pretty.

JOHN POLK: What does she look like?

ASHBE: Let's see…she's, ah, well, Myrtle had acne, and there are a few scars left. It's not bad. I think they sort of give her character. Her hair's red, only I don't think it's really red. It sort of fizzles out all over her head. She's got a pretty good figure—big top—but the rest of her is kind of skinny.

JOHN POLK: I wonder if she has a good personality.

ASHBE: Well, she was a senior when I was a freshman; so I never really knew her. I remember she used to paint her fingernails lots of different colors—pink, orange, purple. I don't know, but she kind of scares me. About the only time I ever saw her true personality was around a year ago. I was over at Kay's making a health poster for school. Anyway, Myrtle comes busting in screaming about how she can't find her spangled bra anywhere. Kay and I just sat on the floor cutting pictures of food out of magazines while she was storming about slamming drawers and swearing. Finally, she found it. It was pretty garish—red with black and gold-sequined G's on each cup. That's how I remember the name—G.G.

Aunt Dan and Lemon

Wallace Shawn
1985

Scene: a dance floor

Man and Woman

Raimundo (30s) a slick man-about-town and Mindy (20–30) his last
date, a hit-woman.

Raimundo fancies himself a bit of a playboy and has allowed him-
self to be taken in by Mindy, an assassin who has been hired to
kill him. Here, they dance to the doomed man's favorite music.

RAIMONDO: *(To Mindy.)* What absolutely wonderful music—really
delightful—
MINDY: Yes—isn't it?
RAIMONDO: It reminds me of—er—Brasilia Chantelle—do you know
that group?
MINDY: No—
RAIMONDO: They have a vibraphone, a banjo, a sax, and a harp. Not
your ordinary combo—eh?
(They laugh.)
MINDY: You seem to know a lot about music, Mr. Lopez.
RAIMONDO: Well, music is one of my passions, you see—you know, I'm
afraid I didn't catch your last name.
MINDY: Er—Gatti.
RAIMONDO: Italian?
MINDY: On my father's side Italian. My mother was English.
RAIMONDO: She's no longer living?
MINDY: Yes—she died last winter. A terrible illness.
RAIMONDO: I'm very sorry.
MINDY: Oh, thank you, really. Do you like this wine?
RAIMONDO: It's delicious. It's special.

MINDY: Yes, it's Italian.—The sparkling wines of that region are always—

RAIMONDO: You picked it?

MINDY: Yes.

RAIMONDO: You like wine, don't you?

MINDY: Not *too* much, no—

RAIMONDO: I didn't say *too* much—

MINDY: You were thinking it, though—You were thinking I look like the kind of person—

RAIMONDO: *Every* person is that kind of person. I'm a student of the subject. Ha ha! Believe me. But I like it, too. When a wine is good—and the company's amusing—

MINDY: When the company's amusing, *any* wine is good.
(They laugh.)

RAIMONDO: You're single, then, Miss Gatti? That's almost Italian for cat, isn't it? It's the same word in Spanish—

MINDY: Yes. Yes. I'm single. Miss Cat, if you like.

RAIMONDO: Yes—yes—I'll call you Miss Cat.
(They laugh.)

RAIMONDO: And when you put that fur around your neck, I'll bet that you look like one too, Miss Cat.

MINDY: Oh come on.

RAIMONDO: No, I mean it. Your smile is a little bit catlike too.

MINDY: You've just got the idea in your head, Mr. Lopez.

RAIMONDO: What idea? Now what idea do I have in my head?
(They are both laughing.)

RAIMONDO: Are you telling me what ideas I have in my head now?
(They both laugh loudly.)

RAIMONDO: You're a very unusual woman, Gatti. I think you can *put* ideas inside people's heads if you really want to.

MINDY: Say—now what in the world are you talking about? Eh?

RAIMONDO: If you only *knew* the ideas you've put in my head.

MINDY: I think you're crazy! That's what I think, Mr. Lopez—I think you're absolutely mad!

RAIMONDO: I think you're a witch! I think you're a devil!

MINDY: *(A roar of laughter from the other side of the table.)* Say—it looks like Marty is flirting with your date!

RAIMONDO: My date? Are you crazy? That's not my date! That's a friend of Freddie's wife, a very close friend of his family, Gatti!

MINDY: Oh she is, eh?

RAIMONDO: Yes!—she is! A friend of his family!

MINDY: Really!

RAIMONDO: Yes!

MINDY: Well, all right, Mr. Lopez, then I think Marty is flirting with a very close friend of Freddie's family.

Imperceptible Mutabilities
In The Third Kingdom
Suzan-Lori Parks
1989

Scene: a kitchen

Two Women

Charlene (18–20) and Molly (18–20) two friends with interesting communication skills.

Molly has been expelled from school because of her refusal to express herself in "proper" English. Here she tells best friend Charlene the story over breakfast.

CHARLENE: How dja get through it?
MOLLY: Mm not through it.
CHARLENE: Yer leg. Thuh guard. Lose weight?
MOLLY: Hhh. What should I do Cho-na should I jump should I jump or what?
CHARLENE: You want some eggs?
MOLLY: Would I splat?
CHARLENE: Uh uh uhnnnn.
MOLLY: Twelve floors up. Whaduhya think?
CHARLENE: Uh uh uhn. Like scrambled?
MOLLY: Shit.
CHARLENE: With cheese? Say "with" cause ssgoin in.
MOLLY: I diduhnt quit that school. HHH. Thought: nope! Mm gonna go on—go on ssif nothin ssapin yuh know? "S-K" is /sk/ as in "ask." The-little-lamb-follows-closely-behind-at-Mary's-heels-as-Mary-boards-the-train. Shit. Failed every test he shoves in my face. He makes me recite my mind goes blank. HHH. The-little-lamb-follows-closely-behind-at-Mary's-heels-as-Mary-boards-the-train. Aint never seen no woman on no train with no lamb. I tell him

so. He throws me out. Stuff like this happens every day y know? This isnt uh special case mines iduhnt uh uhnnn.

CHARLENE: Salami? Yarnt veg anymore.

MOLLY: "S-K" is /sk/ as in "ask." I lie down you lie down he she it lies down. The-little-lamb-follows-closely-behind-at-Mary's-heels...

CHARLENE: Were you lacto-ovo or thuh whole nine yards?

MOLLY: Whole idea uh talkin right aint right no way. Aint natural. Just goes tuh go. HHH. Show. Just goes tuh show.

CHARLENE: Coffee right?

MOLLY: They—expelled—me.

CHARLENE: Straight up?

MOLLY: Straight up. "Talk right or youre outa here!" I couldnt. I walked. Nope. "Speak-correctly-or-you'll-be-dismissed!" Yeah. Yeah. Nope. Nope. Nope. Job sends me there. Basic Skills. Now Job don't want me no more. Closely-behind-at-Mary's-heels. HHH. Everythin in its place.

CHARLENE: Toast?

MOLLY: Hate lookin for uh job. Feel real whory walkin thuh streets. Only thing worse n workin sslookin for work.

CHARLENE: I'll put it on thuh table.

MOLLY: You lie down you lie down but he and she and it and us well we lays down. Didnt quit. They booted me. He booted me. Coundnt see thuh sense uh words workin like he said couldnt see thuh sense uh workin where words workin like that was workin would drop my phone voice would let things slip they tell me get Basic Skills call me breaking protocol hhhhh! Think I'll splat?

Four Baboons Adoring The Sun
John Guare
1991

Scene: here and now

Man and Woman

Philip (40–50) an academic archaeologist and Penny (40–50) his second wife.

> *Penny and Philip used to date in college but drifted apart and eventually married other people. Years later they meet again and fall in love. Here, they tell the story of their second wind romance to their children.*

PHILIP: Penny, I am an archaeologist who never got into the field. I am head of an archaeology department, and I have never been in the field.

PENNY: But you could take your computer anywhere!

PHILIP: My wife. My kids. No. No Sicily there. You should go. You had a wonderful knack for the field. That dig in Pennsylvania.

PENNY: We dug up a seventeenth-century sleigh!

PHILIP: Hated the seventeenth century. Too recent. No, the past Past!

PENNY: The blessed beautiful past!

PHILIP: You said you wanted to marry an Etruscan.

PENNY: Mel is a wonderful man. Just does not possess one drop of Etruscan blood. I love him. Our kids. The most *wonderful* kids. I'm happy. Don't tell the kids this part. I snapped the stem of his wineglass. The wine spills over our hands. I mop the wine from his lap with my napkin.

PHILIP: Wouldn't it be crazy if we started up again?

PENNY: You live out west! Don't tell the kids this part. I kissed the napkin.

PHILIP: This can't be my life. I feel like some mutilated Greek statue sitting at a desk. No arms. No face. No legs. No phallus.

PENNY: Oh, but you have a phallus! Don't tell the kids this part.

PHILIP: I hate my life.

PENNY: I hate my life.

PHILIP: Don't tell the kids this part. My wife has a series of lovers. Drugs. Liquor. She's got her own permanent bed at Betty Ford. They won't even take her back anymore.

PENNY: Mel cheats. Womanizes. Why is that the most derogatory word? Womanize. He cheats. I'm stranded. Don't tell the kids this part.

PHILIP: My kids—what's going to become of them? Motorcycles. California.

PENNY: The values. The emptiness. The promise they'll all be on crack. I want my kids to have a life.

PHILIP: We all have these secret identities hiding inside us.

PENNY: We don't know who we truly are.

PHILIP: What myth we all belong to.

PENNY: Occasionally, if we're lucky or grace hits us, we're transformed, and our true self shines through.

PHILIP: Is there a moment when all our lives are *mythic?* Are touched by grace—by God—and we start life? Is it now? Don't tell the kids this part. Penny, look at me.

PENNY: I don't dare.

PHILIP: We have to dare.

PENNY: I've got to get home. Exit four—

PHILIP: We've been given a gift.

PENNY: I just came into town to have lunch. Come to the museum. Things like this don't happen. Not to me.

PHILIP: Not to me.

PENNY: I hate my life.

PHILIP: I hate my life.

PENNY: Philip put a travel folder on the table. It read: Welcome to Sicily.

PHILIP: *Hurray!* It's a year later and we're in Sicily!

PENNY: Married! We made it! We got our divorces! A snap! Kids! Be happy.

PHILIP: To do what you dreamed of! All those years behind a desk!

PENNY: We were married in Paris! We had dinner on a *bateau mouche* sailing around the Seine by night—a moon—

PHILIP: We had some work to do in the archaeological department of the Louvre.

PENNY: We saw our favorite piece in the world.

PHILIP: Four Baboons Adoring the Sun—like this—twenty-fourth dynasty.

[THE MESSENGER: *(Sings.)* Four Baboons Adoring the Sun]

PHILIP: But it's from a different period.

PENNY: Egyptian.

PHILIP: We're Mycean.

PENNY: But you should see these four baboons, palms upward, eyes agog.

PHILIP: It looked like our divorce, Penny. Me. Your father. Your wife. Four baboons.

PENNY: Now it's just us two baboons.

Keely and Du

Jane Martin
1993

Scene: a basement

Two Women

Keely (20–30) a pregnant woman kidnapped by a militant pro-life organization and Du (50–60) her captor.

Keely is being forced to carry an unwanted pregnancy to term against her will by the pro-life group that is keeping her chained in a basement. Here, she squares-off with Du, the simple and well-meaning woman who is her keeper.

DU: What about your father? *(A pause.)* What about your father? *(Irritation.)* I think you're spoiled rotten, what do you think? You care for your father, and you think that's hard? It's a privilege to do that, young lady. You work two jobs and think you're put upon? There are millions suffering because they can't provide. Your husband forced himself on you? You should have gone to the police. You want to end the life of the baby you are carrying? It's contrary to God's will, it's murder, it's not necessary, it's as selfish an act as you could conceive, and we will not allow you to harm that child or yourself. You are better than that, you know you are, and how you feel or what trouble you might have is not so important as a life. Now grow up and talk to me. *(A pause.)* What about your father?

KEELY: My father? He can move his right arm and the right side of his face.

DU: I'm sorry.

KEELY: He's a cop who got shot being held as a shield during a drug bust. You mess with a cop's daughter, they will skin you alive.

DU: I am truly sorry.

KEELY: You know what you get for kidnapping?

DU: Well, not to the year I don't.

KEELY: All you've got left. All of your life.

DU: I'm a bible Christian, Keely, and you can have my life to stop the slaughter is my perspective, I suppose. Not that I could take the prison, Lord, I don't even like low ceilings. I don't know what I'd do. But...Isaiah 44:24, "This is what the Lord says—your Redeemer who formed you in the womb: See, I set before you today life and prosperity, death and destruction, now choose life, so that you and your children may live." *(A pause.)* I don't know if you care anything about the bible.

KEELY: *(Flaring.)* Hey, I didn't choose to have this baby.

DU: And the baby didn't choose, honey, but the baby's there.

KEELY: And I'm here. I don't have, you know, bible reading to hold up. I'm not some lawyer, alright, with this argument, that argument, put in this clause, fix the world. I can't do this, take care of my dad, get myself straight, take on a baby, I got, you know, night-mares, stuff like that, I start crying in supermarkets because they're out of carrots is where I am because, I could get messed up, who knows, killed by who impregnated me, not to mention I might, I don't know, hate this baby, hurt this baby, throw the baby or something like that, I'm not kidding, what's inside me. Now, do you have some bible quotes for that, or am I just beside the point, handcuffed to this bed, carrying the results of being fucked by my ex-husband while he banged my head off a hard-wood floor to shut me up?

DU: I'm sorry.

KEELY: You're sorry?

DU: That was the act of an animal at that time.

KEELY: At that time? I could tell you many times. Many times. You don't know who I am, and God knows you don't care, with your scram-bled eggs and your grandma act, either let me out of here or leave me alone, do you understand me? I wouldn't eat I don't know what if it came from your hands, I wouldn't touch it, I wouldn't let it inside me. You're filth. I don't care what church you come from or who your God is. You're criminal filth, and I will see to it you get yours. Now, leave me alone.

(She turns away. There is silence.)

DU: I can't leave you alone, honey. Nobody wants to be left alone. Not really.

(The lights fade.)

Stops

Robert Auletta
1993

Scene: here and now

Man and Woman

Jeff (60–80) an old man with a new truss and Mattie (30–40) a troubled woman.

Mattie is driven by inner demons to seek salvation or damnation on the streets. Here, she encounters Jeff, who explains how he has achieved happiness.

JEFF: I'm Jeff.
   (She takes two steps toward him, then stops.)
MATTIE: I know no Jeff.
JEFF: Like Mutt and Jeff. Like the comic strip.
   (She takes two steps toward him, then stops.)
MATTIE: I know no comic strip.
JEFF: I wander about.
   (She takes one step, then stops.)
MATTIE: Touch me, anyway.
   (Jeff laughs.)
MATTIE: Don't do that!
   (Pause.)
JEFF: I've bought a new truss. *(He fiddles with his truss.)*
MATTIE: What?
JEFF: A new truss. At a sale at the surgical store.
MATTIE: Is it a great improvement?
JEFF: Huh?
MATTIE: Is it more comfortable, durable, lighter, more sanitary, does it give you greater freedom?
JEFF: It makes me happy.
MATTIE: Then it's all those things and more. Then it's a good truss.

JEFF: Huh?

MATTIE: Rejoice.

JEFF: I shouldn't wander about.

MATTIE: No.

JEFF: It's bad for me. I can get overexcited.

MATTIE: What?

JEFF: *(Getting overexcited.)* I can get overexcited.

MATTIE: I think I heard you the first time.

JEFF: It's bad for me.

MATTIE: I can see why. *(Pause.)* Tell me what you know, Jeff?

JEFF: I know I shouldn't get overexcited.

MATTIE: Yes. Yes. If only I could have known that. That's truly something important. But what else do you know?

JEFF: I know how to make ends meet.

MATTIE: How does one do that?

JEFF: By cutting corners.

MATTIE: And how does one accomplish that?

JEFF: By doing without.

MATTIE: By doing without what? Exactly what, Jeff?

JEFF: By doing without whatever is not absolutely essential.

MATTIE: And what is the result of all this…denial?

(Jeff laughs.)

MATTIE: Come now, tell me, in your own words.

JEFF: The result is…

MATTIE: Spit it out.

JEFF: Happiness.

MATTIE: Complete happiness?

JEFF: Yes.

MATTIE: Has it worked for you? Have you attained…

JEFF: I am completely happy.

MATTIE: *(Calls off into the distance.)* Why haven't I been told this before? *(Pause; to Jeff.)* It probably would not have worked for me.

JEFF: It works for everybody.

MATTIE: How do you know?

JEFF: I've seen it with my own eyes.

MATTIE: I hope you don't mind me saying this, Jeff, but you don't look completely happy to me. In fact, you look downright miserable.

JEFF: Inside I am a different man.

(He fiddles with his truss. It starts to get dark.)

MATTIE: And your shoes are not highly polished.

(A siren is heard in the distance.)

JEFF: Inside I'm altogether different. *(He exits.)*

The Family of Mann

Theresa Rebeck
1994

Scene: Los Angeles

Two Women

Belinda (30s) a former academic hired to write for a television sit-com, and Sally (30-40) her co-worker.

Here, seasoned writer Sally feels out the new kid on the block.

SALLY: You must miss teaching.

BELINDA: Well, yeah, I guess I do. There actually was something really comforting about discussing Victorian novels for twelve hours a day.

SALLY: I'm sure it was a much more intellectual environment.

BELINDA: Oh, no—I mean, yes, of course, but—

SALLY: We read too.

BELINDA: Oh, I know. I didn't—I really don't miss it that much. I was constantly broke and the politics—I didn't actually fit in.

SALLY: Oh, no. You're lovely! I'm sure you fit in everywhere you go.

BELINDA: Well, thank you. But I never actually felt comfortable as an academic. I mean, I loved teaching, but the faculty...I felt like a populist in elitist heaven. I prefer Dickens to Henry James.

SALLY: Really.

BELINDA: Yeah. And I just thought, writing for television, if Dickens were alive today, that's where he'd be, so—

SALLY: Well, you're very lucky to be with us on your first show. This is one of the best places to work in Hollywood. Ed is one of the few truly decent and supportive people in the industry, and he really does want you to consider this a home. You're lucky.

BELINDA: *(Cautious.)* Everyone's been great. And I really am thrilled to be here.

SALLY: Well, good.

BELINDA: Of course, it's pretty different than I thought it would be. I guess I thought it was going to be sort of like the *Dick Van Dyke Show,* and, you know, it's really not.

SALLY: It does get a little rough sometimes. You must find that hard, coming from your ivory tower.

BELINDA: Oh, no. I love three hours of fist up the ass jokes. We used to kid about that all the time back at the old ivory tower. In between all the drugs we did.

(Sally looks at her. Belinda smiles. After a moment, Sally smiles back.)

SALLY: My first job, on *Happy Days,* the first day I was there, one of the other writers unzipped his pants, put his cock on the table and told me to suck it.

(Pause.)

BELINDA: You're kidding.

SALLY: I was the only woman in a room of ten. They all thought it was hilarious, of course. I was twenty-four years old.

BELINDA: What did you do?

SALLY: Well, I certainly didn't oblige him. I laughed in a slightly uncomfortable way. *(She demonstrates.)* After a month or so the joke wore thin and he went on to something else. The whole trick is going along with it, but not really. You know.

BELINDA: I don't think I do.

SALLY: You can't protest, because that would get in the way of the room's energy, but you also can't just pretend that you're one of them. Because, we're not. Are we?

BELINDA: Apparently not.

SALLY: Anyway, you don't have to worry about the really overt stuff here. Ed wouldn't tolerate it.

BELINDA: He wouldn't.

SALLY: Absolutely not. He's actually rather traditional.

BELINDA: Traditional?

SALLY: On the last season of *Family Business,* we had a staff writer, a woman, who told the filthiest jokes in the room. She also tried to play basketball with them in one of their pickup games. She didn't last the season.

BELINDA: *(Pause.)* Are you warning me about something?

SALLY: I'm just trying to help. Ed is a complicated person. I hope you understand that.

BELINDA: You're kind of complicated yourself, aren't you?

SALLY: Not really. All I want out of life is to make a lot of money. More money than I can count. So much money that everyone will have to kiss up to me, and I can treat anyone I want like dirt. *(She laughs.)* More tea? *(She pours. Lights change.)*

Medusa's Tale

Carol S. Lashof
1995

Scene: a well

Two Women

Medusa (16–18) a young girl in her pre-gorgon days and Girl (16–18) a local.

Medusa has agreed to help Chrysis to carry water from a well. As she waits for her friend by the well, she and a girl of the village discuss love and marriage.

GIRL: I don't know what girls are like where you come from, but around here your father would beat you for talking to men in the street.

MEDUSA: My father's much too busy to worry about that sort of thing. He's responsible for the whole of the Aegean sea.

GIRL: Really? What does he do?

MEDUSA: Oh, everything. He manages all the riptides and whirlpools, tends to the undersea forests, stuff like that. When I was a little girl, he used to let me help him. Once I sunk a ship by mistake and I cried and cried, but he just laughed and got the men to shore somehow.

GIRL: I don't believe you really sunk a ship.

MEDUSA: Well, hardly anybody was drowned.

GIRL: Would you show me something?

MEDUSA: Actually…no, I can't. I never learned to do much of anything by myself. I just did what Father told me to. And when I got older, he didn't ask me to help him anymore.

GIRL: But he lets you go anywhere and talk to anyone?

MEDUSA: I haven't even seen him in months.

GIRL: But that's horrible. Who will arrange a marriage for you?

MEDUSA: I don't want to get married. At least not until I'm much older, maybe twenty-five or thirty.

GIRL: Nobody will want to marry you then. *(Pause. Whispering.)* Do you suppose the wedding night is fun?

MEDUSA: Probably not half so much fun as being courted.

GIRL: What's fun about that? The man looks you over, he asks your father about the dowry...

MEDUSA: I don't mean that part of it.

GIRL: What else is there?

MEDUSA: Oh, you know.

GIRL: Tell me...

MEDUSA: Well...say for instance, when a man catches your glance in the marketplace and you look away and then look back and he's smiling and you can almost feel his eyes on you.

GIRL: But I would be afraid to look at a man that way.

MEDUSA: Or suppose he pretends to notice that your hair comb is slipping and he buries his strong fingers in your locks and his breath warms your neck.

GIRL: I'd better go. I thought you were chaste or I would never have spoken to you.

MEDUSA: Of course I'm chaste. I'm as chaste as Diana or Athena. I don't want to be stuck like other girls, nursing babies and fetching water. Like that girl, what's-her-name? Chrysis. *(Poseidon approaches, whistling a sea song.)*

GIRL: But if you're chaste...Oh!

MEDUSA: You needn't stand there gaping. It's only Poseidon.

GIRL: Only Poseidon!? Don't you know what they say about him? He's famous—infamous, I mean—for ravishing women. *(Pause.)* He's looking at us. Oh, dear. I think he's coming over here.

MEDUSA: Are you running home to your mother?

GIRL: You should run, too.

MEDUSA: Why? Athena will protect me.

GIRL: Look, he is coming over here.

MEDUSA: *(Calling.)* You forgot your pitcher.

You Belong To Me

Keith Reddin
1995

Scene: a living room

Man and Woman

Larry (30–40) and Joyce (30–40) a married couple in dangerous waters.

Here, Joyce indulges in a dark fantasy while she watches her husband read the paper.

LARRY: Huh.
JOYCE: What?
LARRY: That property on Wilshire is on sale. *(Goes back to reading paper.)*
JOYCE: Larry...
LARRY: Yeah?
JOYCE: You ever think about killing me?
LARRY: What?
JOYCE: I mean did you ever imagine killing me?
LARRY: No.
JOYCE: You ever think of how you would kill a person?
LARRY: You thinking of killing me?
    (Pause.)
JOYCE: No.
    (Pause.)
LARRY: You're talking about like after we have a big fight or something. Like that?
JOYCE: Yes.
LARRY: No, I can't say that I have. *(Thinks.)* Uh no.
JOYCE: Not ever?
LARRY: *(Smiling.)* No, Joyce. Why would I want to kill you?

JOYCE: I mean imagining. Like if I took out a gun. *(She takes out a gun.)*

LARRY: Uh huh.

JOYCE: And I pointed it at you?

LARRY: Hey, where'd you get that gun, Joyce?

JOYCE: You know, we're so close, it'd be kind of impossible to miss you.

LARRY: Is that a real gun?

JOYCE: It's loaded, I checked right after dinner.

LARRY: Okay, I don't get the joke, Joyce.

JOYCE: I want you to beg me not to kill you.

LARRY: Are you still mad at me about yelling at you about the American Express bill, is that what this is about?

JOYCE: Come on, Lar, beg me. Beg for your life.

LARRY: I wasn't really mad.

JOYCE: I want you to crawl on your belly and say, don't kill me, Joyce. Come on, crawl.

LARRY: Okay you don't have to pick me up after squash this week, I'll get Ted to drive.

JOYCE: Oooh, this gun is getting heavy. It's getting so heavy Larry I might have to make it lighter by emptying a few bullets out of it.

LARRY: Joyce…

JOYCE: Shut up, just shut your face.

LARRY: Joyce, stop this. Put the gun down. You don't want to shoot anybody.

JOYCE: Where'd you get that line, Larry, some repeat of T.J. Hooker?

LARRY: I'm your husband.

JOYCE: I bet you wish it was you holding the gun right now. You wish you had me in your sights, just a little pressure on the trigger and you blow me into next week. *(She starts waving the gun.)* Come on, start crawling.

LARRY: No.

JOYCE: I'm serious.

LARRY: I'm not going to crawl.

JOYCE: Now!

LARRY: I don't think you can really do it.

JOYCE: Oh no?

LARRY: I don't think so. Nope. *(Goes back to reading the paper.)*

JOYCE: Put that paper down.

LARRY: I haven't finished.

JOYCE: I said…

LARRY: I heard you.

JOYCE: Okay, you are dead.
> *(She fires the gun at Larry. Pause. Then Joyce sits and puts the gun away. Larry lowers the newspaper.)*

LARRY: Anything the matter?

JOYCE: What?

LARRY: You got all quiet.

JOYCE: I was just thinking.
> *(Pause.)*

LARRY: I love you, Joyce.

JOYCE: I know.

LARRY: And? And?

JOYCE: *(Softly.)* I love you too.

One Flea Spare

Naomi Wallace

1996

Scene: a quarantined house in London during the Black Plague

Two Women

Darcy (40s) the lady of the house and Morse (10–15) a young girl
trapped inside a strange house.

*Here, Darcy acquaints herself with Morse as it seems they may be
spending quite a bit of time in one another's company.*

DARCY: Stand here, child.
(Morse nears her.)
DARCY: Closer. Let me feel your breath on my cheek.
(Morse moves closer.)
DARCY: The breath of a child has passed through the lungs of an angel.
That's what they say.
MORSE: My mother said to me that once a tiny piece of star broke off
and fell from the sky-while she slept in a field of wheat and it
pierced her, here, *(Motions to Darcy's heart but doesn't touch
her.)* and from that piece of star I was born.
DARCY: And your father. What did he say? That he molded you from a
sliver of moon?
MORSE: My father is dead.
DARCY: I know. But what did he say about his little girl?
MORSE: My father was born dead. He stayed that way most of his life.
DARCY: I met your father, at the Opera, once. He seemed a decent
man.
MORSE: My father hit the maids. I saw him do it. Sometimes twice a
day.
DARCY: Well. Then he kept order. A household must have order.
MORSE: He used a piece of leg from a chair. He kept it in the drawer of
his writing desk.

DARCY: Sometimes servants misbehave. That's not your father's fault.

MORSE: Do you hit your servants?

DARCY: My servants are dead.

MORSE: Did you hit them?

DARCY: No, I didn't. But when they did not listen, I told my husband and he dealt with them as was necessary.

MORSE: Can I see your neck now?

DARCY: No, you cannot.

MORSE: Can I see your hands?

DARCY: My hands are private.

MORSE: I'm not afraid to die.

DARCY: You don't have to be; you won't die.

MORSE: I already know what it's like. To be dead. It's nothing fancy. *(She moves away from Darcy. She takes the hem of her dress in her hands.)* Just lots of nothing to see all around you and nothing to feel, only there's a sound that comes and goes. Comes and goes. Like this:
(She slowly tears a rip in her dress, up to her waist. We hear the sound of ripping cloth.)

MORSE: Have you heard that sound before, Mrs. Snelgrave?

Picasso At The Lapin Agile

Steve Martin
1996

Scene: the cafe Lapin Agile

Two Men

Pablo Picasso and Albert Einstein, two really famous guys.

> *Here, the painter and the theorist meet and bicker in a French cafe.*

EINSTEIN: I work the same way. I make beautiful things with a pencil.

PICASSO: You? You're just a scientist! For me, the shortest distance between two points is *not* a straight line!

EINSTEIN: Likewise.

PICASSO: *(Still dancing.)* Let's see one of your creations.
> *(Einstein pulls out a pencil. Picasso stops dancing, gets a pencil. The others back away as if it were a Western shoot-out.)*

PICASSO: Draw!
> *(They start to draw on the napkins. Einstein finishes first.)*

EINSTEIN: Done!
> *(Einstein and Picasso swap drawings.)*

EINSTEIN: It's perfect.

PICASSO: Thank you.

EINSTEIN: I'm talking about mine.

PICASSO: *(Studies it.)* It's a formula.

EINSTEIN: So's yours.

PICASSO: It *was* a little hastily drawn…yours is letters.

EINSTEIN: Yours is lines.

PICASSO: My lines mean something.

EINSTEIN: So do mine.

PICASSO: Mine is beautiful.

EINSTEIN: *(Indicates his own drawing.)* Men have swooned on seeing that.

PICASSO: Mine touches the heart.

EINSTEIN: Mine touches the head.

PICASSO: Mine will change the future.

EINSTEIN: *(Holds his drawing.)* Oh, and mine won't?

(Sensing victory, or at least parity, Einstein starts to dance with Suzanne. Picasso stands befuddled.)

PICASSO: Maybe you're a fake.

EINSTEIN: And maybe you're an *idiot savant.* And hold the *savant.*

(Einstein continues dancing. Gaston watches.)

Life Under Water

Richard Greenberg
1999

Scene: Long Island's southern fork, summer

Two Women

Amy-Joy (18–25) and Amy-Beth (18–25) best friends on vacation at the shore.

Here, Amy-Joy confesses to terrorizing a little girl who is terrified of sea monsters.

BETH: So tell me.

JOY: You'll die. I'm bad, I'm so bad.

BETH: What did you do?

JOY: You will just die.

BETH: And what if I don't?

JOY: I'll be very disappointed. But it's not gonna happen, it's just not gon—

BETH: So you went out to allay her fears…

JOY: I went out because the little one, the girl—

BETH: Yes, I know who you mean.

JOY: *Isolde?* Shit, what kind of people name the kids Tristan and Isolde and the dogs Brian and Susan? I mean—

BETH: Your uncle.

JOY: Uncle *Andre,* wouldja believe? Andre Vinegrad as in Abe Weingarten. I mean, the whole family.

BETH: And you went out to allay her fears.

JOY: 'Cause she thinks she sees a sea monster. I find out. I go there, I find it out. The other kid—

BETH: Tristan, this is.

JOY: Tristan—you believe that? A name like that he's gonna have serious trouble dating.

BETH: And then what happened?

JOY: And then what happened is like the other kid's a one-of-those-kids-he swims-like-a-fish...water baby! Like this article in *People* magazine, and he's in it naked. So he's cool about the whole deal, he's working on her, saying there is no such thing as a sea monster, you know?

BETH: Mm-hm.

JOY: And he's got her just about I would say *half* convinced. And I'm watching and I'm thinking, well nothing for me to do, a child is more likely to respond to a sibling, anyway—I took this family planning course—

BETH: Things are going smoothly.

JOY: Things are going smoothly. And I think—I don't know what came over me—I see this little child, five years old—I see this kid, she looks so goddamn innocent, and I think—wouldn't it be kind of neat to scare her shitless?

BETH: You didn't.

JOY: I did.

BETH: Of course you did.

JOY: Who knows why?

BETH: Sea monsters exist.

JOY: In a big way.

BETH: Amy-Joy—

JOY: Shame on me, I know, I know. But you should see this kid. Too dumb for life. Her eyes look like—

BETH: A simile?

JOY: ...Big. Very big. The eyes are very big. 'Cause I tell her these sea monsters in the sea—and they eat anybody's ever been in the sea so too late now—and they especially eat little girls who someday intend to have expensive nose jobs—'cause already they're planning it, you can tell. And they especially *especially* eat little girls with stupid names. And they got these big, humongous—this is the best part—these big, humongous—

BETH: Jaws.

JOY: Jaws, you said it. 'Cause like she's got the lunch box? with the shark? with the mouth? with the kid? with the blood?

BETH: So right now she's—

JOY: Right now she's shitting her pants. But the beauty part is even if she never goes back in the water again, I fixed it so she's terrified. I traumatized her.

BETH: Why?

JOY: Why? Because. It was something to do. I was bored. Because her father's a fairy antiques dealer.

BETH: I wonder what she saw actually…

JOY: Probably Tristan's little zorch.

BETH: Would that have scared her?

JOY: It scares you, doesn't it?

BETH: I'm another story.

JOY: You're telling me…Hey.

BETH: *(Pause.)* Yes?

JOY: You're all right, aren't you? I mean…You're all right.

BETH: I'm all right.

JOY: Good. Let's do something tonight.

The Ornamental Hermit

Jocelyn Beard
1999

Scene: Revermead Plantation, South Carolina, 1860

Man and Woman

Joe (20s–30s) a abolitionist masquerading as a slave and Mehitable (18–20) the woman he loves, a slave.

Joe and his partner have been helping slaves escape via the Underground Railroad all over South Carolina. When they feel their luck is about to run out, they plan one last daring escape. Here Joe begs Mehitable to come with him, though not daring to confess that he is in fact, a northern abolitionist.

(Joe enters dragging an unhappy Mehitable.)

MEHITABLE: I will not listen to you anymore, Joe!

JOE: You have to! Tonight's the night, Delilah. It's now or never. Come with me. Leave this place!

MEHITABLE: And go where? There ain't no place else!

JOE: You crazy, girl? There's a whole world of someplace else!

MEHITABLE: And we'll be killed tryin' to get there!

JOE: We won't!

MEHITABLE: Joe! Last month four slaves from Green Hill was caught tryin' to run and they…

JOE: I know what happened!

MEHITABLE: Then why do you want to run, Joe?

JOE: Because I am a man! I need to…why am I explainin' this to you? Why don't you want to run? Don't you want to be free of all this? Live like a person with a life worth livin'?

MEHITABLE: Because my life ain't worth nothin' if I'm swingin' from a rope!

JOE: You ain't gonna swing from no rope. We got it planned…

MEHITABLE: We? We, Joe? Who's we?

JOE: I can't talk about that.

MEHITABLE: Who you draggin' with you, Joe?

JOE: No one! We already…

[LILY: *(Off.)* Mehitable!]

MEHITABLE: It's Lily. Joe, promise me…

JOE: *(Savagely.)* This is good bye.

(*Joe pulls her into an embrace, kisses her and then disappears into the night.*)

MEHITABLE: Joe!

THE ACTOR'S NIGHTMARE Copyright 1981 by Christopher Durang CAUTION: Professionals and amateurs are hereby warned that performance of THE ACTOR'S NIGHTMARE by Christopher Durang is subject to royalty. It is fully protected under the copyright laws of the United States of America, and of all countries covered by the International Copyright Union (including the Dominion of Canada and the rest of the British Commonwealth),and of all countries covered by the Pan-American Copyright Convention and the Universal Copyright Convention, the Berne Convention and of all countries with which the United States has reciprocal copyright relations. All rights, including professional, amateur/motion picture stage rights, recitation, lecturing, public reading, radio broadcasting, television, video or sound recording, all other forms of mechanical or electronic reproduction, such as CD-ROM, CD-1, information storage and retrieval systems and photocopying, and the rights of translation into foreign languages, are strictly reserved. Particular emphasis is laid upon the matter of readings, permission for which must be obtained from the author's agent in writing.The stage performance rights in THE ACTOR'S NIGHTMARE (other than first class rights) are controlled exclusively by Dramatists Play Service, 440 Park Avenue South, New York, NY 10016. No professional or non-professional performance of the Play (excluding first class professional performance) may br given without obtaining in advance the written permission of Dramatists Play Service, and paying the requisite fee.Inquiries concerning all other rights should be addressed to Helen Merrill Ltd., 425 West 23rd Street, New York, NY 10011. Reprinted by Permission of: Helen Merrill Ltd. on behalf of the author

AM I BLUE? Copyright 1982 by Beth Henley CAUTION: Professionals and amateurs are hereby warned that AM I BLUE? by Beth Henley is subject to a royalty. It is fully protected under the copyright laws of the United States of America, and of all countries covered by the International Copyright Union (including the Dominion of Canada and the rest of the British Commonwealth), and of all countries covered by the Pan-American Copyright Convention and the Universal Copyright Convention, the Berne Convention and of all countries with which the United States has reciprocal copyright relations. All rights, including professional, amateur/motion picture stage rights, recitation, lecturing, public reading, radio broadcasting, television, video or sound recording, all other forms of mechanical or electronic reproduction, such as CD-ROM, CD-1, information storage and retrieval systems and photocopying, and the rights of translation into foreign languages, are strictly reserved. Particular emphasis is laid upon the matter of readings, permission for which must be obtained from the author's agent in writing. Reprinted by Permission of William Morris Agency on behalf of the author. Contact: William Morris Agency, Inc. 1325 Avenue of the Americas, NewYork, New York 10019 Attn: Gilbert Parker

ANTIGONE by Sophocles Translated by Sir George Young Dover Publications 31 East Second Street Mineola, NY 11501.

AUNT DAN AND LEMON Copyright 1985 by Wallace Shawn CAUTION: Professionals and amateurs are hereby warned that AUNT DAN AND LEMON by Wallace Shawn is subject to a royalty. It is fully protected under the copyright laws of the United States of America, and of all countries covered by the International Copyright Union (including the Dominion of Canada and the rest of the British Commonwealth), and of all countries covered by the Pan-American Copyright Convention and the Universal Copyright Convention, the Berne Convention and of all countries with which the United States has reciprocal copyright relations. All rights, including professional, amateur/motion picture stage rights, recitation, lecturing, public reading, radio broadcasting, television, video or sound recording, all other forms of mechanical or electronic reproduction, such as CD-ROM, CD-1, information storage and retrieval systems and photocopying, and the rights of translation into foreign languages, are strictly reserved. Particular emphasis is laid upon

290

including professional, amateur/motion picture stage rights, recitation, lecturing, public reading, radio broadcasting, television, video or sound recording, all other forms of mechanical or electronic reproduction, such as CD-ROM, CD-1, information storage and retrieval systems and photocopying, and the rights of translation into foreign languages, are strictly reserved. Particular emphasis is laid upon the matter of readings, permission for which must be obtained from the author's agent in writing. Reprinted by permission of Random House, Inc. Contact: Random House, Inc. Permissions Department, 201 East 50th Street, New York, NY 10022

LOOK BACK IN ANGER Copyright 1956 John Osborne CAUTION: Professionals and amateurs are hereby warned that performance of LOOK BACK IN ANGER by John Osborne is subject to royalty. It is fully protected under the copyright laws of the United States of America, and of all countries covered by the International Copyright Union (including the Dominion of Canada and the rest of the British Commonwealth), and of all countries covered by the Pan-American Copyright Convention and the Universal Copyright Convention, the Berne Convention and of all countries with which the United States has reciprocal copyright relations. All rights, including professional, amateur/motion picture stage rights, recitation, lecturing, public reading, radio broadcasting, television, video or sound recording, all other forms of mechanical or electronic reproduction, such as CD-ROM, CD-1, information storage and retrieval systems and photo copying, and the rights of translation into foreign languages, are strictly reserved. Particular emphasis is laid upon the matter of readings, permission for which must be obtained from the author's agent in writing. Reprinted by permission of Helen Osborne Representing the Estate of John Osborne. Contact: The Hurst Clunton Craven Arts, Shropshire, SY7 OJA UK.

THE LOTTERY Adapted by Brainerd Duffield from a story by Shirley Jackson Copyright 1953 by Brainerd Duffield CAUTION: Professionals and amateurs are hereby warned that performance of THE LOTTERY by Brainerd Duffield is subject to royalty. It is fully protected under the copyright laws of the United States of America, and of all countries covered by the International Copyright Union (including the Dominion of Canada and the rest of the British Commonwealth), and of all countries covered by the Pan-American Copyright Convention and the Universal Copyright Convention, the Berne Convention and of all countries with which the United States has reciprocal copyright relations. All rights, including professional, amateur/motion picture stage rights, recitation, lecturing, public reading, radio broadcasting, television, video or sound recording, all other forms of mechanical or electronic reproduction, such as CD-ROM, CD-1, information storage and retrieval systems and photocopying, and the rights of translation into foreign languages, are strictly reserved. Particular emphasis is laid upon the matter of readings, permission for which must be obtained from the author's agent in writing. Contact: Linda Hapjan, c/o The Dramatic Publishing Company, 311 Washington Street, Woodstock, IL 60098

THE MADNESS OF HERCULES by Seneca, Translation Copyright 1995 by Dana Gioia CAUTION: Professionals and amateurs are hereby warned that performance of THE MADNESS OF HERCULES by Seneca translated by Dana Gioiai subject to royalty. It is fully protected under the copyright laws of the United States of America, and of all countries covered by the International Copyright Union (including the Dominion of Canada and the rest of the British Commonwealth), and of all countries covered by the Pan-American Copyright Convention and the Universal Copyright Convention, the Berne Convention and of all countries with which the United States has reciprocal copyright relations. All rights, including professional, amateur/motion picture stage rights, recitation, lecturing, public reading, radio broadcasting, television, video or sound recording, all other forms of mechanical or electronic reproduction, such as CD-ROM, CD-1, information storage and retrieval systems and photocopying, and the rights of translation into foreign languages, are strictly reserved. Particular emphasis is laid upon the matter of readings, permission for which must be obtained from the author's agent in writing. Contact: Aron Zimmerman, Permissions Manager, Johns Hopkins University Press, (410) 516-6968.